ANATOMY & GEOGRAPHY

Dedication

To William Heyen, whose writing I admire
most from among his renowned contemporaries

&

For my Loved One of three & a half decades,
Kathleen

ANATOMY & GEOGRAPHY
Copyright © 2025 by Robert Gibbons
ISBN: 978-1-960451-20-0

First paperback edition published by Stalking Horse Press, October 2025

www.stalkinghorsepress.com

Cover painting: Francisco de Goya, *The Colossus*
Sheet music, score for *Sound of the Downward* by Marilyn Crispell

Design by James Reich

Stalking Horse Press
Santa Fe, New Mexico

PRAISE FOR ROBERT GIBBONS

"Gibbons' collection of poetry is a well-crafted homage to memory and influence. Each poem on its own is a glimmering gem, but together they are a cool constellation under a dark Colorado night. To read this work is to trace your finger along the gorgeous and gritty Front Range, a journey as much nostalgic as it is cutting edge. *Under the Great Divide* is more than just a timely invocation of the nomadic spirit of Ed Dorn, it serves as a reminder of a bygone poetic era, while forging forward with its own distinct voice and concerns. This book is a relevant and compelling collection that like the rest of Gibbons' work will no doubt stand the test of time."
    — Tim Z. Hernandez, *American Book Award-winning poet*

Gibbons has allowed himself to be schooled by Kerouac, Olson, Creeley, Ginsberg, and here, Dorn, author of the groundbreaking *Slinger* (1975) and quintessential poet of the American West. With his acknowledgment of Dorn as predecessor and model…Gibbons is paying homage to a lineage of which he is—in this reviewer's estimation—the fulfillment.
    —Richard Hoffman, review of *Under the Great Divide with Ed Dorn*, in *Jacket2*

"*The Book of Assassinations* is a remarkably skillful updating of the *Illuminations*, full of odd turns and surprises; *Streets for Two Dancers* is a repository of unusual insights, moving observations and getting it absolutely right. Gibbons's is a very intriguing oeuvre."
    —Marjorie Perloff, author *21st Century Modernism: The New Poets*

"[*Of D.C.*] is admirable, and astonishing. You are where Rimbaud was when he got to the *Illuminations*…What poets have preceded you in the D of C: Whitman, Pound, Olson!"
    —Guy Davenport, author of *The Geography of Imagination*, letter, June 4, 1992

"In his verse, Gibbons sees things others miss, extracting gains from the ruins of powerlessness in which the average citizen lives, offering then, a therapeutics for the public sphere."
    —Jim Feast, *Evergreen Review*

ANATOMY & GEOGRAPHY

ROBERT GIBBONS

STALKING HORSE PRESS
SANTA FE, NEW MEXICO

CONTENTS

ANATOMY & GEOGRAPHY
BOOK I

ANATOMY & GEOGRAPHY
BOOK II

...CONTENTS

ANATOMY & GEOGRAPHY
BOOK III

CODA

POSTSCRIPT

"Writers, in a way, are like beggars. They are continually begging to be heard..."
—**Henry Miller**, *Open Letter to Small Magazines*

"Should we have stayed at home and thought of here?"
—**Elizabeth Bishop**, *Questions of Travel*

"The book, the idea of a book or the image of a book, is a symbol of learning, of transmitting knowledge... I make my own books to find my way through the old stories."
—**Anselm Kiefer**, *The Secret Life of Plants*

"I have learned much in my life
from books
            and out of them
                        about love.
                                    Death
                                                is not the end of it."
—**W. C. Williams**, *Work in Progress*

PREFACE TO BOOK I

Writing a preface to a book by Robert Gibbons is essentially unnecessary. If the aim of the preface is to give the reader some kind of way-in to what follows, then I can assure you that all the keys to understanding and feeling Gibbons's writing are there, in that text. If the preface is meant to persuade uncertain readers to read on, you're better served skipping on a few pages to the real stuff. If the preface gives validation, or an aegis for the writer's work, Gibbons's poetry needs no protection from enemies or the elements. The long poem sequence that is *Anatomy & Geography* stands up for itself, and the poet has put everything of himself into it, and everything that the reader might need to read it.

So I offer these few words because writing about Robert Gibbons's poetry involves thinking about and experiencing it, going over or repeating the mental and corporeal sensations that it causes. But it also forces the secondary-writer — or critic — to ask those questions of her or himself again that the poems put so firmly the first time round. You can't be a spectator to *Anatomy & Geography*.

For those who've read Gibbons's previous works — and if you haven't, do, soon — there's an immediate surprise or even shock. Most of his writing over the last few years, at least since I met him in 2006, and from reading his collected poems from before then, came in the form of prose poems. These were rectangular blocks of intense and highly rhythmic language. The poet shared his daily life, his dreams, his past, his reading, and his music. All passions.

Anatomy & Geography is different. Instead of the uniform shape — albeit of varying length — we see snaking, shifting, shapes on the page. The inverted triangle, the long thin column; interruptions of prose including extracts from other writers or letters he's received (here I must show my hand — one of my messages, about a philosopher we've both read, appears here verbatim). The poems are sinewy, muscular, and flexible.

This shape relates to a central image or even presence in the poems: the solar plexus. The solar plexus is a nerve centre, in the middle of the torso. It's vital to much of the body's functioning but also, as anyone's who's ever been hit there knows, a point of great weakness. The phrase appears and reappears at intervals in the sequence, re-establishing the physical presence of the poet in the verse.

It's analogous to Gibbons's practice: the visceral being of the poet in the work, but at risk, offering up his twin strength and vulnerability to the reader. César Vallejo wrote about the "blows in life so hard...I just don't know." Closer to the present day, Cristian Aliaga, from Argentina, talked about "God's knockout blows." Gibbons's writing takes on this threat.

So we come back to the body, the anatomy of the title, as it moves through space and time: the other half of the title, geography. The poet in his hometown, the poet visiting friends, the poet years earlier travelling Mexico or Europe. Memory, dream and fiction collide in jazz concerts in Paris or car crashes outside Cuernavaca. "This is fiction, right?" Gibbons asks, though it's not clear it is.

Jazz runs throughout these pages: the moment that anything that can happen, the perfect note or chord, the epic solo, the catastrophic failure: the artist risking everything to be completely there in time. Reading Gibbons on jazz is damn close to as good as listening to the thing itself. When he writes about theory, or literature, the same unpredictability, the same improvisation, runs through his discourse. Thinkers like Kristeva, like Deleuze, shine in these pages. Likewise the poets he loves: Olson, Cavafy, Mallarmé, to name three here. All of them have in common a sense that at the moment of writing, everything is at stake. For Mallarmé, that was the roll of the dice. For Deleuze, it was the real game, not the rigged game, but the game that can change rules at each play. For Kristeva it's the essential, pre-linguistic pulses of desire that underlie human existence.

Gibbons is a political poet, on two levels. Firstly, he speaks politically, speaks his truth and accepts the risk that comes with it: on US politics, or Gaza, on war. Secondly — linking back to his anatomical presence in the work — he is operating with a clear ethics of writing.

Cervantes wrote that the greatest temptation the devil could send to a man was to persuade him that he could write a book and make profit from it. Gibbons has worked all his life, often in hard, unrewarding jobs. Poetry is not a rarefied escape from that. Poetry isn't meant to make money. An Argentine poet once said, "La poesía no se vende porque no se vende" — literally, poetry doesn't sell because it doesn't sell, but, better, "Poetry doesn't sell because it won't sell out."

Nicanor Parra, the great Chilean who'll be 100 years old later this year, wrote that "Everything is poetry except Poetry." That capital P, of prizes, judging panels, logrolling, creative writing programmes and, yes, academia (so writes an academic) is just what Gibbons is kicking against in every line. He makes an ethical challenge to the reader to reflect on what s/he does with writing, if it's honest, if it takes up the gauntlet, if it evades the comfortable and convenient.

Anatomy & Geography is Gibbons opening his guts and his mind to the reader. This is a trimmed down, focused, intense Gibbons. It's a call-out to anyone who opens its pages. Put as much of yourself into reading as the poet has into writing.

But you don't need me to tell you that. Just read on.

—*Ben Bollig, Oxford, August 2014*

ANATOMY & GEOGRAPHY

BOOK I

ANATOMY & GEOGRAPHY

*He does not turn to Paris or Rome for relief
from the monotony of reality. He turns to himself…*
—Wallace Stevens

All that walking
only to return
to alone.

No ideas,
but in
anatomy.

Along with its
accompanying
geography.

Vagabond in flight.

At this moment, "All
we have is today,
right now,"
she said,
a day
or two
ago.

I'm in Bremen.

Axel expresses interest
in theories of writing: internal
motivations, anatomical, & external,
geographical. Precursor, back there
in 1967, of Julia Kristeva's *choric* vessel

filled with preverbal vibrations. Travel
then, at twenty, even now, contributes
to understanding her notion of internal
organs as divinities.

In touch with the center
of my being, the Solar Plexus,
that nerve distribution center
located behind stomach,
in front of aorta &
crura of diaphragm.

Reverberating…
in silence
& language.

I've become almost slender at this age,
this stage, & writing reflects it like that lodgepole
pine outside our hotel window in Golden, Colorado.

Yellow & black-
ringed snake
digesting
bluejay
whole
in shade
of an open field
between five round hills.

Stomach still
has its say.
Lung heart kidneys,
a chorus.
Duo of bladder,
& pancreas.

I've asked a lot of the liver, as if it were
Oracular.

Solo vocal chords.

Or, all at once now,
cerebral cortex chiming
in with primitive brain stem
calling forth Schönberg on
6 A Cappella Choruses in G Major.

No, not there in Salzburg, Austria
with Charlotte Appleton,
but here, today,
right now.

So,
alone
isn't
always
the case.

With someone other
in Genoa,
or an old friend,
& new acquaintance,
along with total stranger, all three
on Capri.

These aren't stray ideas,
but flesh & bones
& largest
organ
of all,
skin,
recalling.

Alone,
now, after
another long walk
only to return, not
with any regret,

but acknowledged
inevitability
to solitude.

Hell, today
I'll put black
Danish socks on
on purpose just to reimagine
streets & sounds, silence in fjords
of Aalborg... or,

One night, strolling along
rue Sainte-Jacques
in the shadow
of Rimbaud,
a group of solitary
Algerians surrounding me
in my unconscious
stupor.

Off rue Jacob
the woman back
at the hotel prayed
hard I hadn't drowned
in my derangement
in the Seine.

Schönberg still playing
with that chorus
of women
sopranos,
in tune
with multiple prayers
of the woman in Paris.

6 A Cappella Choruses in G Major,
in a way, accompanying
her litany.

Years later peered
through the shop
window at
sundown
on rue des Rosier
just in Time to see
a man light the ninth
(*eighth*) & final candle
of the menorah
coinciding
with the last evening
of the year & millennium,
2000.

Skin
remembers
the cold, eye
the light illuminating the dark
inside
& out.

::::

Sped across the Texas panhandle.

Touched the Sound at the edge
of downtown Olympia.

To say I'm slim is an imagined exaggeration
similar to Charles Olson dreaming,
riding the back of an elephant
moving through mountains,
or any other obstacle.

Again, Mt. Rainier first seen
from Route 5 in Seattle.

Again, in Bremen, often,
Axel asking
trenchant
questions
on theories
& motivations
of writing like walking
in Dublin & Berlin
only to return to
alone.

It's not that one desires
simply to sit
with a cup
of coffee,

unless, there
are pen & paper & windows
or vistas at hand,
to potentially
jot down
a word,
phrase,
fragment,
sentence
expressing
the experience
as best one can.

Say the difficulty
of getting the Hell out
of Belgrade on foot & by plane?
More difficult than arriving by bus.

I'm in Belgrade.

Walk the whole day to the airport,
when a kid comes out of the woodwork
asking if I'll send music,

(speaking no English,
other than titles & lyrics
of The Beatles),
back to him from America,
if I ever get
home.

Or, where I've not gone,
but want to go,
& so long to, so do
go in a sense, & have
gone: Havana, Madrid, Barcelona,
Göteborg, Bergen, & the outskirts of Oslo.

Asheville, to visit an old friend before both of us
disappear.

Maybe we'll smoke & talk
& he might even get up
& walk?

Grudgingly, New Orleans by train
only in order to write in that
matter of fact rhythm
the way Edgar Degas
observed geography
in 1872 all the way
down there from
New York,

writing home to a friend of his in Paris
suggesting he locate an atlas in order
to get an idea of the distance
between both cities,
where for him
he found,

"Air – there is nothing
but air–…"

For freedom,
language, & experience,
add to anatomy & geography,
please, let me see the Badlands
& Grand Tetons, far & away off-
season from crowds & chatter
of thousands of
tourists.

More likely, again, only to return
to alone.

Or, let me head out anywhere with her,
for wasn't it Freud who called desire
to travel the same as that to explore
the body of a woman?

Here we are again at the juncture
of the bulbs of the vestibule
entering the cathedral
of Vezelay, or Moissac.
Romanesque: Madaleine & Pierre,
respectively.

Bath of passion.

"Sex & Death,"
(the Dead), said Yeats,
the only valid subjects
make me think
of Freud's
notion
of the hidden
desire
to return to
inorganic
matter.

So dust & ash are,
or are not any
longer
anatomy,
& the grave is
a different form
of geography.

::::

Standing over Yeats' grave
under Ben Bulben
I knew his
epitaph
urging
us to "pass by"
had been written
while reading Rilke.

Hovering above these two words in the open
dictionary below me: *liberty* & *libidinous.*

Neither one far
from *libation.*

Frédéric Gros, French author of **A Philosophy of Walking** says, in an
interview:

*All we call 'progress' represents an additional mediation
to eliminate the body's efforts. Technology is what allows us to
not have a body, to escape from fundamental characterizations
of the body: gravity, opacity, thickness, slowness, finiteness,
mortality, wear. Cyberspace, the virtual world is transparent,
light. On the other hand, we can note all around us an immense
apology for the body. To have a perfect body is more important
than to have a soul without sin.*

So at this age, at this stage in life, in the past year,
in fact, I have lost over one fifth my body
weight, forcing me to be more
in touch with the center
of my being,
the Solar Plexus,
that nerve
distribution
center
located behind the stomach
& in front of the aorta & crura
of diaphragm.

(There are the *crura,* also, of penis
& clitoris.)

That's it now, as O'Hara made plain
from experience & geography
of New York City,
You just go on your nerve.

Philosophy of walking, then, that makes sense.
I'm thinking about Charles Olson now,

not only because he appeared
in a dream just last night,
when I was interested
in what his poem,
"The Lamp"
meant,
in which he writes,
(although I couldn't recall it
in his presence in the dream, exhibiting
great patience with me as he did):

...there is that point that the whole thing itself
may be a passage, and that your own ability
may be a factor in time, in fact that
only if there is a coincidence of yourself

& the universe is there then in fact
an event...

He must have dropped by the house
in order to set the record straight
regarding his view of philosophy
itself, because I'd been trying
to digest just what he was
getting at regarding
D. H. Lawrence's ability
to resist the high temptation
of the mind,
as unlike
Plato & Schopenhauer,
both deathly afraid of *the unruliness*
of the sensual...
in favor of
The aridities of the mind.

Words come up & out of the Grand Central
nerve distribution center: Solar Plexus
located behind stomach & in
front of aorta & crura
of diaphragm.

Diaphragm, both rhythmic
& percussive.

Jazzy & spontaneous, say, like *Four Hands*
coming out of KMHD radio in Portland,
Oregon at this moment Mingus
on bass, Teo Macero on tenor,
John LaPorta, who wrote it
with Mingus, on alto,
Clem DeRosa
drums.

Just like that. From
way down deep
inside,
the nerves…

Internal chorus with anatomical vocabulary,
collected as *The Jazz Experiments of Charles Mingus*,
1955, released on the Bethlehem label.

One page over from the definition of crura,
my eye lands on that of cry: *10.*
An inarticulate vocal sound
characteristic of one
of the lower animals;
as, the cry of a hawk;
the cry of wolves.

Jazzy, rhythmic, passionate…

Olson complained of poets with no passion other than for that
of words.

::::

Skin & bone & wound.
Letter by letter back
home documenting
experience.
The second life
of writing, as intense,
or more so, than living.
Aesthetic based on the tactile.
The chew of the word. A certain taste,
not always familiar.
I'd film words like Godard,
if I could, chant like Coltrane,
if need be, paint a sign like Kline,
however one has to get it down,

send it out, make a note.
Thrust & parry,
the battle &
pleasure.

Attention, here, given
to the resonance
of silence

advancing toward her,
an audience of
one.

It's difficult to hear silence
resonate.

The next-door carpenter enjoys his
hammer blow
as opposed
to Brahms' *Choral di St. Anthony,* quiet echo
of Haydn streaming across water
from Venice radio
as if it were
Prelude
to the hymn
Pilgrims sing in procession
toward Padua on his feast day
exactly three days from now, resonant
reverberation.

Only now
track down
& pick up stray
pages by Zukofsky,
who asks to become deaf
in order to hear, what, fire
& lost speech of ancestors?

He traces Bach's family tree
back to a meeting of
the lute with a mill
wheel grinding.

Listen: ash
silent
fire.

I run across ... *the indweller,*
who is the only builder... as Thoreau
puts it in **Walden**, & imagine the skin
as the body's largest organ housing
Divinities, including Solar Plexus.

Imagine Bach's lute
& the mill wheel
grinding as if
it were Time
itself.

Two stones propped up
properly, or askew,
can make an
altar, even
a cairn.

For that matter, two blue-tinged bottles
standing, clear, except for the image
of Emerson seen through
the other side, sent as
message recently
from a fellow
poet
can
act
as

talisman.

Americana
Emerson, dwelling on Beauty,
found himself "above the region of fear."
Two blue-tinged bottles, c. 1880 –
dwell on these poet, to remember.

                        —William Heyen

Brockport, NYL Poemlet Press / 2014 #8/27

I'm in Cabo San Lucas.

Just off the overnight ferry from Mazatlán across the Gulf of California
with friend, Brad Fuller, making our way further south as south can
go, where at land's end shore's edge is peopled by stones only,
evidence of which is in / the form of photographs taken
with heavy Sinar 4X5 view camera bartered for
& lugged all the way down here hitched
to a three-legged tripod.

Look, a bit of sand, but mostly
igneous stone theriomorphic
& anthropomorphic forms,
the crowded beach, where
various waves of ancient
man had plenty of Time
on his hands at this
land's end.

Reminds me of the Time I held
the rope for another man
in order to rappel
& descend
mammoth
stone to
read
the **K** etched,
recondite,
at cliff's
edge.

Is it any wonder, now, to return to find the French
philosopher, Frédéric Gros, alluding to:

The appeal of transgression, the call of the great outdoors
are easily found in the writings of Kerouac and Snyder:
throwing off moronic conventions, the soporific security
of four walls… boredom of the Same, the wear of repetition,
the chilliness of the well heeled and their hatred of change…

The decision to walk (to head somewhere far off, anywhere,
to try something
else)…

There's an answer
to the question, "Where to go
from here?"

"Anywhere." We tramped (tranced?) across

the unnamed desert.

Open randomly to pages in Portuguese notebook jotted
down on plane from København to the opposite
end of the earth from Cabo San Lucas =
Aalborg, no less, only to find
Whitman my traveling
companion on
8/29/2013
saying:

You road I enter upon & look around, I believe you are not all there is here,
I believe that much unseen is also here…
Now I reexamine philosophies…
may prove well in lecture rooms… not… at all under spacious clouds…
landscape & flowing currents…

Whoever you are come travel…
find what never tires…
The earth is rude, silent, incomprehensible at first…

Dawn saw you
naked. Flesh
dressed in light.

I'm in Mexico City.

After a month in Zihuatanejo,
where across the dirt main drag,
Adrianna Page, all of say 6'3" of her,
walks right up to me asking if I'm a Kennedy,
what with the 'Fitz' of Gerald & Gibbons (my own
stolen at Ellis Island) linking us ancestrally in physiognomy
& geography back there as Normans & Irishmen, "No, but I get that
all the time."

She's a star in Manuel Ávila Camacho's films.
Can we come up to the Hotel Presidente
tonight at 7:00 to watch them film?

Hell, ya, is not what I said, but Hell, ya,
struck right in the Solar Plexus on
a hot day in the middle of
nowhere.

It's a long story: Manuel
(just yesterday I saw event
inside eventually) came down
from the hill, where his hotel
perched, to visit our $40-a-month
shack with burlap cots & no running
water our cliffside digs above the bay,
marveling at the stack of books lining one
wall, & he compared the room to van Gogh's.

You heard right, & not far off, the poverty so
evident before a millionaire's eyes.

"Call me when you're back in Mexico City."

I'm in Mexico City.

Latest spot: another one room (this current phenomenon
interests me, in that I don't dwell on the past,
but dwell in the present, so in a sense,
[innocence] during this walk Mexico
City rises up to kiss a sixty-seven-
year-old man on the lips)
only in a boarding house
room bordering on
Zona Rosa.

God,
how Grandmother Roseanna
rises up now, too, as she did then
in an abandoned building diagonally
across the street in with her kittens,
all of which we fed scraps
from the local butcher
fascinated as he was
by my superstition
that Roseanna
visited me
there
in the center
of Mexico City
in the form of a stray
cat with kittens!

How long's it been since I recalled that!?

Adrianna answers the phone:
"Manuel wants to know
if you would like to go
with us to see
Ray Charles
tonight?"

"Hell, ya."

We see (& hear) Ray + the Raylettes!!

Afterward, go to the oldest restaurant in the city,
then the burlesque, where there is no age
discrimination: mature women on stage.

They lock the doors behind us.
The place is packed, except
for four empty seats four
rows from the stage
to which we're
ushered,
& where
a man is pulling a string of hundreds of razorblades out
of his mouth.

Further, afterward, that same night, Adrianna
smashes into a taxi with her VW Bug.
Cops arrest her for not having license
or registration, along with Manuel,
whom they call a murderer for
his politics = grandfather
president of Mexico
during WWII,
he's now
attaché to current
president, Echheverria.

We hang with them, if only
as eyewitnesses.

Manuel pays off the cops.

Invites us to live in his
mansion. Hell, ya.

This is fiction,
right?

In Oaxaca,
Manuel, then
thirty-one-years-old,
having lived the previous summer
in Paris at Orson Welles' house, clad in leather
jacket, motions right-hand index & middle fingers across
the high mountain air saying, "Robert, if anyone ever betrays you"
(fingers mimicking scissors) "even once,
cut them out of your life."

Which I've done
many more
than once.

Julia Kristeva, whom I also met recently
& correspond with now & again,
wrote, *Indeed, love knows*
nothing of fiction.

Loved Manuel,
one of my first
mentors, part
of my Harvard
& Yale,
passed away
a few years
ago at age
sixty-five.

Vast,
these juxtapositions
for a kid who had to fight
his way out of Peabody, Massachusetts.
Hello, Sidney Goldfarb.

Don't care about the past, except how it affects
the present
moment.

Until now.

When jotting this
down the two merge.

Past & Present are One.

Within these lines with no borders,
I'm anywhere I want to be, when I'm here
within the Solar Plexus, situated,
(bundle of nerves, distribution
center of the torso) behind
stomach, in front
of aorta & crura
of diaphragm.

I'm here within.

I'm in Braintree.

At our daughter's new apartment with old New England wooden floors.
Far cry from her earlier place: complex with 400 tenants & onsite
building managers, no, I'm here looking out kitchen
window with lace curtains & view of hickory
tree museum/arboretum quality & bottle
of Napa cabernet on the writing table
reading Frédéric Gros on Rimbaud's
meanderings, always broke,
mentions places I've been
at the same age:
Brussels, Paris, London, Genoa, Marseille, & even now, no
kidding, the unnamed deserts of Aden.

It's difficult when you have no money.

I know a great deal about that, which in effect,
has saved my life from all penchants
& addictions, but this wine,
listen, to this wine
my daughter promptly opened upon arrival here
at her new home in Braintree: Napa Angel,
2007:

Exploring the terroirs outside
his native Chile, Aurelio Montes,
after venturing to Argentina
decided to tackle America's
best-known wine region,
the Napa Valley. Aged
in French oak for 10
months, gains hints
of black currents,
red berries &
a touch of
vanilla.

The hickory tree & I are friends.

Gros cites Rimbaud walking to Stuttgart,
where, of course, I'd also been, at twenty,
visiting Mrs. Tauber (& her older sister)
{at my grandmother's request}, who
worked hard there as cook
at the nursing home on
Montebello Road
in Boston just
down from
the Hi Hat
where
Miles
played.

I'm not kidding,
this French philosopher, Gros,
now says that in *1877 Rimbaud left
for Bremen* = Hello, Axel, wherever
you are, I hope
you still are!!

*But ended up in Stockholm
as a ticket collector on
a circus turnstile =*
one of my first
jobs out of 54
& counting, if
someone ever
hires me,
again?

LONDON: "You look suspicious," Marina Abramovic said
to an older couple standing at the side of a room
in the Serpentine Gallery… There is nothing
in the galleries except lockers, where
visitors can put their bags &
electronic devices.

"That is the point,
the public is my
material."

I'm in Indianapolis.

Alone.
At the bar/poolroom
at booth table with a drink,
reading.

Could have been the unnamed man
in **Notes from Underground**
reflecting on his days
at twenty-years-old:

"My chief occupation…
was reading…
I gave myself up to dissipation…
Once, passing a cheap tavern, I saw through
the lighted window some gentlemen fighting with billiard cues,
and one of them was thrown out the window."

Must have given off both air & aura of obvious naïveté
exhibited by Prince Myshkin, coupled with infernal
rage of Raskolnikov, when the blonde Lithuanian
woman asked permission from her husband,
(seething at the bar), to come over to me
& say, "You remind me
of Dostoevsky."

Danger followed me
in those days
like Fate.

Back at the Kitchen performance space in Chelsea, where
Opera Cabal's production of Georg Friederich Haas's
Atthis, based on fragments of Sappho is
a monodrama performed by soprano,
Ariadne Greif, while agonizingly
stripping silver duct tape from
her naked torso.

Ms. Greif, singing, accompanied by eight instrumentalists
from the American Contemporary Music Ensemble,
tears tape from skin, an act symbolizing
the anguished passion of Sappho.
Pain made more than merely
dramatically real.

"I kept thinking," she said,
[while tearing tape from her naked skin]
"I'm in the Marina Abramović school!"

Chance, Time's half-brother, led him
to another area
of music.

Where in Africa
would I be
walking
listening
to Coltrane's *Kulu Sé Mama* alone,
or with Elvin Jones,
Pharoah Sanders,
McCoy Tyner,
(whom we saw
in a tent
on the Mall
with our kids,
for free,
the day before the first Clinton inaugural),
Juno Lewis, who wrote the poem
the tune is based on
playing hand drum
blowing conch shell
& chanting,
Frank Butler on drums & vocal,
both bassists, Jimmy Garrison & Donald Rafael Garret

+ JC!!!

I don't know
the geography,
but the anatomy
is my own, influenced
entirely by ritual atmosphere
with headphones & shades on
in the cellar on the treadmill next to the room
with asbestos flooring we haven't had enough bread
to get rid of properly eyes closed palms overhead shade
hot sun on the path well worn by long-distant ancestors wilderness
long trampled down into the ground by dance & anger rising from lower

depths of crura of diaphragm into chords of throat
reed of sax string of bass originally invented
to drive out evil spirits walk over an hour
starting with *Dusk Dawn* for a change
along with alternate take
what with Time being
just three days
away from
Solstice
at 6:31 A.M.
this Saturday
into *Kulu* or *God Sees Mama*;
Vigil, Kristeva calls a Feminine act,
& Coltrane emphasized as "watchfulness
against elements that might be destructive –
from within or without";

Welcome, with its "peaceful, tranquil, hard-won repose
achieved after struggle"; into
Selflessness,
where the ground
of my imagined Africa merges
with the next-door asbestos flooring
& I am NOTHING
but two feet legs arms astride
Solar Plexus nerve distribution center
located behind stomach in front
of aorta & crura of
diaphragm

silent
for a change turning
all this walking into a return
to alone renewed, emptied.
yet no less curious as to how one
makes this corporeal inner
drive at language
redemptive?

::::

Would that one could cross a river
as nimbly confident as
the Great Blue Heron
we saw ten minutes
ago over the Fore
in Portland.

Chance, [*Trance?*] *Time's half-brother =*

Trane's success,
it seems to me,
is based partly though inadvertently on a sort
of musical hypnosis.
                              —Nat Hentoff

Made a point today, midmorning, of reminding my wife
that Coltrane's grandfather, fire & brimstone minister
of the African Methodist Episcopal Zion Church,
(& with whom young John lived as a kid
in High Point, NC,) was a Blair, just
like our own grandson's other
grandfather, giving her
some added hope
& maybe faith
as Levi's
first
birthday
approaches less than a week away.

By Chance,
I suppose, I chose Coltrane's
Live at Birdland to listen to in order
to walk on the treadmill down cellar next
to the room with asbestos flooring
we can't afford to remove
on a poet's economy
eyes closed shades

43

on-going nowhere
other than
Birmingham,
Alabama,

which latter name
becomes the most monumental
tune on the album with Tyner's left
hand rolling its initial chord like wooden horse-
drawn wagon wheels of caisson carrying bodies of four
young girls blown up by a box of dynamite with Time delay
placed under the steps of 16th Street Baptist Church
on September 15th, 1963.

Less than a month later
Coltrane's in New York City playing
his own quiet tenor, when asked whether
specific tragic events triggered the composition,
answers just as quietly:

"It represents, musically something I saw down there
translated into music from inside me,"

prompting poet, Amiri Baraka, to add on liner notes,
a sentence that has always struck me:

"One of the most baffling things
about America is that despite
its essentially vile
profile,
so much beauty
continues to exist
here."

In the cellar on *Afro-Blue* I saw/heard the music
rise up above a map of Africa like an unnamed bird
I'm unfamiliar with, at the same Time trying to conjure
just how difficult
it is to fathom

the depth
of courage
rose up
out of the struggle racial strife
murderous hatred that was the city
& state Birmingham, Alabama, 1963.

Chance [Change?] *Time's half-brother, led him*
to another area of music. —Cuthbert Ormond Simpkins,

No
money
is a kind
of poetry.

The New York Times, in
print, is a kind of poetry, epic
& tragic, even fashionably dramatic,
but money is not any kind of poetry, although
many of my contemporaries
treat it as if it were
coterminous
with it.

Olson said poets need
take a vow
of poverty.

Poverty is a subject for poetry
for Baudelaire, Pavese, Vallejo…

When I return
to myself
& Coltrane,
Chance leads
me down
in the direction
of the cellar
next to the room

with asbestos
flooring
in order
to walk
quickly
for over
another
hour, this Time
listening to
John Coltrane Live in Paris
with the Quartet
of Jones
Tyner
Garrison,
at *Salle Pleyel* +
two cuts
from the Antibes Jazz Festival
the day before the Paris gig, July 27 & 28, 1965,
respectively.

I walk along alone accompanied by the Quartet,
first on the great, loving *Naima*.
But, what I'm trancing along alone
for with the Quartet, eyes closed, shades
on, is the spectacular *Blue Valse*, third track
after *Impressions* in which I see Pissarro Renoir
Monet painting colors of the wind as Coltrane does
there in the Cote d'Azur in the heat where the audience is
decked out lounging in Bermuda shorts & bikinis the band is
dressed to the Nines sweating in black-tie tuxedos just as the bandleader
demanded.

But *Blue Valse* is something altogether
different, & weighing in at 22 minutes 32 seconds
the longest version of any Coltrane composition I know.

Fact that it's played at *Salle Pleyel* in Paris in 1965 has me there today
with twenty-something daughters at the turn of the millennium
roaming streets, visiting galleries, they take taxis on their

own to gym to work out, nights walk to dance the clubs,
but listening today to *Blue Valse* with its scratches
left over from analog transcription I'm at
Musée d'Orsay, where oldest daughter
21-year-old cannot abide Manet's
Olympia, "Screwed up!" she
responds, maybe objecting
to the black maid, for all
I know, what with her
own half-black skin
she labors to carry,
a skin she says
surprises her
in front of
the mirror,
often.

No, too, I'm enthralled listening here to
Blue Valse, not there in Salzburg
tripping with Mozart, but here
next the room with asbestos
flooring you know
the rest.

::::

First full day of summer leaf shadow against (what
a great word *against* is today!) the back stockade
fence is as deep & real as branch & leaves
themselves. Yesterday on the Solstice
spent in front of wharf poles
on the waterfront listening
to Coltrane's Paris
version
of *Blue Valse*, timing the whole thing from beginning
to end, including perhaps the most brilliant Jazz
bass interlude of all Time = Jimmy Garrison's
(gratitude, I just took ten seconds from

this expression to offer the sky
a long summer's moment
of gratitude for so
much, including
the word
against)
exactly
7:00-
solo
starting at the 8 minute 30 second mark & ending at the cymbal-crushing
tap
by Elvin Jones.

Garrison's Bach-influenced bowing & strumming
thudding percussion high-pitched & low
digging of the bass with fingers & bow
as if he were tearing up & throwing
out an entire roomful of asbestos
poisoned flooring against
all the powers that be
finishing there at
Salle Pleyel
at the 15:30
mark, so

Coltrane could reemerge
challenged by such brilliance
to take off, Man, take the fuck off
into the astro-musical stratosphere hovering
above CHAOTIC SUBLIME…

Now I've heard Coltrane almost all my life
& as my friend Brad would say Coltrane is God, but nothing
compares to this Black Man in Paris returning to the stage
I mean Jazz legend has Garrison's extended solo based
on the fact that Elvin Jones gets pissed at something,
maybe having to wear the tux demanded by
the bandleader, who the Hell knows,
but he's off stage trashing drum

paraphernalia out of a trunk
while Garrison covers
for him with such
incredible
improvisation it brings tears to the eyes
& upon the bandleader's return skyrockets
into that realm I'm telling you has never been
reached will never be reached again *against* such odds
on July 28th 1965 in Paris, France, he wouldn't quit flying up
there in a realm difficult to comprehend
the muscularity of throat & vocal
chords pushing through tenor
sax reaching down
to Solar Plexus
that complex
of nerves
located geographically
that day in Paris & anatomically
behind stomach in front of aorta & crura
of diaphragm Coltrane is God my friend claims
& during this 22 minutes & 32 seconds of *Blue Valse*
on that night in Paris, I too, could
believe it's true.

Nowhere to go from here
except by Chance
to Bach,
when
down
Thames
Street
along the waterfront next to the International Ferry Terminal
I ask her to play track 5,
which turns out to be
{she suddenly reads}:

…the great D-minor Chaconne (or Ciaccona, according to Bach's manuscript):
a massive set of variations on a repeated four-bar ostinato "bass," or ground…
Such an imposing & emotionally weighty fifth movement inevitably draws

attention to the number five… five is the number of Christ's wounds & thus
is linked closely with the idea of suffering & death… newly composed
in the second half of 1720 some commentators have speculated that Bach intended
the Ciaccona to be a tombeau – or musical memorial - for his first wife.

Through broad smiles of joy on the first full day of summer
come tears at this extended lamentation
we see Chance tossing in front of us,
as if it were dice thrown by Mallarmé,
I tell her referring to his grand experiment
in which he spells chance in large caps:
CHANCE

Drops
      the quill
            rhythmical suspending of defeat…

Broad smiles led by CHANCE itself, I tell her
I felt as though my life had recently turned into a poem,
a phenomenon similar to the way
Mallarmé describes it
in a letter to fellow poet Théodore Aubanel
on July 16, 1866:

Never in all my life have I worked so hard as this summer;
in fact I have worked <u>for</u> all my life.

I have laid the foundation for a magnificent work.
Every man has his own special secret.

Many die without having discovered it, & they will not discover it
because, when they are dead, neither they nor their secret will remain.

I died, & I have risen from the dead with the key to the jeweled treasure
of my last spiritual casket… I am working on everything at once; I mean that
everything is so well ordered in me that each sensation is transformed at birth
& simply handed over in a given book or poem. When a poem is ripe, it will fall.

You can see that I am imitating the natural law.

Ten years later he'll write *L'Après-midi d'un Faune*, another thirty
to complete *Un Coup de Dés Jamais N'Abolira Le Hasard*.

:::

Back now from another long walk
reminds me of Olson digging down
so low, writing late in life he favors
the *animate/aboriginal*, touching the
prehistoric, as if that bison etched in
stone, that mountain lion, that black
bear, bird-man, that dancer beyond
Colorado, Gloucester, or Conduché
present the instant ever alive & moving
as ever alive as that hare I saw scurrying
along for better grasses today in summer
redolence, every image & color shimmering
down there where Olson said form was to be
found *in the downward* my animated trek filled
with a wild animate menagerie of objects in
the bright summer wind
coming down

Warm &
Westerly.

O: ...(*man as a man the "stone," and himself as self the tool, chisel, or
whatever, brush if he be silk*)... *-silence, as the thing from which-and against
which-all speech plays, if a man talked steadily his whole life long he'd only
chip at, it is so buried, so much as the earth out of which any stone comes, to be
carved. And so much the fact of rhythm, that, in speech it is silence which is the
interstice, the space, the variants of stress, the thing that we mean when we say
(say Dostoevsky) he gets it all in.*

Summer
comes in filled
with the shimmering
Animate of all things breath
of wind gives added movement to
trees grass flowers fences walls roofs
clouds sun sky, internal images of that bison
etched in stone, mountain lion, black bear, bird-man,
dancer beyond Colorado, or Conduché, or even here, instant
ever alive, an acoustic resonance Susan Howe applies to visual
or written marks she hears, or feels the charge of.
I pick some flowers including peonies
blue flags & chives gone
to bloom.

Suddenly,
Francis Ponge's ***The Making of the Pré*** enters the scene:

recall sending the book to Guy Davenport down in Lexington, KY
for his birthday wondering what year that was sifting through a number
of letters before finding his response written on November 22, 1988
& postmarked the next day on his actual birthdate at sixty-one
so young & wise:

"Bullseye. Meadows
stole my heart years ago,
and still have it. And for the makings
of <u>anything</u>, I'm the ingredients man in a roomful
of people… I haven't had time to study this lovely book;
looking through it, however, promises so much that I long to get
at it.
              A page of Bach as meadow!
                              I wish I'd known
this when writing my 'Meadow' (in the ***JV Steam Balloon***);
I would have worked harder.
                              And the Closerie des Lilas at
the beginning of it (where Ponge was made to remember Rim-
baud's 'harpsichord of the meadow') and where I once spent
an evening with Sam Beckett.

's a grand present."—GD

::::

A grand present?
Such was it ever to open
the mailbox to find a letter
from him, & now returning
to that Time no different finding
him as gracious as a man could be
to a fledgling poet signing a missive
three months earlier in the Greek manner
he loved as much as the Danish approach
to life,

VIII 24 1988:

"I write from a miasma of the world's worst summer
cold... Heat and drought like Hell itself. So don't expect anything.

RIP George Butterick.

Have not written since Denmark? A lovely, good month there.
We've danized ourselves since: reading Nexø, Grundtvig, Brandes,
whichwhat. The weather was indeed beautiful. One rainy day only,
and then we took in "My Life as a Dog" in Swedish, with Danish
subtitles.
            Isak Dinesen's grave at Rungsted (simple granite slab
under majestic beech in a forest).
                              Was allowed to stand at
Kierkegaard's desk. The archivist who showed us around the K
room instructed me (I asked) in the proper pronunciation:
kyear-keh-gore. I never quite got the Søren to his taste. As
with van Gogh, there are no photographs of SK.

        Balthus has read my "Balthus" and liked it. Said I should
be "encouraged". I am encouraged...

Xaipete!   [Always Hello?]

Guy

::::

CHANCE leads
in the direction of a stray
volume hanging around here,
there, everywhere, resurfacing now
& again, renewed twice at the library:
Karol Berger's, **Bach's Cycle, Mozart's Arrow**
wonderful cover of Tiepolo's, *The New World*, 1791,
housed in Ca' Rezzonico, Venice + the book's own humble
subtitle, **An Essay on the Origins of Musical Modernity**.

Try my best to take in nuances of the music, especially the author's
notion of how Bach approaches Time. Berger is clear that a fugue
like the *Well-Tempered Keyboard* combines atemporal, as well
as temporal aspects, but says the atemporal dimension is what
really matters. His language even more definitive addressing
St. Matthew's Passion. The ending chorus's aria fused
into a single phrase makes simultaneous what should
be successive: "abolishing the succession
of past, present, & future, in favor
of simultaneity of the present…
neutralizing the flow of time
in favor of the eternal
Now."

::::

To return to meadow,
or pré, as Ponge would
say, as if to return to the self,
or open field of self, where in *accent
aigu* over the word he sees a bird measuring
the meadow by its flight.

To return to the text
after all these years,
to pages I found
so unique,
profound,
I purchased three copies.
Gave one immediately to Brad
& waited to send another
to Guy close to his
birthday. With
fresh eyes
now I see
that the
book
begins
with
a fragment
of a letter
written to
"Ph. S"
whom
I now
recognize
as Philippe Sollers,
author of the novel **Femmes**,
friend of Barthes & Lacan, & married
to Julia Kristeva, whom I met last October,
& whose own work so influenced my own
over the years, especially her theories
of preverbal *chora* + internal erotic
charges turned language she
calls cathexion.

Took Ponge four years to make/write/compose **The Pré**.
Chagall's *pré* is there in the cold Paris room or studio
on that first day of October 11, 1960 + a speck
of pointillism, azure gray yellow mauve.

Look at this: animals emerge, & as if
chance & inspiration are inseparable
forces, "From this point on my page,
a gallop. The gallop of writing, as
inspiration leads it."

In between, October 11th & the new page
composed on the 12th is an illustration of
sheet music: Johann Sebastian Bach's,
Harpsichord Cadenza.

October 12th, 1960, Paris is the page I love best, & the one I fell upon
prior to tracking down Guy's response to the gift of the book, where
Ponge mentions his beginning progress on the poem to Ph. S.
out there on the terrace of Closerie des Lilas, & Sollers utters
Rimbaud's phrase from **Illuminations'**, "Soir historique,"
la main d'un maître anime le clavecin des prés / harpsichord
of the *prés…*

The poet tells his companion to <u>*be quiet*</u>.

::::

Guy Davenport saved my life
between the first year I wrote
to him in 1987 & for the next
sixteen years we corresponded:

"I talked to Hallam Movius on
the phone one Sunday morning
when I was writing 'Prehistoric
Eyes'. Marshack had given me
his number and said I should
talk to him…

…

I'm into insects again. Swarming.
Mating rituals. There's one little
bug that gives his wife a fig seed
and takes advantage of her while
she's eating it. No insects, no
oxygen. We don't have that
importance. Let Kierkegaard
put that in his pipe…"

"…to counteract making a study of
Mies van der Rohe, as I don't
think I really like the modern
in architecture. Rietveld, OK,
but what after? Modern houses
have spirit but not character.
And spirit needs character for
a ground, jo? A roof is a hat.
Hat is rank, prestige, role.
A flat roof is an abnegation
of responsibility; besides, they
leak." 29 April 1988

Guy Davenport needn't have told me
about where he met Beckett.
Knew Guy's **Geography
of the Imagination**
forward & backward
before making the outreach
back there in '87, backward & forward,
where in the final essay on Max Ernst, whose
retrospective I sought out at the Guggenheim in '75,
Guy sees *modernity in terms of its discovery of the specific.*
                          "Things," Proust said, "are gods."
Guy saw: *my best hope of a sustained reality
would be one like Max Ernst's world,
which is always
of verifiably
real things…
not… where
they are supposed to be…*

Max Ernst, who like Joyce, discovered that quotation
can be eloquent beyond its original statement,
and can release meanings
concealed in the original.

Guy compares gathering the montage of specifics
in his writing to the foraging of the Dogon in Mali.

For his piece, "Au Tombeau de Charles Fourier,"
the author says he needed seven elements
of what he termed *involucra,*
which had to include
something said
in conversation
about Joyce
by Beckett.
…this poignancy belonged to the pattern
I was making and not to autobiography.

So now, the recollection & confirmation of his claim
in that early letter, *…for the makings of <u>anything</u>,*
I'm the ingredients man in a roomful of people…:

Thus, Beckett to Davenport on Joyce
at the East-Side Terrace of Closerie des Lilas
(in chairs once occupied by Apollinaire, Joyce, Picasso, Jarry, Braque)…

::::

The brandnewness of a summer's day might include certain tactile
memories of similar hours in childhood adolescence young adulthood
middle age maturity, yesterday, when I took Rimbaud with me
downtown, & certainly an immense amount of Now. Huge & Light &
Timeless.
Filled with Light & Shadow weighing heavily on senses, while
Solar Plexus distributes all the nerves of internal corporeal
goings on & on one is mostly unaware of except on any
season's day may include a certain tactile memory

of similar hours of childhood
adolescence young adulthood middle
age maturity, or a yesterday in Paris or Portland,
when I took Rimbaud downtown, not to scold him
like his old lady constantly, nor up to the attic
like the idiotic father of Anaïs Nin
who begged him not to spank her
on her bare bottom out of earshot
of her mother, who would have
intervened, no, & certainly
an immense amount
of Now, Huge & Light
& Timeless.

I have held the summer dawn in my arms. —Arthur Rimbaud

Timeless?
Yes.

Put it this way: when I walked into town with the Poilâne bag
we got in 2000 at 8 Rue du Cherche-Midi, Paris, France,
I carried that drawing…

Wait a minute now, Times silence is worth the word =
I have heard the echo of the silence
of the dead.

(There's a moment round the 14-minute mark
in Bach's *Ciaccona*, when lamentation
is so pronounced, harking/echoing
back to the Silences at both
halfway point &
dénouement,
that it brought up from the Solar Plexus,
rather than cerebrum, Benjamin's
Trauerspeil, or mourning play:
A tragic death is an ironic
immortality…)

the drawing Rimbaud sent to Ernest Delahaye in May 1873 from Roche.

May, the month exactly two years earlier, when he sent
the more famous *Lettres de Voyant* to Paul Demeny,
Georges Izambard. I like both letters immensely.

The current letter, May 1873, alludes to his
Pagan Book, his **Black Book**, which will
become his self-published ***A Season in Hell***,
he'll not have enough money to pay for.

It's this poverty intrigues me
as motivation &
foundation to
writing
poetry.

Poverty &
poetry. Poetry
& poverty.

Never
made
more
than
29
grand
a year.

Rimbaud
can't send
his first three
stories from the
manuscript, quoting
a constant phrase from
his mother, *"It costs too much!"*

Can you imagine the current value
of the first three stories sent from Rimbaud,
not sent?

My fate depends upon this book...

Damn,
I met Rimbaud
a couple of times.

Once on rue Monsieur-le-Prince, Paris.
The other in a dream, both hallucinatory,
as he demanded the poet get to via derangement
of the senses. Seriously, what another great teacher
like all the others who <u>RARELY</u> ENTERED A CLASSROOM
= Whitman, Pound, Williams, Kerouac, Ginsberg, Baudelaire, listen
to the SEER = "Baudelaire is the first seer, king of poets, a real god!
[May 15, 1871, Rimbaud to Demeny from his mother's home in
Charleville

= I have decided to give you an hour of new literature... —Here is some
prose on the future of poetry—...
...I is someone else.
If brass wakes up
a trumpet, it's
not its fault."

I saw Miles in 1969, front row,
Lennie's on the Turnpike in Peabody,
Massachusetts, on stage & at the bar where
his whiskey matched the color of his trumpet,
& his anger came damn well close to Rimbaud's
& my own:

"If old imbeciles [they fill classrooms] had not discovered
only the false meaning of the Ego, we would not have to sweep
away those millions of skeletons, which, for time immemorial!
have accumulated the results of their one-eyed intellects by claiming
to be authors."

So, out of Venice Radio over airwaves & ocean waves
comes Robert De Visée's, *Entrée d'Apollon,* =

Rimbaud, "I am present at the birth of my
thought: I watch it and listen to it: I draw
a stroke of the bow: the symphony
makes its stir in the depths, or
comes on stage
in a leap."

Followed by Carl Philipp
Emmanuelle Bach's *Sonata for
Flauto & Clavicebalo* & Johanne's
Concerto Brandenberghese in Sol.
Hell & Heaven, I'm suddenly in East
Berlin, again, where atop the towering ruin
of the Brandenberg Gate a small tree grows.

"...the poet is truly the thief of fire," As I steal this from him,
he'd gladly approve, as he did in the dream, listen =

GIVING RIMBAUD A LIFT (MAY 24, 2007)

I.

He arrived after midnight from a forgotten photograph, or one never
taken, a composite of those seen throughout years of reading: Rimbaud,
black, charred. Didn't recognize him in the dream, fearing an arsonist
ready to spread accelerant on the floor, light it with spark, or word. Twice
he approached in African guise. Had I known it was him I wouldn't have
yelled in terror, but in my recoil, the dread of being burned alive, my wife
had to shake me out of this potential Hell.

II.

I believe it was Rimbaud. In the morning I looked up his death date to see if that were the occasion for his ritual visit, knowing full well the day of his birth. If that weren't it, what about the worse fate: amputation? That's it! Three days from this calendar date well over a century ago two doctors & two interns with knives & a bow saw lopped off his right leg thigh-high. No writing equals that cut. Rimbaud in the dream, no mask. Arrived in the port of Marseille on the twentieth of a merciless May, 1891, gangrenous leg incinerated exactly one week later.

III.

Of course many people will doubt this claim, "Why would Rimbaud visit him?" For years I've imagined such possibility, hoping for cordial handshake on rue Monsieur-le-Prince late at night, half-deranged, hallucinogenic with his ghost. But no, he shows up the incendiary, criminal invalid! Rimbaud still needs help. When I told my wife about meeting him, & the reason for the scream from which she woke me, she said she'd been dreaming, too, that I was driving with my foot. Driving the car with my foot on the steering wheel!!

:::::

He goes on in one of the *Lettres des Voyant* sounding so much like Olson,
you know where the latter says, "…the downward is the place
where form is
to be found…"

Rimbaud =, "The poet… is responsible
for humanity, even for the animals; he will
have to have his inventions smelt, felt, and heard;
if what he brings back from *down there* has form, he gives form;
if it is formless he gives formlessness. A language must be found."

So glad that Marilyn Crispell
put my poem, "Sound of the Downward"
to music. I wish you could hear her:

Hi Robert-

I got a disc made for you (and one for me) today by my engineer friend - will send it to you in the next days along with a copy of the score. I dedicated the piece ("for Pessa Malka") to a relative of mine (and her family) who were killed at Sobibor (I just found out about it a few years ago) - Thank you for the inspiration of the poem - Much love, Marilyn

Sound of the Downward

I) slow, freely

1)

2)

Play line 1, line 2   Play Retrograde line 2, line 1

Inversion

3)

4)

Play line 3, line 4

#) Forte Hold pedal down

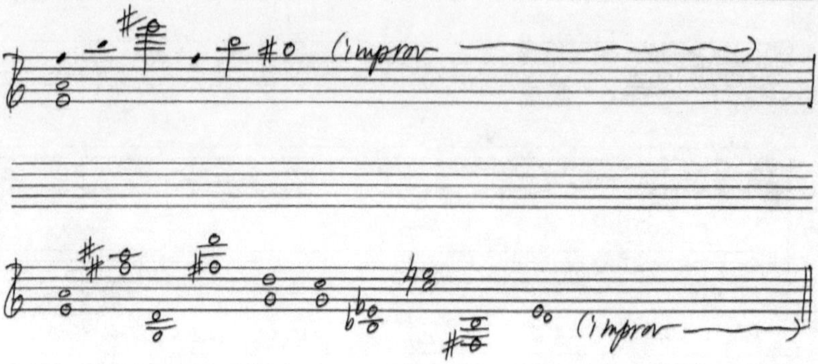
(improv)
(improv)

Electronics: Ingrid Lee Engineer: Adam Adhiyatma

For Robert, Love, Marilyn

11/2013 (for Pessa Malka Amber-Strosz)

SOUND OF THE DOWNWARD

...the downward is where form is
to be found... —Charles Olson

I.
Driven forward in life,
back in memory.
The river one dives into, eyes open,
where water moves,
stones remain still.

Desire & loss
in realms of dream & real worlds, together,
in a dance above the grave.

If only silence could climb to a whisper...

II.
Praise the anonymous dead.

The shame
to be without names.

Bending down,
our eyes
in awe.

III.
Haunted by the image of the river below a stand of trees
walked through to sleep by the riverbank
reminded me of one day,
felt like a dream,
when Heaven & Death shot past faster than language...

& later, music filtered down
through an actual dream in the form of a solo instrument,
& the one word
dream libretto
echoed:

Dachau..........

IV.
Begin again, as if in a new world, vivid, confident, knowing, free.
But not deathless.
Death's underlying presence
from the get-go
to the end
linking desire & loss
to the possibility of the new world,
named & unashamed.

V.
Geography of Bach, unseen, but heard
in the bells
of a distant church.

Death of Celan.
{Scream of Erinyes... Trees, alternately, furying & unburying
the silences.}

Returned redeemed, an eternal spar
thrust upward toward the sky
from depths of the Seine.

VI.
Shades of nothingness,
overheard...

VII.
Black sky, grey trees. Grey sky,
black trees. What is it one sees
during moments of one's life?

VIII.
Memory to the point of haunting.
A woodcut by Anselm Kiefer *Untitled (The Rhine)*, where the river is
an undercurrent & dark reflection.

Explored the nave & stained glass
of the cathedral at Köln,
then walked through its sculpted portal through columns of trees
to sleep under stars visible & invisible.
Named & unnamed.

The architecture pictured in his woodcut
is not Köln Cathedral, but symbolic of structures erected to the Time
that contributed to the shame
of no names.

IX.
Sustained, extended refrain: If only silence could climb to a whisper… to
say
what it has to say...

X.
Sound of the downward,
brought up.

::::

Rimbaud: "Poetry will not lend its rhythm
to action, it *will be in advance.*
These poets exist. When
the endless servitude of

woman is broken, when
she lives for and by
herself, man –
heretofore
abominable –
having given her her
release, she too will be a poet!
Woman will find some of the unknown!
Will her world of ideas differ from ours?
[Hello, Julia Kristeva, there in Paris discovering
the Unknown!] She will find strange, unfathomable,
repulsive, delicious things; we will take them, we will
understand them."

I poor terrified one who for seven months have not had a single copper!

::::

From out of the blue a new terrain
shoved through the letter slot
by the mailman.
It's a postcard view
of Kardamyli, Greece,
where Chris Ziagos thought
enough to share his experience there:
swimming in the Bay, hiking in the hills,
downing wine & ouzo.
He even wonders
what day it is,
Saturday?

That's the way to travel.
Sit at a café, write home
to someone you know will
appreciate the venue, at least
vicariously. Adds that "Mycenae
is amazing!" [Love that pun!]

...

One day
I go into town
for a bottle of gin
at Sweetgrass Farm
tasting room at the corner
of Pearl & Fore Streets, walk
down Gold & call Geoff & Angelina
from a bench on Silver across from Northpoint.

They suggest we get a drink. Mention happy hour at
Petite Jacqueline. They offer to pick me up, but I say
I'm writing a long poem on walking, so I'll see
them there. "Did you get my email suggesting
we meet for a drink downtown, Bob?"
"No. I guess CHANCE sent me
in your direction."

Next day I'm thinking of heading the same way
as the day before, bearing left
on Woodford, however,
a sign reminds me
of Friends
of Portland Public Library
book sale at the Catholic girls
high school down Stevens Ave
to the right. Members' preview on
Thursday night, so a day & a half later,
don't expect much, but get 10 books for
10 bucks. What I'm totally knocked
out by are 2 vintage pieces
of sheet music
published by *Propriete de l'Editeur Moscou chez A. Gutheil*,
13 Preludes pour Piano par S. Rachmaninow. Op. 32 Complet
[date unknown] numbers 5 + 12
of the original 13.

Specifically, ask the woman who priced them what she charged
for the Rachmaninow = [she originally patted her heart
when she saw it, miming the words, *I love him.*]

& said, "Nothing. I gave them to you.
I don't know whether they're worth
a quarter, or fifty cents, or
a hundred & fifty dollars."

Thanked her profusely.

Packed the other ten books in my black canvas bag, carried sheet music
barehanded along Stevens Ave next the long wrought-iron fence
of the convent, glad no one could see me,
weeping tears of joy to the unheard
music inside the pages.

Just so happen to have a stray manuscript titled,
Rachmaninov's Last Concert in Boston,
the event witnessed by Mrs. Wright,
[from the high rise, where I was
doorman], then a student
at the Conservatory,
claiming she sat
in the front row,
paid a dollar.

::::
::::

Terrain itself contributed to her epiphany.
Took our 2nd Bloody Mary down to the edge
of Crescent Beach in Cape Elizabeth, where
the path led to a stand of ancient windswept
pines, trunks hard as iron, while a bit further
on she spotted the doe right-front leg held
mid-step in the air sizing us up, then moved
on in silence, but turning head back toward
Kathleen through foliage couple more times
before disappearing, but her visage, the doe's,
will remain fixed as part of her resolve, along

with the old pine tree propped up by younger
oak entwining its own limbs as sun & sky allowed.

Her epiphany has something to do with motherhood,
the deer, the tree, & the freedom she found down
there at the edge of the beach at the cross of the path
on a rare Monday off from work.

Saw the snake slither from sun to shade of grass.

She heard it.

She was quick to tell me, I'd reached out
to her in the early morning indoor July air
in bed, she dreamt of buying me a new pair
of skis for Christmas, it being November in
her night world, she looked for a card at the
Dollar Store, but all they had were birthdays.
She knew my October date passed, but purchased
one with a baby on the cover, the inside saying,
"Let's keep trying!!"

Loving,
generous,
erotic.

One of the ten books for a buck struck gently
at the Soul, what with so few
books of poetry,
one-third of
a table
compared to hundreds
in the girl's gymnasium fiction.

In fact, the dowager I first asked about a section
on poetry was sure they had some, yet had trouble
locating that third next grammar books & dictionaries = there,
much to my delight: *A Poet's Journal: Days of 1945-1951*
by George Seferis, from which, many Julys ago

I took note of an exchange between the poet
& a fisherman (often a mythological
encounter) & wrote:

How Far Back does Desire Reach?

Onshore wind producing excavating waves revealing stones unseen for
years. Desire & light. Ancient desire. Desire reaching back to the oldest
image of boats on Aegean seals: high prow forging over spiraled water,
low stern, keel projecting beyond. Square sail. Vessels capable of voyages
from the Cyclades or Crete to Syria & Egypt. A world washed in new light.
From the beginning I wanted to turn the object of my desire (my wife),
into the image of a small boat. Lacking technical skills, but not desire.
How far back does desire reach? Desire born of the marriage of Night &
Day. Not excessive desire, which kills desire. The image of a small boat,
her ribs into those of a canoe, say. Then one morning in 1946, the year
I was born, George Seferis, after chopping wood, swimming, watched a
fisherman pass, who offered fish from his boat he called a *kourita*. He was
from Asia Minor. The boat originated in Smyrna. The beautiful old wood,
the carving on prow & stern recalling icons from the past. He observed
this boat with much joy. Poem of desire. A small boat, her ribs. This image
based on the sculpted stone *kourai*, whose sail is the carved *chiton* lifting
her body. The sailor riding the image of the memory of the woman until he
returns to the real thing. Ultimately reminding one of the other stone boat:
the foundation plinth for Nike of Samothrace at the top of the staircase in
the Louvre!

::::

In Paris, at the Théâtre de la Ville, at the beginning of the performance
of Pina Bausch's "Palermo Palermo," an almost-pure-dance
piece she was to create in the years before her death
in 2009, unlike the darker theatre-based "Viktor,"
based on a sojourn to Rome, nothing happens
for twenty seconds, then a resounding crash,
when the large brick wall falls to rubble.

Immediately, the tall, blond,
Julie Shanahan, crawls out

of the dust & stands in
high-heels, saying,
"Hold me! Kiss me!"
as two men
respond in kind,
"Throw tomatoes at me!" (Palermo, after all!)
"Harder! In my face!" Dancers throw trash on the floor.
A woman kicks a man violently. The atmosphere is somber
& the mood filled with suffering.

A nearly catatonic woman seems
to urinate from a bottle of water
onto the stage floor.

However, by the end of three hours
trees full of pink petals are lowered
to the stage. Beauty, hope, love;
all possible, it's Palermo after
all! [—Roslyn Sulcas]

::::

Another book among the ten
WITHDRAWN
July 6, 1977
from Portland Public Library: modern version
of **Canterbury Tales**, & look, again, how Poverty
fares in *The Tale of the Wife of Bath*:

"The poor man, when he walks
along the way, / Before the robbers can sing & play… / a stimulant to
busyness; / A great improver, too… / poverty's an eye-glass… /
Through which a man his loyal friends may see."

With the image of Kardamyli, Greece, Aegean Sea in foreground,
mountain there beyond orange roofs of town, I want to give
the sender, Chris Ziagos, a copy of one of these ten books
for ten dollars from the Friends of Portland Public

Library: Lawrence Durrell's, *The Greek Islands*.
Beforehand, randomly turn to:

"Poet & wayfarer alike have always appreciated Cos for its green
abundance & quiet."

Snakes that are not venomous
(which is true of those on
Crete) are easy
to play with.

Look, here, Durrell is generous enough to quote Nikos Kazantzakis:

"This Cretan landscape seemed to him like good prose;
well-fashioned, economical, shorn of excessive riches,
powerful & controlled… It said what it had to say
with manly austerity. But between its austere
lines you could discern an unexpected
sensitivity & tenderness –
the lemons & oranges
smelt sweet in
sheltered hollows,
& beyond
from the boundless sea,
came an endless stream of poetry."

Kathleen doesn't need remind me that back in college she proofread
the manuscript for translator, Michael Antonakes,
Kazantzakis's, *Russia: A Chronicle*
of Three Journeys in the Aftermath
of the Revolution.

::::

I'm in Split,
then still part
of Communist
Yugoslavia.

Want to rent an apartment, chronicle
my own journey thus far: London, Dover,
Calais, Arras, Brussels, Rotterdam, Den Haag,
Amsterdam, Bremen, Hamburg, København, Helsingør,
Berlin, Munich, Stuttgart, Salzburg via train to Rijeka, & now
just off the $5 overnight mailboat, where we slept on deck under panoply
of Adriatic stars.

Instead, we move on
to Belgrade by bus, where
I'll write a long Rimbaudian letter
back home to mother abandoning literature
for what I imagine at the Time, Forever, then
fly to Venice.

I dig Proust.
If I understand
them, contemporary
French philologists & philosophers,
theorize the real as nothing other than pain.

In that way, the sign for the real, what is it, R,
or Emptiness itself? becomes a calling to arms,
as Guy Davenport once wrote about them in a letter,
that they write, including Lyotard, perhaps his most egregious
example, not only about nothing, but nothing, so in defense I would
say that to have found the subject <u>nothing</u> means a great deal & doesn't
diminish the writing of it. Zero, on the other hand, as Barthes would have
us
believe is far more than nothing, not any minus
or negative, but a positive force
in the Universe.

As if it were
the default
to Death
itself?

Not the best line regarding the city,

just stumbled upon *centuries of rubbish piled in Split...*
in William Bronk's, **The World, The Worldless**, at 3:00 a.m. July 3rd, 2014.

But rather here, that: *Grace lies in the way life takes its will with ruins...*

Sun also unexpected this morning out bay window in kitchen,
but welcome, what with newly formed Hurricane Arthur
tossing threatening remnants up & down the Atlantic
coast most of yesterday, & forecast for the rest
of the Independence Day weekend.

Freedom, no doubt, must be
fought for one way or
another. Hate parades
& fireworks!!

Today, am in touch with that central
nerve distribution center, the Solar Plexus,
located in thorax like Grand Central or Union
Station or even Gare de l'Est, Paris to Reims, when
the Fourth of July seems to mean more there in France
than here in terms of finding & savoring real Freedom.

Solar Plexus located
behind stomach, in front
of aorta & crura of the still
resonating diaphragm.

I'm walking down the unknown
road, unnamed/mundane road for the sole
purpose of purchasing a bottle of *Agua de Piedre*
Malbec from Argentina at the local corner store, when
this image enters the cerebral cortex, now, granted, I'd walked
for forty minutes on treadmill, punched punching bag for three
three-minute rounds, & dreamt the night before of two birds
with golden feathers piercing their beaks into letter slots
looking for mail, then turning into two women.

Before turning into two women, I asked
Ed Conway, who used to punt
on the football team,
"Ed, what kind
of birds are
those?"

& the word
resounding
somewhat
like the flightless
cassowary
echoed around
the dream,
but when
the two women
emerged someone
said they were ugly,
& granted, one had purple
scales on her face, but I objected
to that term, that designation, believing
no woman is ugly.

So, on the Fourth of July I'm walking down the unknown road,
unnamed/mundane road for the sole purpose of purchasing
a bottle of *Agua de Piedre* Malbec from Argentina
at the corner store, when this image enters
the cerebral cortex, now granted,
I'd walked for forty minutes
on treadmill, punched
punching bag for
three three-
minute
rounds,
& dreamt
the night before of two birds,
but here's Marcel Duchamp inside my head,
mid-morning, noon, in fact, smiling without cracking it,
working secretly on *Étant donnés* (*Given: 1. The Waterfall,*

2. *The Illuminating Gas*) in the last years of life, smiling,
but unsmiling underneath the unbroken smile,
giving us the secret
of the Feminine.

Look, peep, if you will,
how this image of Marcel now
smiling, but unsmiling underneath
the unbroken smile, giving us the secret
of the Feminine entered the cerebral cortex.

Now granted, I'd walked on the treadmill, punched
punching bag, & dreamt the night before of two birds,
become two women someone said were ugly, & granted, one
had purple scales on her face, but I objected to that, believing no
woman is ugly.

I'm either here
or in DC or driving
down 295 to work at L. L. Bean in order
to sew monograms of kids' names on backpacks, or
dogs' names on blankets, at 57-years-old, along with women
even older & doing a HELL of a lot better job than I, quicker & finer
on the machine, which is, in fact, so much like a treadmill
with its buttons & contraptions, except you better be in
front of that sewing machine before 6:00 in the morning, logged in,
or else,
just as it was at the meat factory in Lynn, MA, so long ago
still resonates, still,
resonates, dig?

You? You ever worked in a meat factory
with undocumented Greeks, who dare
not make a peep, or leather
with similar silent
Puerto Ricans?

Is this the subject
of Poetry, Academics
who never did, nor ever would
work in meat nor leather nor sew
kids' & dogs' monograms will ask?

I'm in D.C.
scoping out
lay of land on
the first day from atop
Washington Monument
with view of Ellipse, which
during Lincoln's Time was stockyard,
or walking down Constitution Ave. on lunch
hour from National Gallery of Art Library past FBI,
or on way back to work, Archives,
where friend, David Ferriero,
now presides.

Skeptical of everything.

Cynical of nothing.

Still in D.C.

Get this package
in the mail today
from Peter Anastas
in Gloucester, MA,
with the EXACT contents,
gift of a slender book sending
me back to the first month we're
in D.C., where I'm at a desk at The Library
of Congress requesting, among other things,
one of the few books by Charles Olson I'd never
even seen before = **New Man & Woman**, which

<u>call-slip</u>

I recently found among papers thanks to Bill Heyen
suggesting that I organize 40-years-worth for possible
acquisition by the Beinecke at Yale:

<u>call slip dated: 9/11/1990</u>

New Man & Woman marked **X** on slip =

<u>Not on shelf</u>.

Talk about initial
disappointments!

Damn,
Library of Congress
staff can't LOCATE the book
I want to examine in the first month
of four long years of my extended apprenticeship there!!

Where the Hell am I then?
What environment,
geography, locale?

It's a swamp.

Just ask Gill Scott-Heron:

"Symbols of democracy, pinned up against the coast
Outhouse of bureaucracy, surrounded by a moat
Citizens of poverty are barely out of sight
Overlords escape in the evening with people of the night
Morning brings the tourists, peering eyes and rubbernecks
To catch a glimpse of the cowboy making the world a nervous wreck
It's a mass of irony for all the world to see
It's the nation's capital, it's Washington D.C...
                    Punishment is capital in Washington D.C."

Survived that PLACE,
that swamp.

Peter's gift, the book with wings, is a gift, a godsend,
something David C. Driskell, who knew Langston
in Washington, would call Divine Intervention.

There's a mourning dove in the distance
with that low treble sound of a *deus ex machina*
warming up at about the same Time I say to her,

"Let's not be distanted."

::::

July 2, 2014
Dear Ben,

I'm interested in whether I can extract something, methodologically
speaking, from your quote by Deleuze:

"The more our daily life appears standardized, stereotyped and subject
to an accelerated reproduction of objects of consumption, the more art
must be injected into it in order to extract from it that little difference
which plays simultaneously between other levels of repetition"

It's that phrase "between other levels of repetition…" that interested me,
& it stayed with me initially as "interruption of repetition…"
would that be sound?

I'm also interested in Walter Benjamin's two essays on *Trauerspeil*, which
first one ends with "The nature of repetition in time is such that no
unified form can be based on it… The mourning play… is inherently non
unified drama… the mourning play represents the transition from
dramatic time to musical time."

I am interested, in some ways I guess, in what Baudelaire heard
as he strolled on the outskirts of Paris = the Lamentation of the World.

Wondering if I should be listening for the "interruptions…"

July 3, 2014
Dear Robert,

If it's interruptions, it's perhaps not in the sense of a blocking or stopping; more (I guess) as a disruption, an alteration. That fits with the irregular-rhythmic musical time of the mourning play.

The extrapolation from Deleuze is that when industrial production can start
introducing something that seems like difference through repetition -consumer specification, -your name on a coke can, your own colour combination of trainers - art becomes even more important because of the non-profitable, unpredictable, challenging (threatening) sensations it creates. Deleuze says on the same page,

"Art [...] discovers underneath consumption a schizophrenic clattering of the jaws, and underneath the most ignoble destructions of war, still more processes on consumption." Then, over the page (366) talking about what art can do, with reference to cinema,

"the novelistic manner in which little modifications are torn from the brute and mechanical repetitions of habit, which in turn nourish repetitions of memory and ultimately lead to repetitions in which life and death are in play [...]"

The examples are Butor's *La modification* and *Last Year at Marienbad*). My friend Aliaga talks about the "tombola without any prizes" in analogy to his writing of poetry...

All best to you,
Ben

Mourning dove continues to resound
in distanted
distance.

::::

Stopped by RSVP to thank wine guy, Chris Ziagos,
whose sent postcard from Greece arrived
the day before yesterday,
telling him it immediately went into the long poem
I'm working on. He goes on about the history of Mani peninsula,
Spartans, & wars against Turks, trying to describe the geography
on the back of his hands, & widespread five fingers.

I said,"Ya, I tried
to get an Atlas
from Bowdoin,
just for that purpose,
but they're all in Reference."

He said, "I have an extra one,
I'll give it to you. A friend gave it to me,
& I have one just like it."

Told him I told the reference librarian
I'd have to pick one up at a used bookstore.
Chris is bringing it into work tomorrow.

::::

Next day, Chris returns to his office, once I arrive with the Durrell in
hand,
in order to retrieve the massive **Atlas of the World**,
National Geographic Society,
Washington, D.C., 1981,
close to 400 pages,
reminding me
right this
second

of bumping into my old school chum
from grad school, Alphonse Vinh, on Dupont Circle

as he strolled out for his lunch hour as reference librarian
at National Geographic headquarters,
& how we had such a grand afternoon
at the wine bar/bookstore on Connecticut Ave,
talking books & poetry, along with his desire to become
a Southern Writer, of all things.

Wishing him luck in whatever his undertakings, that was the last
I ever saw of Alphonse, much to my own chagrin,
as they say.

But hold on for a second,
I don't want to leave Alphonse
behind just like that. I'd written earlier
about that chance meeting, & come to think
of it, it had to do with the gift of another volume
documented in this prose poem & translated
into Danish by Bent Sørensen in our bilingual
book, *Jagged Timeline*:

HANDED DOWN

The new book of calligraphy & scroll painting from the Yuan Period in
the 14th century may well have fallen into my hands because of that other
massive tome of collected Haiku printed in Tokyo at the turn of the last
century, which I gave to Alphonse Vinh upon his second utterance of awe
& admiration for it. It wasn't difficult to let go of that way, knowing he'd
appreciate it even more than I, what with his father professor of physics,
as well as poet in Saigon before the war, & pilot during the debacle.
Alphonse, Yale for two years before the family couldn't afford it, then
Michigan, where his father taught. We bumped into one another in DC
once after grad school in Boston, spending an afternoon at the wine bar up
past Dupont Circle. The literati of the Yuan painted the scroll, then added
calligraphic inscriptions amounting to the lovely, bitter tandem of stroke
& lettering I'm beginning to envision attached to my daily landscape view,

where roots & straws & vines drawn across rock faces begin to speak in choral harmony, a nostalgia I quickly deny, penetrating further the literal facts of geologic strata giving nutrient to root, weed, grass, flower complex variegation. *Then listen, again.* The entire enterprise could be taught & handed down. Wang Meng depicted scholars, legs folded, talking quietly in a circle at the entrance to a cave in *The Orchard Chamber*, another figure at a distance walking toward them balancing a tray of wine cups. It's not the same as two barstools on Connecticut Avenue in DC, but Alphonse & I ought to start a school.

::::

First thing I do with the Atlas
with its intimations of the weight
of the World reminding me of the mythological
character, who held sturdy the celestial sphere: crack
it open to the Mani peninsula, where sure enough on the map
I can make out a similar topography jutting into the sea Chris Ziagos
used his hands to formulate,
when initially attempting
to portray the rugged,
Spartan landscape.

::::

At Trader Joe's waited in John's line, who
has all my books, just to wish him a Good Fourth.
When asked what Kathleen & I were doing tomorrow,
replied, "Staying close to home,
off the roads."

To which the Black Woman
in the turned-up felt-green
hat behind me said,
"& pray."
Turned toward her saying,
"Did you say Pray?"
"Yes," came the muddled answer
out of a mouth with one top tooth,

none below,
or vice-versa.

I said, "That's just what I'll be doing at some point tomorrow, "

& she said, "Yes, in the shower."

I said, "You're pretty perceptive, that's exactly one place I pray."

"Don't forget to chant."

I asked her her name,

"Red."

"Did you say it was Red?"

"Yes, it's really Scarlett, but people call me Red."

I said, "I love the name Scarlett, & Red, too!! Have a Grand Fourth
tomorrow!!"

::::

Blue chickweed flowers under blue sky
& white clouds, so animate
at the corner of India
Street & Fore.

Resonant?
May I hear the music
of the flowers, their green stalks?

WCWilliams' asphodels?
Resonating?

Zukofsky interrupts: *An animate still-life – night.*

...

Writing to Bill Heyen reasons for aversion to my own handwriting
(prefer to hit the keyboard) reminds me of Rimbaud saying
he'd never own his own hands.

Kathleen takes Time on the holiday to read aloud
from *James Baldwin's Turkish Decade:*
Erotics of Exile
by Magdalena J. Zaborowski:

"What Turkey could teach America, he insisted idealistically, was 'a kind
of sense of other people & how to deal with other people' that it learned
after having ceased to be an empire, a sense
that the United States could not yet
attain, bent as it was on
building its own.'"

"A survivor of the ghetto & of police brutality in Harlem, young Jimmy grew
up vulnerable not only because of his skin color but because of his sissy looks,
a way of walking with a definite 'switch' that was caused
by scoliosis, & sexuality that he never hid."

"I... know, in my own flesh...
in the scars borne by many of those dearest
to me, the thunder and fire of the billy club, the paralyzing
shock of spittle in the face; and I know what it is to find oneself
blinded, on one's hands and knees, at the bottom of a flight of steps
down which one has just been hurled."

::::

The day after the day after the Fourth, & I'm still seeking
& experiencing Freedom
in the sense of
resonance
& animation
of EVERYTHING:
stones, their polytopes,

inchoate, innate, or expressive lines
Olson would call them; the air
the very air itself winding around
corners down streets across
ocean waves;
that fish
cloud
swimming across the very sky;
& earth come up to meet my every step.

Clouds kissing, wanderlust...

We get in out of the daylight for a quick tasting at Shipyard Brewery, &
who
does Fred introduce me to at the bar, but Jesus himself from Chihuahua,
Mexico, & we hit it off immediately, even forget about the beer,
just talk.

He works for a nonprofit in Boston, wears two hearing aids,
knew Stanley Jasspon Kunitz
past his hundredth birthday.

I let him know my life
has recently turned into a poem
& he goes, "I know, I saw that in the way
you entered the door, the walk, the linen jacket,
the [blackthorn Irish] Shillelagh
(believe me,
there was no swagger,
just a sense of resonance & animation
at the core of Solar Plexus, central nerves
located & vibrating behind stomach in front
of aorta & crura of diaphragm)
that during my three months
in Mexico in 1974, I met
the poet Ali Chumacero
at his home,

& who when Googling his name just now, one day *after* alluding to him
in conversation with Jesus, (you know, pronounced the Mexican way,
Hāsoos),
shocked to find this announcement of his death
the day *before* uttering his name:

Latin American Herald
Caracas, Monday [today!]
July 7, 2014

Mexico City – Mexican poet & editor Ali Chumacero Lora died of natural
causes in Mexico City, the National Arts & Culture Council, or Conaculta
said on Saturday. He was 92. {Kathleen corrected this as 95}

Conaculta in a communiqué lamented the death of the poet, born in the
town of Acopaneta in Nayarit state on July 9, 1918, who "dedicated his life
to his love of poetry & books with generosity & devotion."

A wake will be held Saturday for the writer at the Gayosso Funeral Home
on Calle Sullivan in the San Rafael neighborhood, Conculta officials said.

Later, the organization will gather to offer a group tribute, the president of
Conaculta, Consueloa Salzar, said on her Twitter account.

His poetic work comprises three books: "Paramo de Sueños" (*Plateau
of Dreams*), "Imagenes Desterradas" (*Images in Exile*) and "Palabras en
Reposo" (*Words at Rest*), which were published between 1944 and 1956.

He also published a book of essays entitled "Los Momentos Criticos"
(*Critical Moments*) in 1987, and in 1997 he produced the CD "En la
Orilla del Silencio y Otros Poemas" (*On the Edge of Silence and Other
Poems*) recited by the author.

The late Mexican Nobel laureate in literature, Octavio Paz, considered Ali
Chumacero "the magician and teacher of Mexico's modern poets."

Among the honors he received were the 1984 Xavier Villarrutia Prize
for Literature, the 1986 Alfonso Reyes Prize, the 1987 National Prize for
Science and Art in Linguistics and Literature, the 1993 Amado Nervo

State Literature Prize and the 1996 Belisario Dominguez Medal of the Senate of the Republic.

In 2008 he received the Fine Arts Gold Medal as a tribute to his 90 years.

When the program of national tribute in his honor was announced, Ali Chumacero told reporters:

"I would like that when I go with music
to somewhere else, they remember me
as a man who came from a small village
called Acaponeta, in a small state called
Nayarit, looking for his own place in the world."

:::::

For its part, the FCE publishing house "deeply" regretted in a communiqué the passing of "one of Mexico's most important poets."

The publishing house recalled that the same writer said in 1987 that "to create something that survives us comes from our wish to leave a mark, a sign, a signal, etched on the fragile sheet of time: an ambition spurred by intelligence, lucidity, the imagination, and also, by the opportune symphony of silence."

:::::

Jesus from Chihuahua,
it was a pleasure
to meet you.

Señor Chumacero,
I remember you,
vividly.

:::::

Finally get a chance to delve into this gift
from Peter Anastas arrived the day after
the Fourth, a pleasure to open Olson's
New Man & Woman to hear
him address the importance
of METHODOLOGY
as the discipline
to arrange
materials,
& cites
dance
as foundation,
ground,
kinetic,
adding "geography – equally, though here maps & experience of
walking…"

Seriously.

Charles is
deadly serious.

"'Our class' – the non-class – the a-class – the expressors, solely now
have the responsibility to restore expression to such prime place. To be
distributable — in this sense, that all men and women are 'creative', that
they are capable of 'expressing' themselves.
                           Dig? I mean value! Let's talk! Words are
value, instruction, action. And they've got to become social action. The
radicalism lies from our words alone…
                           It is unbearable what knowledge of
the past has been allowed to become, what function of human memory
has been dribbled out to in the hands of these learned monsters whom
people are led to think 'know'. They know nothing in not knowing how
to reify what they do know. What is worse, they do not know how to pass
over to us the energy implicit in any high work of the past because they
purposely destroy that energy as dangerous to the states for which they
work, which it is, for any concrete thing is danger to rhetoricians and
politicians, as dangerous as a hard coin is to a banker…"

::::

…states for which they work…

::::

*Desire is always revolutionary because it wants more
connections & assemblages.* – Gilles Deleuze

Vast vortex of Mani's geography, spelled
out abstractly on the back hand of a man I respect,
doubling with that of the Atlas, where land resembles hand,
& gift of Olson's tract sent by someone who knew him well;
or Seferis, there on one of the islands; Guy Davenport reminding
us that he, too, cared for real *things* in the manner of Proust,
& found that like Joyce or Ernst a quotation cited beyond
original context can reaffirm & lift meaning into another
realm.

Reminds me of something I wrote EXACTLY 12 years ago
to this day & week, which saw the light of day only
in an obscure online magazine in Switzerland,
of all places, & of course then, barely
seen or read:

SMYRNA, DELPHI, HELIOPOLIS, HADES, GLOUCESTER

Let no thought pass incognito, and keep your notebook
as strictly as the authorities keep their register of aliens.
—Walter Benjamin

I'm in my Greek mode, reading Seferis's journal, thinking about heat, warm water, Retsina, olives, Homer, etc. So if I write, it may be laying foundation stones, not necessarily anything finished. I return to this little book on occasion. It is, it's like gathering things words phrases for a future work, one Rilke refers to in one of his pieces. In that way it's expansive, the *moment* I thrive in, because it is intent on a future creative modal it extends out there in space, & because it's the Greeks also reaches back, sifts up the past like an archaeology, to be examined first-hand, like an old stone implement. Look at how that damned thing was fashioned, what technical skills, what precision, what a love for Time.

7/3/02 Heat rose up quickly, tactile before the sun, like her under sheets, out of dream. In the house she's the center of attention. Fans swirling, coffee on, weather report, computer booting, shades lifted, hands washed, it's still her skin, her body, her mood which carries anything of significance: the body's language, furrowed brow, languor, vigor, *intime*, vocal, silent, internal…

Sun through skylight contains a similar, if substitute presence.

I've always been fascinated by the laconic honesty of George Seferis especially in his *Journal: Days of 1945-51*. It's refreshing. "Friday, October 18: Yesterday after lunch I cut wood. The body functions more easily; the animal is more relaxed; no elation. That's it. The head is empty, emotion settled down. Not at all in a poetic mood. It doesn't matter; for the time being it's better so. Don't forget that you must leave & return. Shut up rooms warp you with bad habits; the room I lived in recent years was stifling. I think of nothing now… I don't want to be anything today, tomorrow, we'll see." [1]

He's as fascinated by small boats as I am, their sculptural/functional appeal. "This morning: wood, swimming. A fisherman passed & offered fish; [just this morning I sent someone in CA a copy of Olson's "The Company of Men," with its lines

...the generosity

can come only

from those

who have fish'] [2]

his boat is a <u>kourita</u>. Here people do not know these boats. Those I asked said 'something like a gondola.' I, too, ask him; 'What do you call your caique?' 'Korita,,' he answered. I understood that he was from Asia Minor. 'Without a keel do you use leeboards?' 'These don't need leeboards; with the sail, their side serves as a keel... From Smyrna to here?... This one went to Egypt in 1913 with four or five others; she's the only one that came back. They took them to the Nile and sold them. Look at her warped planks.' I looked. I was pleased with the workmanship. The beautiful old wood. The carving on prow and stern recalled icons from my past. I observed this boat with much joy." [3]

Yesterday I attempted a poem of renewed desire. It didn't work. Failed at the end, (perhaps from the beginning), when what I wanted to do was turn the object of my desire (my wife), symbolically, into the image of a small boat, her ribs into those of a canoe, say. But I couldn't construct an image that would account for the way a man rows a boat, without counterpart in sexual position. But this ancient image, where the construction of the kourita is based on the sculpting of stone *kourai*, the sails the carved *chiton* lifting her body, the sailor riding the image of the memory of the woman until he returns to the real thing...

She's nine minutes late ten twelve fourteen with the goods, the food, her fruit, her good. I've got my Greek sense of patience on. I'm waiting out Darius.

7/4/02 The rose I picked for her with one flower, three buds, nine leaves, dancing on its stem in the water of the Spanish rosé bottle in front of the circulating fan is a bad actress, mimicking her every move, missing her lines.

Down to the shoreline before 11:00 A.M. Take watch off. Step into the 5th century BC with my canvas shoes, the ones I got married in, the ones with rawhide laces, & Herodotus.

7/5/02 On my brief vacation I've had time, merely, to delve into Herodotus. Nothing in depth. In a cast of thousands it's difficult to ally oneself, identify the true heroes. If I tried to identify any, surely Themistocles, with his ability to interpret the Delphic oracle, in order to plan strategies to defeat the Persians at Salamis.[4] Choric honesty there, colluding with deepest resources of unconscious. The two remain today the most powerful forces in the world, not Persians, nor Greeks, but the expression of the unconscious, & the art of its interpretation.

"In essence, the poet has one theme: his live body." [5]

7/6/02 Dream last night: party, lots of friends & relatives in a vast house, during which I introduce most to all, but my mother thinks I forgot about my cousin, so I drag him around re-introducing him to everyone. At some point exploring the rest of the house I reach a floor where a whole section is boarded up tight, (a host of nails, wood fragments, shutters, some metal, a veritable artwork), I assume for renovations of the addition behind it. When I wake up that's what I decide to do. Embark upon a renovation project. Less wine, for a change, more exercise, a renovation project for the body.

I took my notebook along on my new walking regime. There, piled up between the Caterpillar & the Bucyrus-Erie cranes, Olsonian congeries of stones, dolmen, & hieratic heads ready to shore up the seawall against Boreas, in-law of the Athenians. North Wind, alias Hellespontine, which sunk 400 Persian ships during a four-day blow off Magnesia. [6]

At the same time, across the street, perched in the branches of the staghorn sumac, the red-wing blackbird practicing singing keeping his timbre strong.

7/7/02 Out before sunrise. Rain overnight helping the birds & flora back to life. Mountainous grey cloud over the horizon, some of it burning from the star underneath, burning the way Arizona & Colorado wish things burned, metaphorically. Take along my little telescope to get a closer look. Many fewer boats, in fact a lone skiff. Alone, too, on land with only previous civilizations insinuating themselves in tracings. Phalanxes of cormorants. Sun fully up by 5:17. I can't help thinking of Ra, knowing it's such a cliché, but when I walk back home, past the morning glories, the doves, the street sign where I live has somehow dropped its "S," it's "E," its "C" & "D," leaving only "ON," the Egyptian name for what the Greeks called Heliopolis, City of the Sun.

7/8/02 Last day of vacation together, facing the threat of chores put off: inspection sticker for the car, trash to dump. Somehow, in-between, we manage time to get the little fiberglass boat we bought two years ago down to the rocky shore & OUT ON THE WATER! The shore stones baking, & today humming with flies, we escape! Oh, Aegean, Seferis, whom we read together to each other, "Clashing Rocks – those stones that strike you, now on the head, now in the heart, now in the kidneys. Ultimately they never finish you off. You rise half-dead and keep going, a foolish visionary in the golden light of the sea." [7] In the meantime, I've let my fishing line rest in the water, which bogus lure at the end of it couldn't trick any fish. But wait, as I reel it in, "I've got something," something long before any sign of the plastic lure, a crab, holding on for dear life to the 40-pound nylon test. "Look, she laughs, he's a trapeze artist!"

At night I can't let go of the Greeks. Go to Book XI. Odysseus speaking with the dead: Elpenor; Anticlea; Tiresias.

7/9/02 Back to work via ferry.

7/10/02 I recall Book XI has a special reference for the blood ritual of speaking to the dead, but I can't recall it. Knowing Olson referred it I go to the index of George Butterick's, **A Guide to The Maximus Poems of Charles Olson**, under Homer. But there are only two references, one which astonishes me. Butterick says it's a story Olson either recalled or invented, but that it was written on a notepad just ten months before his death. "...I'd like to live to die as Homer did – or at least as I have that story of how [he] did die at Smyrna, I mean the story of his last day, that he got so interested watching two boys fishing he was careless about taking care of himself, and fell out after the chill of evening where he [found?] himself on the road and was found there in the morning wrapped out [inadequately] in a rug for his sleeping..." [8]

Story contradicting the legend of his blindness?

I'm struck by the reference to Smyrna, where the boat Seferis was in awe of came from. Seferis watching the fisherman. Of course, while reading this, I recall the Greek word for the rite of blood given to the dead of Hades in order to speak to them, *Nekuia,* which isn't indexed here, & recall the dream last night in which a bunch of us were looking for someone reported dead. The only evidence we could find was his hat. The only sentence I wrote down: "They found the hat in the mud." I thought of it as Adam's, or some other ancient civilization's "first man."

When I lived in Gloucester I heard stories of Olson in his last years just as he described his vision of Homer, "in his own Zarape or whatever heavier roll or blanket he did have wandering as it seems he was..." [9]

::::

[1] George Seferis, *A Poet's Journal: Days of 1945-1951*, translated by Athan Anagnostopoulis (Cambridge, MA: Harvard UP, 1974) p. 50.

[2] Charles Olson, *The Collected Poems of Charles Olson*, ed. George F. Butterick (Berkeley: University of California Press) p. 423.

[3] Seferis, p. 60.

[4] Herodotus, *The Histories*, translated by Robin Waterfield (Oxford; Oxford UP, 1998) p. 453.

[5] Seferis, p. 62.

[6] Herodotus, p.471

[7] Seferis, pp. 74-75.

[8] George F. Butterick, *A Guide to the Maximus Poems of Charles Olson*, (Berkeley: University of California Press, 1978) p. 735.

[9] ibid., p. 735

::::
::::

I had a difficult time finding, or even imagining beauty, that is, what *is*.

::::

Granted, wind out of the south was warm off the water, but people seemed
automatons, or zombies, & I'd seen all that flora a hundred times,
no new flora at all, then a political jolt showed up in the form
of a white Coast Guard van with blackened windows,
which stopped on its return trip, where I peered
inside the driver's half-open window curious
as to the nature of their duty now on land,
& recognizing in their sizing up of me,
with ripped jeans, bedraggled, long
hair, disheveled, but unwarranted,
that blatant snarl by the driver,
that this was now an added
Authority to the mix
of Surveillance
& Repression.

"Power has no essence; it is simply operational.
Even a 'thing' like prison is seen as an environmental formation… a form
of content (where the content is the prisoner). But this thing or form
does not refer back to a 'word' designating it, or to a signifier for which
it would be the signified.
It refers to completely different words and concepts, such as delinquency
or delinquent, which express a new way of articulating infractions,
sentences, and their subjects. Let us call this new formation of statements
a form of expression.
    —Deleuze, ***Foucault***

I'm in Nice.
First day in Nice, France,
July 1967, having hitchhiked
with a 24-year-old woman artist
from Rome in three days. So we hit
the beach immediately, greeted by other travelers,
in our case mostly bearded young Dutch men gravitating
her way. It's not long, however, before two gendarmes come
down the stairs yelling, "Passports, passports, passports!" just
as the armed soldiers had on the train prior to Rijeka, Yugoslavia.
So I dig mine out simply to comply.

Guy doesn't even open it, demands I follow him
with a group of others back up stairs & straight
into paddy wagon.

Mostly Germans on the benches, they ask if I'm American.
Offer reassurances that I'll be let go, but they'll be deported.
In the cell of the jailhouse there's a lot of apprehension
among every detainee, (& granted nothing of this
incident can compare to the Hell
& repression Gaza is
today, July 9,
treachery
Mosul,
chaos
eastern Ukraine,

catastrophic childhood
immigration Brownsville,
Texas, nor the day-to-day hardship
experienced by those not in the elite's
deterritorialized
world)
& yes,
they
let me go,
find my way
back to where
my backpack seemed
untouched in the doorway
of by-then closed American Express.

After all I'd already been to Rimbaud's Stuttgart,
& all there was inside were dirty clothes
& a copy of Erich Fromm's,
Escape from Freedom.

::::

SOCRATES: And if he had someone with him, he would put what he
said to himself into actual speech to his companion, audibly uttering
those same thoughts, so that what before we called opinion has to
become assertion…
Whereas if he is alone he continues thinking the same thing by himself,
going on for a considerable time with this thought on his mind…
It seems to me that at such times our soul is like a book. in Derrida,
Dissemination

*I prefer, faced with aggression, to retort that contemporaries don't know how to
read—*
*Unless it be in the newspaper; it dispenses, certainly, the advantage of not
interrupting the chorus of preoccupations.*
To read-
That practice-…

Stéphane Mallarmé, quoted in Derrida, **Dissemination**

::::

Suspected the tenor
of the day might lighten up
a bit after going eye-to-eye with local
Coast Guard Authorities, reading about lack
of essence in such entities, (*it is simply operational*)
& reminded of an earlier confrontation on the first day
in France in 1967 at twenty, but I never expected this coincidence
the day after mentioning Gaza,
when she & I walked
down the trail along
the waterfront just
short of the high
chain-link fence
of Portland
Yacht
Services
at the edge
of the foliage,
seeing the kid
with a fishing rod
on the rock ledge balancing
precariously on the stones carrying
both rod & a plastic bag with something
moving (Damn, in all my meanderings out
here over the years, I've never seen anyone
catch a thing, years ago even stopped a couple
of older guys walking forlornly down the path,
rods in hand, "Catch anything?" One guy stood
silent, the other answering, "No, there's nothing
out there anymore!")

& that's proved true,
until I glimpsed this kid
balancing both rod & plastic
shopping bag above the high ledge,
so ambled along the space between
chain-link & foliage, asking, "Did you catch
something, what a mackerel?" I was excited for
him, & he could tell, trying to get the wriggling,
lively thing out of the plastic, while balancing both feet
on those stones, I said, "No, don't show it to me, don't lose
it!" Just then he got another bite. "Step on the bag, don't lose
that fish." He lost the bite, but stepped on the bag I could tell
held a good-sized mackerel, "I never saw anyone catch anything
here!"

"I'm good!" pointing to himself in the Solar Plexus, the kid
with orange basketball shirt & baseball cap turned backwards
on his fourteen-year-old-handsome-innocent head, & I said:
"You are, what's your name?" "Abbas!!"
Yes, Abbas, some angel straight
out of the confines
of Palestine
& Gaza!!

When she & I turned around, <u>heading back the other way</u>,
I caught another glimpse of him, & he of me, I yelled,
"Did you catch anything else?"

Same broad, proud,
innocent smile
pointing
toward
the bag
now
secured
further
up the bank away
from the brink,

104

"Ya, I got four more!
I have five!!"
Holding up all five fingers as if waving
in Peace.

"You're the man!!" I yelled out
before turning down the trail
wondering about all the gifts
the universe offers, possibly
equaling all the chaos
of its horrors.

20 A...

confusion of the two

with interruption of the open ground   *or = ***
                                                the action in
                                                the background
                                                -taking up where
                                                one leaves off-...

notes by Mallarmé, cited by Derrida in "The Double Session"

Derrida says Mallarmé *reads,* [his italics]
that he writes while reading... Now, I just wrote
to Bent Sørensen that I was reading "The Double Pleasure"
adding immediately that I left out words *Session* & *with,* [insert after
Double above] so that there & here are proof of the twin
Pleasures, when one writes, while reading combining
to form an obvious Freudian Helix.

[He licks,
what, to read,
& write?].

Well, the gist of "The Double Session",
or connection between Socratic & Mallarméan
beginning & end of writing, that marriage of beginning

105

to end, both philosopher & poet noting the closeness of Soul
to Book, is the weave of the hymen, or virginity
of blank page, that approach to whiteness
with the penetration of the letter, word,
line, sentence, paragraph, volume.
Oeuvre as wife?

Between the two Sessions, a letter from Philippe Sollers
is necessarily inscribed.

Tear myself away
from the work to the walk,
when I saw Abbas & can't think
about his name without the double
association with Abyss & his distance
here in Portland, so far from that place
I mentioned on the same morning before
catching a glimpse of him later in the afternoon
between the high fence of Portland Yacht Services
& the embankment of scrub foliage & sumac: Gaza.

So, open my notebook to see what else got jotted down
briefly, other than his name, & find across the bay,
tanker, *Cap Felix* of EURONAV Line flying
Belgian colors came all the way from
Ceyhan, Turkey. A few other minor
details like the kindness of wind,
waves, all the eyes of cliff
ledge stones, but stumble,
too, on previous notes
where someone else
is making Books.

It's Anselm Kiefer using materials such as ashes & lead
to compose those Books so close to the Soul,
in this case a number that include titles
from words in lines of poems
by Paul Celan.

I didn't mean
to go here,
didn't mean
to go anywhere
other than to a page
in a notebook where I knew
I'd find the spelling of the name
of my young hero, Abbas, noting
the constant similarity to the notion
of Abyss & the distance at which I met
him here in Portland, Maine, & the image
of the land I may well have imagined him
as victim earlier that same morning referring
to "the Hell & repression at Gaza", the irony
now of stumbling a few notebook pages before
that to find Kiefer making books with materials
such as ash & lead, oil & emulsion, twigs & resin,

[Please allow me to insert here,
while proofing, that the lead
Kiefer uses in his "Books"
comes from renovation
of the roof of Köln
Cathedral, through
which portal
I walked in
1967,
then
down through a path in the trees to sleep on the banks of the Rhine.]

pencil & plaster, earth & hair in order to co-author
with the deceased poet a collaborative future oeuvre
based on themes by Celan: darkness digging straw ruins
depth, whose writing, it's obvious was always in mourning.

:::::

Should I wake up wondering which direction chance will lead me, & a
simple turn
      toward
            a different room
                with yet another
                    myriad stack of books,
                        hands it to me,
                            oak library table
     from Sterling at Yale
          Jean Fields & her late
              husband picked up
                  for free when he studied
                    architecture there in the 50's,
  & she thought
          I'd make the best use
             of it, downsizing
                her living quarters, not wrong
                  for me to imagine terrain under
    my feet, that direction led
        by chance, as letters on pages
            as much as geography of sand, pebbles, roots =

                Derrida, no less juxtaposes
                  anatomically the ring of circumcision,
      [*shhh shibboleth*]
                    in his discussion of Celan,

to the hymen in connection
       between Socrates & Mallarmé,
            beginning & end to writing
                seeming to validate the date
                    = Friday, July 11, 2014
                        & Time 8:33 a.m.,
                            Eternity,
                                today.

Before
I open
a book
this
morning
with all
of its thisness
(its haecceity)
allow me to address
the overnight dream
in which the young woman
painted an ecstatic work, large,
abstract. *The blue purple banner*
hovering above the right-hand corner
hinted festival, many many swirling marks
of color underneath, yet a lone, darker-than-
the-rest, oval-shaped hieratic head close to the center.

Told her I liked the painting because it was based on the dance.

Whereupon others, theretofore unseen in the dream, agreed.

Miles is playing on the mix now down by the waterfront, where
I recorded the dream above, now Coltrane chimes in while the sun,
granted, well-up at that 5:34 a.m. marker down Forest Avenue slides
another line across the calm Atlantic.

What can we expect from today, when yesterday was so Eternal, in fact,
so Eternal it's part of today, what with having taken that direction
toward Derrida on Celan, the former citing the importance

of the door in his work, & first thing this morning
after dreaming the above regarding a festival painting
by the young woman whose own hieratic head appeared amid a ton
of activity, my own one eye open caught the predawn light streaming through
the doorway, which I critically evaluated at least as important
as the door itself, threshold & doorway in a predawn light
at least equal of door & door-handle.

I went through it as if in a lovely festival dream alone,
& find myself down here by the waterfront with the sun streaming

a shimmering beam across calm sea.

:::::

After a trek down Widgery Wharf in Portland past
all the little lobster shacks
on boards made
of oldest Maine
timber, after
an afternoon,
which she
can finally
afford
to take
off from work,
we decompress
on the foothill at the bottom
of Munjoy overlooking islands
& ocean, I return home to rearrange,
consolidate three-rooms' worth of books
& sources, maps, sheet music, notebooks, liner
notes from cds, congeries of stones Olson might
say, into one space in the backroom on Yale library table,

whereupon the invaluable source
taken out of Bowdoin library so long ago
with cover of James Ensor's, *Figures*, **Untimely Beggar:**
Poverty and Power from Baudelaire to Benjamin
reemerges, only to find on the very first page
a reference to, no kidding, seriously,
Stéphane Mallarmé writing,
"the true state of literary
man is poverty."

All I can, at the moment,
add, without lashing out
against rich, or well-off
in current/contemporary
literary scene I view from
a distance, no, won't lash
out here, although I could
name a list of those who've
even BOUGHT their way in,
no, here is all I have to offer:
after a working-class undergraduate
degree, one semester costing $275;
graduate degree in library science
took four long years, one semester
at a time, & the aforesaid, lamentable
54 jobs during career as poet = pockets
empty much much more more often
than NOT.

I'm in Viby, Denmark.
At Manna's & Søren's,
11:45, friendly greeting,
amazing library, invite
Paul, Manna's son, to look
at a photograph of him
at piano, "What were you playing?"

Shrugs, "No idea, I was in the second grade."

Explore further the vast library on both sides
of living room past **Danmarks Historie** by Palle Lauring,
past Adorno's **Minima Moralia**, Barthes', *The Rustle of Language*,
Justine, Durrell, even Bakhtin's, **Problems of Dostoevsky's Poetics**, & Eliot's,
Complete Poems & Plays to Zukofsky's **A**:

where I open randomly to two lines:
> As Bach calls to composers & writers of my time. /
> If Paul loves Bach I need not tell him....

reminding me of a game Camelia played
with Kathleen, where they picked a number,
opened a page & read the word 12 lines down
in answer to a question the latter asked about
the conference where I presented the Keynote:
Kerouac & the Ecstatic Act of Writing,
in their case landing on the word, *please.*

We have some plum schnapps from Romania,
Smörgåsbord, Danish ale, French red, & talk
about third-party psychology via puppets & Tarot
cards. Their digs the obverse of American style,
which suits my aesthetic to a capital **A**.

::::

The rarity	Suppose if I were
of say 3 days running	if the mind were
the weight of misery	born or trained
hunches the shoulders	that way, then
while reading	I would once
over those who've	conceiving of a
gone before over	thought try to
poetry's sharp shoals	ratchet it up
so you don't have time	into a lofty
to jot down	conception,
a single word	but it doesn't,
to match that	it's not, it won't,
misery.	which other is a mere

It remains silent.
Unaccounted for
for three days
running,
but the getting
through somehow
proves the worth
of such silence
in those rare
instances
against what
would have been
some bleak amateur
wailing.
To reiterate:
the misery
of three days running
deserves nothing
other than a stoic
resilience
dredged from its
depths.

tramping upon
solid ground like
Ireland or Gloucester
for that matter
reaching down to
ancestors in my
continuing immediacy,
or foreign, say
Venice where it's
not so much solid
ground, but porous
waters buried tree
trunks & basilica
               ceilings mimicking
the sky above them.
No, what happens is
no formal conception,
but an informal
spontaneous, rhythmic
reenactment of
the here & now
of experience
in language.
Sentences with
boots on, letters
shibboleths in rites
of passage.

::::

Sound of the fan on in the backroom,
while maybe the heat has caught up to all that chatter
& racket of the unidentified bird holed up
in one of the oaks. Underneath it
I can hear that silent
lamentation

of the world,
an ongoing mourning,
while earlier, too, I thought I heard
the quiet, reassuring voice of Guy Davenport
rising out of the fireproof strongbox holding his letters.

Letters save lives. This I know.

God Bless Guy.
Bill Heyen, too.
His second postcard
in a few days just arrived,
thanking me for his copy of *TVA*,
after I shared with him my letter to Mark Olson,
who found in some drawer in his Asheville print shop
three copies of *This Vanishing Architecture*, which survived
the flood that destroyed almost all of his inventory, including *Of DC*.

July 10, 2014
Dear Mark,

Kathleen found the package stuck between doors when going out for the papers just now.

I keep asking the mail guy to ring the bell if he has anything beyond the usual junk slipped though the letter slot = Kathleen says maybe we were out walking,
a possibility.

Both copies *of This Vanishing Architecture*, 2001, close to pristine, one definitely so, numbers 65 & 67, respectively, I read the Proust epigraph, she read, "The Little Phrase".

It's probably in this book that I came into my own, raising the bar of the blank page turned art.

I recall the desperate struggle I had with the sequence, when on a roll, I'd been writing 3-4 pieces a week on my commute to work from Scituate to Boston by old red Chevy truck given to me by Brad, ferry to Boston Harbor Hotel, trek thru financial district past the Custom House Tower to the Orange Line subway to NU.

It was at NU that I found an obscure book on Venice with photographs showing Campanile at St. Mark's fallen to rubble, then rebuilt 10 years later with the same stones. [1901-1910, the exact same years for the construction of Boston's Custom House Tower!!]

What the fuck, but in my unconscious insanity, I had to find out more about Venice, (faintly recalling the importance of the Campanile to *In Search of Lost Time*), so I took a number of weeks to strenuously reread Proust.

What a bitch it was to let go of the roll of 3-4 pieces a week to get sidetracked like that!! Like a cul-de-sac!

I began to feel like I made a huge mistake, because I didn't write anything, other than notes, during that entire Time!!

Can't recall now just how long a seeming-hiatus it was, but by the end it felt like, (let's just say it was 10 weeks), the education of spending 10 months in 1981 to read everything I could find on & by Yeats in all the libraries of Boston to write the play "I Am of Ireland," in response to the 14 poems of his put to music by Steve Scotti!!

Drained by that process, emptied, I recall one Sunday loading up the car with a minor hangover, some juice, fruit, vitamins, & maybe even a bit of leftover wine, driving down Oceanside Boulevard to the lighthouse to watch sunrise, determined to write SOMETHING.

Soon after that sun climbed out of the Atlantic, I put felt-tip pen to yellow legal pad & with the help of the light (Proust opened the shutters of his hotel window to his first full view of Venice dominated by the Campanile), I wrote the first of this series, "Twin to the Campanile in Venice".

The rest of the chapbook's contents just rolled up out of the streets, across air & water!!!!!

Well, my bookshelf of books has grown, but I'd given away every single copy of ***This Vanishing Architecture***, but one. So I rarely took it off that shelf.

<u>It's luminous</u>, inside & out, & can't help praising your artistry & generosity!!

As I wrote to you in my previous missive, I OWE YOU!!!!!

Best!!!!!!

Gratefully,
Robert

<u>Letters save lives.</u>

Years during a dearth of correspondence,

(no Bill Heyen in my life back then, no Bent Sørensen
understanding the work, none of the high-level discourse
exchanged with Ben Bollig, no expert reading & critical response
from Peter Anastas, nor incisive reviews by Jim Feast or Richard
Hoffman),

Guy types two pages on Easter, 1989, finishing with
"You can't know what good things, inspirational and informational
(both senses) I've been getting out of the Making of 'The Meadow' book
you so generously sent me."

A month later: "Apollinaire's voice in a Kentucky room
full of late afternoon golden sunlight is what it's all about.
I'd known that he made a recording, but had never heard it.
A true ghost. Blessings on your head."

A year later, June 23, 1990: "Your writing is so radically different
from mine that in order to read it I must reconstruct your poetic
sensibility - - partly Rimbaud, partly Olson. You make me realize with
something of a start that you're writing out of yourself. Your psyche has
a voice. Worth knowing, this. For me, that is. By difference we know. My
perception is scarcely judgmental. I'd love to write like you."

Bless You, Guy.

My own copy of Mallarmé's **Selected Letters** has a lone bookmark
marking the more-than-four-page letter to Paul Verlaine
in which he traces his family ancestry
to a syndic of the booksellers
under Louis XVI.

Admits setting off for England at twenty to learn
English in order to read Poe, an admission
from which one can intuit the influence
of Baudelaire, just as he had been
for Proust.

To poetry, he has given up all vanity, all satisfaction:

"with the patience of an alchemist… as in the past one burned
one's furniture and the beams of the roof, to feed the furnace
of the Great Work… The orphic explanation of the Earth
is the sole duty of the poet and the literary game
par excellence…"

It's Bastille Day.
We take our meal out
of the freezer: kale soup,
some kind of root soup from
as far back as last November
with strong hints of turnip, along
with the last of five bags of cusk
bought a while back at $3.99 a pound.
Ask Ethan at Rosemont for a $5.00 piece
of Roquefort, pair it with some olives, &
Esprit de Sarrail Rosé wine from Carcassonne.

I'm in Carcassonne.
Then, posthaste, I'm outside
walls of Carcassonne, doing the laundry.

While coin-operated machines go round, we down
a bottle of 1664 Kronenbourg at the seediest dive imaginable
with sailor nodding over girl with track marks on both arms.

The bathroom is literally outside, no walls at all.
I love the French, as one can already make out
here: Ponge, Rimbaud, Baudelaire, Sollers, Kristeva?,

Barthes, Deleuze, Apollinaire, Mallarmé, did I mention
importance of Duras?

[Bastille Night, 7/14/2014, Jessica Williams coming over KCSM Radio
in San Francisco with *I Remember Bill,* the way the keys resound,
resound, an obvious homage to Evans.

Earlier in evening sent celebratory greetings to friends
with link to Keith Jarrett's *Live in Paris Concert.*
Vive la… Vive...

I am not critical, [1971 driving down Sunset Boulevard in Hollywood,
pick up only creative young 16-year-old hitchhiking (all legs)
with track marks on her arms, says one of the Chambers Brothers is her
"old man."]

Derrida's Mallarméan example of everything become language,
where:

"the dancer *is not a woman dancing,* for these reasons
juxtaposed that she *is not a woman* but a metaphor summing
up one of the elementary aspects of our form (sword, cup,
flower, etc.) and that *she is not dancing,* suggesting,
through a marvel of short cuts or surges, with her
bodily writing that it would take paragraphs
of prose dialogue to express on paper
a poem freed from any scribe's
equipment… would have to
express the double game: perhaps
the whole adventure of sexual difference!…
whose secret smile seems to pour forth…through

the last veil that remains forever, the nudity of your
own concepts, and silently proceeds to write your vision
in the manner of a Sign, which she is."
-SM "Two Pigeons"

It's near midnight
on Bastille Day in America,
nearer early morning in the Paris
I know with people I know there.
Let's go for a walk. Down Bonaparte,
maybe across rue Jacob, past all the galleries
on rue de Seine. It's not important which way
one chooses, unlike here in the context of the text,
where the vortex of the text governs direction. Across
rough mountain roads of America come sounds out of KCSM
radio in San Francisco doing their best to honor the French I've
attempted
to honor all along with that American art form, Jazz,
including Charlie Parker, *April in Paris*,
Stephane Grappelli *I Can't Get Started*,
Jean-Michel Pilc, *One for My Baby*,
even Quincy Jones, *Evening in Paris*, & now,
I know that voice, on *Baby Won't You Please Come Home*,
Dinah Washington, who Steve Scotti told me tried to get out
of her Roulette Records deal to no avail.
Bastille Day in America?

BASTILLE DAY IN AMERICA

Why I swung toward work enclosures today as I ironed my linen shirt, a shirt
one doesn't wear to work, say, leather factory with its massive dyeing wheels
& dryer belts, or soon enough fish with its saws could cut a man's arm up to
here; then meat, where the difference in temperature between what lands in
& rises out of the plastic vats for dogs & sausages & that of the freezer is the
vast difference between poor & rich, between alienated & privileged. There

are worse things than working in any of these factories, or the textile one I labored at before six in the morning in front of sewing machines counting production & stitching hours at fifty-seven-years old, where others were older. Like not having a job, fending for oneself on the streets of any rough & tumble street in America. I don't begrudge those jobs, in fact thankful today to have them unconsciously rise up in juxtaposition, adding to the immense sense of Freedom I feel inside this shirt, breathing this air where I can come & go as I please, where I can gaze at trees, comparing that Freedom with the first five-minute break we got after an hour & a half of drudgery under the mechanical eyes of sewing machines, five-minutes of regimented exercise, that is, calisthenics to keep young & old limber enough to work another hour & a half before release for a cup of coffee. I'd always sidle up next to the lone window in the place, where the equally lone tree stood outside. It's happening right now up in Freeport, Maine!

Placed
that there
after midnight
on the Fourteenth of July.
This morning rain beat down
heavily enough for me to mistake
it for the whirling of the ceiling fan.
Backyard foliage lush through six windows
& two storm doors of the backroom, but what
I'm thinking of is this totally separate, magical
shrub that marks two special locations close to our
Souls.

Took quite a while to identify, but we gravitate
its way in summer heat for shade at the foot
of Munjoy Hill, or simply for its magnificent
scent circling the entire ring of Niles Pond,
Eastern Point, Gloucester: *Clethra alnifolia*
(sweet pepperbush, Anne Bidwell or summersweet),
is a species of flowering plant in the genus *Clethra*
of the family Clethraceae, native to eastern
North America from southern Nova Scotia
and Maine south to northern Florida,
and west to eastern Texas.

Clethra alnifolia sounds
like a small notebook,
when I say it silently
under my breath.
The blank page.
Unnumbered.
Waiting
as good
friends
wait.

Told daughter over the weekend the anecdote
of walking close to the tombolo,
which separates fresh water
of Niles Pond from salt at Brace Cove
(I own a photograph of Fitz Hugh Lane's pen & ink
drawing of the Cove & Brace Rock from the collection of prints
& drawings at the National Gallery), when after a number of years
seeing this guy feeding crows on the beach, asked him
how long he'd been doing that?
Twenty-something years,
if I recall correctly,
adding that in gratitude one time a crow landed at his feet,
placing a shiny dime
on the ground.

::::

In one sense I forced,
(not without the other sense
of Freedom to choose), return
to Celan, who has a finger tracing
a child's map in order to discover
the endless circle of the Meridian
round midnight to midday to midnight,
again, & Derrida's take on dating such

undertakings as <u>incisions</u>,
<u>cuts</u>, <u>wounds</u> as if <u>on</u>
the body itself
"like a memory."

So there, waiting patiently
in the same small notebook,
written in pencil, (as Mallarmé
pointed out to Verlaine in his letter,
graphite contributed an air of quiet
conversation between friends, away
from crowds with no raised voices),
the jotting record of a short journey
to see an old, good friend, Dan Carr.

Granted, Dan passed away just two years
ago, now, but his work as printer, publisher, poet
lives on. In this case, on 4/17/ 2014, I sought out Dan's
marvelous printing of Celan's **Todesfuge**, 300 copies for
The Limited Editions Club at Bowdoin College Archive, #102,
translated with an *Afterword* by John Felstiner.
White gloves on, waiting patiently for
retrieval of the massive volume =
opening it was close to hug
& handshake.

A quiet reacquaintance.

Dan Carr published my first work, **Yellow & Black**,
under the imprint of his Four Zoas Night House Press, Boston, 1980.

In 2007, as Poetry & Fiction Editor at *Janus Head*,
I'd solicited translations of both Neruda & Celan
from Professor Felstiner.

Ten years ago, I used Paul Celan's quote from "The Meridian" to
demarcate
the second section in the collection prose poems, **Body of Time**:

"Even in a poem's here & now-the poem really only has this one,
unique, momentary present-even in this immediacy and nearness
it lets the Other's ownmost quality speak: its time."

Being in the archive,
it was all quite physical,
sensual, even. At the table,
touching paper, its scent, feeling
incised cuts from Dan's own type,
& of course, words of Celan & Felstiner,
the tactile combined with the spiritual =
here is Mallarmé's BOOK, if there ever was one.

Nonetheless,
it's tough going,
reading this poem
"Todesfuge" damn
difficult as human flesh
begins to incinerate before
your very eyes & ears in lines
such as, *scrape your strings darker*
you'll rise then as smoke into the sky.
The cruel, the brutal, masked by the music.

Yet, Felstiner sheds light
on the darkness of the work.
He points out how images aren't
metaphorical, but actual, "they're
plain fact, survivors claim… ashen hair…
a grave in air…" Then there's Celan's voice
on the accompanying cd bringing taut, staccato
rhythm to the vocal, eschatological composition,
verging on a chant for the end of days אחדית הימים.

I appreciate, too, Felstiner's handing back to Celan,
the final two & a half lines in the original, ending with
"dein ashenes Haar Sulamith."

::::

Not sure I was reminded of an observation
regarding the approach to reading poetry
back there at the archive, or whether
it's surfaced solely here today,
but this statement by Francis Ponge
in his meditation on the work of Braque
haunts the echoes of the silence
of the dead in Celan's poetry:

"…if your corporeal complexion is so constituted that you are present
to that point, *at least* as sensitive to the signifier as to what is signified,
you are a reader for poetry (as I understand it) or for Braque's painting.

The *blood* which is apparently on *page one* is to you, at least I hope it is,
apparent, significant… let us say (for now) in the background, while the
ink
is in the foreground."

::::

CLOSE READING

Bone, skin, teeth, hair, all about to fall down or out.
The rest of the organs comporting themselves as if age
were extraneous. Opposing someone's gossip, or whispers
of their weekly book club, I'm lining up my great ones:
Dostoevsky, Nietzsche, Rilke, to see the relevance they give
fracture, wrinkle, ache, loss, in a larger scheme of things.

It's close to an exhumation, reading the lips of the dead,
their final sighs, last articulations of life. What I've gotten
from them so far is that ink & blood are nearly equal.

::::

My internal GPS.
Global Positioning System,
the Solar Plexus located behind
stomach, in front of aorta & crura
of diaphram.

So where does that leave me, & which direction to take, if at all,
what with all that went on yesterday toward
the eschatological
& Death?

In touch with my Soul there, as if Solar Plexus
were the physical manifestation of the Dream
Image that occurred late that night between
my daughter & myself both seated in
the bus, seats apart: *a rose* floated
from me to her encased in panes
of glass: my Soul as *Eros*.

I stay seated here in the kitchen with no place to go,
no plans for a walk today, for a change,
& by chance, with sun coming out
unexpectedly according to
weather predictions,
return full-circle
to the French
philosopher,
Frédéric Gros',
A Philosophy of Walking,
if only, now, to disagree with his point that
by walking you are not going to meet with yourself.
By walking you escape from the very idea of identity…

Not my experience.

Response to the philosopher's contradictory notion
called to mind the sentence from Olson,
"I come from the last walking period of man."

So write to Peter Anastas, knowing he referred to it in a review
of Maud's, *Charles Olson's Reading*, wondering
exactly where it comes from in the poet's vast oeuvre?

Peter responds that it comes from the last pages of *The Maximus Poems*,
& that if I needed further help to let him know.
Busy with his own work & personal affairs, I tell him I'll find it.

In fact, Peter preferred the phrase, "last walking age of man,"
which Olson used in conversation with him.

After perusing Butterick's *Guide* to no avail, I found it thanks to Peter's tip
on page 222, seven pages from the end of *Volume Three*.

Strange thing is that it was written on this exact day
& date, Wednesday, July 16, forty-five years ago today in 1969.

Told Kathleen about this unlikely coincidence, & she asked
if I saw the obituary today in the *NYT* for an 81-year-old
artist who painted dates on a daily basis, including one
pictured in the paper commemorating the Apollo 11
space shot, & man's first walk on the moon = JULY16,1969.

On Kawara was best known for his "Today," or date painting series:
monochromatic canvases, often small,
whose only images are dates
on which they were made,
rendered in meticulous white letters
that look almost printed against fields
of red, blue, black or gray.

The series began in New York in 1966
-before Conceptual Art existed –
when Mr. Kawara painted that date
on an 8-by-10-inch blue surface.
It continued throughout his life.

On Kawara was born in Japan in December 1932
& raised in an intellectual atmosphere suffused
with Shinto, Buddhist and Christian teachings.

He was a promising student, he said, until
the bombings of Hiroshima and Nagasaki in 1945
left him traumatized and full of doubt about "everything."

::::

JULY 17, 2014 in Honor of On Kawara

::::

"Date as cut or wound, 'incision that the poem bears in its body
like a memory… calendar (year, month, day), the clock
(the hours… - how many times Celan names them
only to restore them to the night of their ciphered
silence…) above all the names of cities…
they mark only insofar as their readability
announces the possibility of a return…

"Not the absolute return of what precisely
cannot come again: a birth or a circumcision
takes place only once… rather the spectral revenance
of that which, as a unique event in the world,
will never come again. A date is a specter…
that which cannot come back will come back
as such, not only in memory… but
also at the same date…"
—**Jacques Derrida**, *Sovereignties in Question: the Poetics of Paul Celan*

Mallarmé in his November 16, 1885 letter to Verlaine considered,
"the present period as a form of interregnum for the poet,
who has no business to get involved with it…"

& yet

William Heyen in his postcard marked 7/12/14 cannot leave out
what the cut & wound of a date entails:

"Here in our village, last evening Han & I sat up at the Erie Canal
& heard country music in idyllic weather, a sense of luck & security
while Hamas – Israel exchanged rockets & death... Blueberry season
here -"

::::

The Mallarméan interregnum is long
gone.

::::

I'm not in Gaza.

But on Wednesday JULY16, 2014, four young boys,
cousins in the extended Bakr family,
are.

Running from a beach shack owned by their fishermen fathers,
Ahed the youngest, maybe 8,
Ismail, 9,
Zakariya, 10,
& Mohammad possibly 12,
are

                                        blasted into
kingdom come
                                        by Israeli rockets, mangled,
burned there on beach sand
                                        in Gaza City, where the map
marks the ancient Mediterranean Sea.

But it's hard to fathom
such a beautiful
combination
of words,
ancient Mediterranean Sea,

in juxtaposition

                    to Gaza burned kingdom rockets bodies
                    mangled strewn beach…

::::

How can I help picturing Abbas there, 7/10/2014, a week ago today
waving, palm open, fingers signaling that, yes, by that time
he'd caught five mackerel on the ledge above Atlantic
waters so far from the Mediterranean Sea, Gaza,
when events of JULY16, 2014 in the future,
had not yet occurred?

::::

Anatomy & geography,
in deed.

::::

When asked what he will miss most about his brother, Mohammad,
Ramzi Bakr, 8, responded in Arabic, "Kul."
Everything.

::::

The future of this moment had not yet occurred,
when I open my book five minutes later, after mention
of tragic geographical & anatomical events in the city of Gaza,

only to find Jacques Rancière examining Rimbaud's poem "Childhood"

[*Enfance*]: "The fine hour is not for tomorrow.
And there is nothing to do but go through
all the characters again, to return to
the child, to the child's fight
with dawn that is delegated
to each of the other
characters and so

on up to the end
of the pier that
has no end,
all the way
to 'the end
of the world
advancing."

::::

Making my rounds 'round town today,
I took note of all the traffic islands
filled with homeless
carrying signs.

At times, they are signs,
like when Malte [Rilke] writes:

> *And how did that small, gray woman come to be standing at my side*
> *for a whole quarter of an hour in front of a display window, showing*
> *me an old, long pencil… I felt it was a sign, a sign for the initiated,*
> *a sign only outcasts could recognize; I sensed that I was supposed to*
> *go somewhere or do something.*

Got out there on the path early enough
to have it all to myself, when suddenly
cliff stones turn into a herd of horses,
lone owl perched, & band of warriors
stand at such riveting attention one knows
a secret is near.
Brand-new staghorn antlers tower
over last year's height.
New England asters appear ahead of
their autumn timetable.
& mullein gives the whole place an added
phallic balance
to feminine Queen Ann's Lace,
stray morning glories,
leaf-veiled raspberries.

Trying to shake Gaza off my mind no easy task.
At cliff's end & East End Beach begins,
& there off in the low-tide distance
are eleven, count em, eleven
people practicing Yoga
on surfboards.

It's stunning in a way: here's America, firsthand,
as far away from Gaza as you want to be,
Yoga at low tide on surfboards, far,
as far away as can be, (other
than New Zealand),
I'm calculating
distance
between

Abbas here
on the ledge over Atlantic in Portland,
& the Bakr boys there
on the Mediterranean Sea?

Wondering, too, what's right & wrong
with this world, & briefly conclude,
one thing: that America can rarely
claim to be a mere innocent
bystander to events in this
Wide World.

                    :::::

Returning home with nothing on my mind
other than the arrival of daughter,
Avry, & granddaughter, Layla,
this afternoon,
KCSM
out of San Francisco
has Thelonius Monk & his

Orchestra at Town Hall in 1959
with Donald Byrd on trumpet, Phil Woods, alto,
of course, Charlie Rouse on tenor, Art Taylor drums,
& Sam Jones bass, as part of the ten-member ensemble,
playing Monk's tune, *In Walked Bud.*

Just walking through a door,
up & over a threshold,
is enough to
offer up
a note
of

gratitude.

7/19/2014

WORKS CITED IN ORDER OF REFERENCE, BOOK I

Stevens, Wallace, "Two or Three Ideas" *Opus Posthumous* (New York: Knopf) 1957.

Kristeva, Julia, *Revolution in Poetic Language*. Trans. Leon S. Roudiez (New York: Columbia University Press) 1984.

Olson, Charles, *'West'* (London: The Goliard Press) 1966.

Perloff, Marjorie J. "Heart Mysteries': The Later Love Lyrics of W. B. Yeats" *Contemporary Literature* 10 Spring, 1969.

Freud, Sigmund, *Beyond the Pleasure Principle*. Trans. James Strachey (New York: W. W. Norton) 1961.

Yeats, William Butler, *The Collected Letters of William Butler Yeats* (New York: Macmillan Company) 1955.

Webster's New International Dictionary, Second Edition (Springfield, MA: G & C Merriam Company) 1959.

Schapira, Michael, Interview with Frédéric Gros *FULL STOP*, 2014. http://www.full-stop.net/2014/06/04/interviews/michael-schapira/frederic-gros/

Gros, Frédéric, *A Philosophy of Walking*. Trans. John Howe (London: Verso) 2014.

O'Hara, Frank, "Personism: A Manifesto" in *The Poetics of the New American Poetry* (New York: Grove Press) 1973.

Olson, Charles, *The Collected Poems of Charles Olson: Excluding the Maximus Poems* (Berkeley: University of California Press) 1987.

Olson, Charles, "D. H. Lawrence and the High Temptation of the Mind" *Collected Prose* (Berkeley: University of California Press) 1997.

Olson, Charles, *Charles Olson & Robert Creeley: The Complete Correspondence, Vol. 10* (Santa Rosa, CA: Black Sparrow Press) 1996.

Zukofsky, Louis, "A: 4" in *America a Prophesy* (New York: Vintage Books) 1974.

Thoreau, Henry David, *Walden and Other Writings* (New York: Modern Library) 1965.

Heyen, William, "<u>Americana</u>" (Brockport, NY: Poemlet Press) 2014.

Whitman, Walt, "Song of the Open Road" *Leaves of Grass* (New York: Doubleday, Doran) 1940.

Kristeva, Julia, *Time and Sense: Proust and the Experience of Literature,* trans. Jeanine Herman (New York: Columbia University Press) 1993.

Sulcas, Roslyn. "An Artist Fills Galleries with Emptiness" *NYT*, June 14, 2014.

Dostoevsky, Fyodor, *Notes from Underground.* Trans. Mirra Ginsburg (New York: Bantam Dell) 1974.

Da Fonseca Wollheim Corinna, "Putting Duct Tape to Another Use: Opera" *NYTimes,* June 17, 2014.

Simpkins, Cuthbert Ormand, *Coltrane: A Biography* (New York: Herndon House) 1975.

Coltrane, John, *Kulu Sé Mama.* Impulse Records, 1967.

Coltrane, John, *Live at Birdland.* Impulse Records, 1964.

Coltrane, John, *Live in Paris.* Charly Records, 1987.

Skinner, Graeme. *Bach: The Six Sonatas & Partitas for Violin Solo, Lara St. John.* Ancalogon Records, 2007.

Mallarmé, Stéphane, *Selected Poetry and Prose,* various translators (New York: New Directions) 1982.

Olson, Charles, "The Animate versus the Mechanical and Thought" *Collected Prose* (Berkeley: University of California Press) 1997.

Olson, Charles, *Olson / Creeley: Correspondence, Vol. 10.*

Grubbs, David, "Shadowy Hush Twilight: Two Collaborations with Susan Howe" *Chicago Review*, Vol. 55, No. 1, 2010. [via Yale Union, http://yaleunion.org/david-grubbs-susan-howe/]

Ponge, Francis, *The Making of the Pré*. Trans. Lee Fahnestalk (Columbia: University of Missouri Press) 1979.

Davenport, Guy, Personal letter sent from Lexington, KY, 11/22/1988.

Berger, Karol, *Bach's Cycle, Mozart's Arrow* (Berkeley: University of California Press) 2007.

Kristeva Julia, *Desire in Language*. Trans. Leon S. Roudiez (New York: Columbia University Press) 1980.

Davenport, Guy, *The Geography of the Imagination,* (San Francisco: North Point Press) 1981.

Rimbaud, Arthur, *Rimbaud: Complete Works, Selected Letters.* Trans. Wallace Fowlie (Chicago: The University of Chicago Press) 2005.

Nin, Anaïs, *Mirages: The Unexpurgated Diaries of Anaïs Nin* (Athens, Ohio: Swallow Press /University of Ohio Press) 2013.

Benjamin, Walter, "*Trauerspiel* and Tragedy" in *Walter Benjamin Selected Writings, 1913-1926, Vol. 1* (Cambridge, MA: The Belknap Press of Harvard University) 1996.

Seferis, George, *A Poet's Journal: Days of 1945-1951* (Cambridge, MA: The Belknap Press of Harvard University) 1974.

Sulcas, Roslyn. "Limping in Solidarity and Leaping for Joy" *NYTimes*, July 1, 2014.

Chaucer, Geoffrey, *Canterbury Tales* (New York: Covici Friede) 1934.

Durrell, Lawrence, *The Greek Islands* (London: Faber) 1978.

Kazanzakis, Nikos, *Russia: A Chronicle of Three Journeys in the Aftermath the Revolution*. Trans. Michael Antonakes and Thanasis Maskaleris (Berkeley: Creative Arts Book Company) 1989.

Bronk, William, *The World, the Worldless* (New York: New Directions) 1964.

Olson, Charles, *New Man & Woman* (Gloucester, MA: Millennia Foundation) 1970.

Scott-Heron, Gil, "Washington, D.C." on *Moving Target*. Arista Records, 1982.

Deleuze, Gilles, *Difference and Repetition*. Trans. Paul Patton (New York: Columbia University Press) 1995.

Atlas of the World (Washington, DC: National Geographic Society) 1981.

Kung-wang, Huang, et al., *The Four Great Masters of the Yuan* (Taipai: National Palace Museum) 1975.

Zukofsky, Louis, "A-5" in *"A"* (Berkeley: University of California Press) 1978.

Rimbaud, Arthur, "Bad Blood" *Rimbaud: Complete Works, Selected Letters/* Trans, Wallace Fowlie (Chicago: The University of Chicago Press) 2005.

Zaborowski, Magdalena J, *James Baldwin's Turkish Decade: Erotics of Exile* (Durham: Duke University Press) 2009.

Deleuze, Gilles, and Parnet, Claire, *Dialogues*. Trans. Hugh Tomlinson and Barbara Habberjam (New York: Columbia University Press) 1987.

Benjamin, Walter, "One-Way Street" *Walter Benjamin Selected Writings, 1913-1926, Vol. 1* (Cambridge, MA: The Belknap Press of Harvard University) 1996.

George F. Butterick, *A Guide to the Maximus Poems of Charles Olson* (Berkeley: University of California Press) 1978.

Deleuze, Gilles, "A New Cartographer" in *Foucault*. Trans. Seán Hand (Minneapolis: University of Minnesota Press) 1986.

Fromm, Erich, *Escape from Freedom* (New York: Rinehart & Co.) 1941.

Derrida, Jacques, "The Double Session" *Dissemination*. Trans. Barbara Johnson (Chicago: The University of Chicago Press) 1981.

Lauterwein, Andréa, *Anselm Kiefer/Paul Celan: Myth, Mourning and Memory* (London: Thames & Hudson) 2007.

Derrida, Jacques, *Sovereignties in Question: the Poetics of Paul Celan*. Trans. Thomas Dutoit (New York: Fordham University Press) 2005.

Greaney, Patrick, *Untimely Beggar: Poverty and Power from Baudelaire to Benjamin* (Minneapolis: University of Minnesota Press) 2008.

Lauring, Palle, *Danmarks Historie,* (København: Carit Andersen) 1968.

Adorno, Theodor, *Minima Moralia: Reflections from Damaged Life*. Trans. E. F. N. Jephcott. London: Verso) 1978.

Barthes, Roland, *The Rustle of Language*. Trans. Richard Howard (New York: Hill and Wang) 1986.

Durrell, Lawrence, *Justine* (London: Faber and Faber) 1958.

Bakhtin, M. M., *Problems of Dostoevsky's Poetics*. Trans. Caryl Emerson (Minneapolis: University of Minnesota Press) 1984.

Eliot, T. S., *Complete Poems & Plays* (New York: Harcourt, Brace & World) 1971.

Gibbons, Robert, *This Vanishing Architecture* (Charlestown, MA: Innerer Klang Press) 2001.

Gibbons, Robert, *Of DC* (Charlestown, MA: Innerer Klang Press) 1992.

Proust, Marcel, *Remembrance of Things Past*. Trans. Scott Moncrieff and Terrence Kilmartin (New York: Vintage Books) 1982.

Mallarmé, Stéphane, *Selected Letters*. Trans. Rosemary Lloyd (Chicago: The University of Chicago Press, 1988.

Jarrett, Keith. *Paris / London: Testament*. ECM, 2008.

Mallarmé, Stéphane. "Two Pigeons" *Dissemination*. Chicago: The University of Chicago Press) 1981.

Celan, Paul, *Todesfuge*. Trans. John Felstiner (New York: The Limited Editions Club) 2001.

Braque, Georges, *G. Braque*. Trans. Richard Howard (New York: Abrams) 1971.

Anastas, Peter, Review of Ralph Maud's, *Charles Olson's Reading: A Biography*, 1996. *Gloucester Times*, 3/28/96.

Butterick, George, *A Guide to the Maximus Poems of Charles Olson* (Berkeley: University of California Press) 1978.

Olson, Charles, *The Maximus Poems: Volume Three* (New York: Grossman Publishers) 1975.

Smith, Roberta, "On Kawara, Artist Who Found Elegance in Every Day, Dies at 81," *NYTimes*, July 16, 2014.

Barnard, Anne, "Boys Drawn to Gaza Beach, and Into Center of Mideast Strife," *NYTimes*, July 16, 2014.

Rancière, Jacques, *The Flesh of Words.* Trans. Charlotte Mandell (Stanford, CA: Stanford University Press) 2004.

Rilke, Rainer Maria, Greaney's *Untimely Beggar.*

Monk, Thelonius. *The Thelonius Monk Orchestra at Town Hall.* Riverside, 1959.

ANATOMY & GEOGRAPHY

BOOK II

PREFACE TO BOOK II

"The city occupies a significant place in the heart of this old ship's passenger and harbor stroller"
—Walter Benjamin on first visiting Antwerp
(Letter to Carl Linfert, late December 1934)

Writing a preface to a book by Robert Gibbons may not be necessary in the traditional sense of doing the reader the service of opening up the book in front of him or her, but it is certainly a pleasurable excuse for the writer of such a preface to engage with Gibbons's work once more and to think about the ways in which he crafts already open texts such as these explorations of *Anatomy & Geography*.

'Open' does not translate as 'simple', by any means. A poem sequence such as this second book of observations on the connections between living and traveling, sensing and feeling, experiencing and writing is of necessity complex. Gibbons's master image for charting the connections listed above is to describe himself as a supplicant before the "vortextual world", a world that one can only enter fully by submitting to the "vortex of writing", that process of transforming memories, dreams, rhythms, visions and thoughts into the stuff of poetry, or life itself. One of Gibbons's many sources of inspiration for this sequence, Julia Kristeva, describes this process as one of 'transubstantiation' in her discussion of Marcel Proust's method of making life into text, and that word is also apt to describe Gibbons's improvisations and mosaics of many stones, letters, signs and animal totems.

The poems in this sequence connect. They interconnect with one another in a textual play that indeed is better described as a maelstrom than as a docile web. But they also connect in other ways, bridging time to time; reaching deep inside to find the spines of bodies as well as books. In this volume the poet remembers animals he has encountered and the lessons they have taught him, bridging those lessons to the ones he has received from literary shamans such as Charles Olson and Rimbaud, musical wizards such as Marilyn Crispell and Bach, and artist magi such as Robert Motherwell and Goya. In the process the poems force us to think in new ways, accepting that writing can make stones float across oceans like ferryboats, connecting ports and people that were not in touch before and would not be in touch but for words such as these that flourish across the pages like wings of migrant birds, the only sentient beings on the planet that travel as far and high as humans.

In a medieval manuscript written to edify its readers on the progression of human life and its peregrinations, we read: "I fly a boue the skyes heyere than eyther heroun or egret" (*The Pilgrimage of the Lyf of the Manhode* – ca. 1450). This same height is attained in Gibbons's *Anatomy & Geography*, and the egrets he tells us about in his poems are direct descendants of those the medieval monk used to instruct us of how to get nearer to God:

Five white egrets on the Back Cove
abreast the coming storm, which I took
as good omen, as my own
will to overcome all
obstacles, & write
this minor tract
acknowledging
Death as one
to overcome.

The white egret is a migrant bird, and the peregrinations of bird and man alike is the great theme of most of Gibbons's work. In these long poem sequences he has developed a new way of floating signifiers across time and space, forging an almost alchemical conjunction of meanings – creating what in medieval astronomy was called a *syzygy*, an event that only occurs when three celestial bodies are perfectly aligned and one eclipses the other. The matter that Gibbons uses most prominently in performing this alignment is blackness – black as in the skin of those that did not choose of their own free will to come to American shores; black as in the palette of Robert Motherwell's elegies for the victims of Fascism; black as the air Rimbaud felt that he breathed; black as the characters in Genet's passion play *Les Nègres* in which Maya Angelou acted when it was performed at St. Mark's Playhouse in May 1961; black as the wine of Cahors gifted to the poet; black as the Voodoo dancers in Maya Deren's *Divine Horsemen* film; black as the eclipsed sun at the center of Harry Crosby's concrete poem "Black Sun", cited as part of the book; black as in the color of the volcanic stones the poet finds off the shore of Maine. Gibbons says: "Black is the color of his & our Time", aligning Goya in *syzygy* with our present. But then there is the matter of those five white egrets, and many other "Signs in flora & fauna"…

As black and white are juxtaposed in Gibbons's text and life, the poems herein juxtapose the fundamental feeling of loss and the many lamentations and names for this emotion that art has offered (such as Lorca's *duende*) with the profound sensation of joy that wells up in us when confronted by the finest endeavors of man. Gibbons quotes the great French prose poet Francis Ponge: *The poem is a thing of joy offered man, made and posed especially for him.* The idea of *posing* a poem as one would a problem to be puzzled out by the use of mathematical or logical formulae and deduction is in a sense alien to Gibbons's way of working. He never poses or posits, but rather *throws* us a poem as one throws a shape out of clay on a potter's wheel (cf. Pound's idea of *Phanopoeia*, or casting the die of images upon our imagination) – just as he imagines in a dream what could happen to his own ancestral clay, his body becoming the luminous shape of the *chora*, or the womb itself.

Thus, while the elegiac undertone of these poems never ceases to resonate, they ultimately fulfill the exhortation of one of the great European peregrinators, Walter Benjamin, who 101 years ago instructed us "our youth is but a brief night (fill it with rapture!)". These poems are not exclusively for the youths of the world, but they would serve as a good introduction for them to connections of ideas and practices from all corners of the world. Gibbons has always balanced Europe and America in his writing, finding many mentors from both those continents. His journey to Denmark plays an important role in this book and I am honored to appear as one of his many interlocutors in these texts. In this book, however, he has extended his global equilibrium to also encompass South America in a tribute to Pablo Neruda, to whose home Gibbons never managed to perform the pilgrimage he had once intended. Instead Gibbons lends the pages of his book to his son-in-law who did manage to visit that famed house in Chile, and who tells a raw, yet affecting story about how he did not know the significance of what he experienced on that trip till much later when Gibbons prompted him to remember it and write it down. If this book by Gibbons and the hospitality its pages offer can make many more young men and women in need of a prompt such as this to write down their portions of the vortextual life, we would all be much the richer for it. For as Gibbons reminds us, time and again, "notes save lives"; letters are necessary – and so are poems.

—*Bent Sørensen, Knäred, Sweden – October 2014*

ANATOMY & GEOGRAPHY

II

*I know that the only people able to renew the world
are those grounded in poetry.* —Guillaume Apollinaire

Want to wander.

Those three words I've been carrying around for days.
To want to wander where, & there I am on the edge
of the continent with a friend,
older, teacher, not the *adult*
Walter Benjamin might have had to warn us about,
who may advocate giving up the dreams of youth, no,
Robert Hellman breaks the silence of the day
with an expert rendering of Mahler's,
Songs of a Wayfarer,
"Isn't this a splendid world,
splendid world?"

How the world did brighten & shimmer,
come to immediate life way back then
in my early twenties, what with him
in his late fifties, teaching me so
many things without the heavy
pedagogic burden Benjamin
warns against in that early
essay, "Experience,"
rather,
when he exclaims parenthetically
"(fill it with rapture!)" I hear the sound
of Hellman's voice breaking the silence

with Mahler's words, "in the sunshine all things
took on color & sound," & that resonance & vibrancy
animated the immediate.

Then Hellman left for Denmark
with his family: wife, former dancer,
Margaret, baby, Miranda, son, J.B., dog,
Jewels, who mistakenly ate a hundred tabs
of LSD, what shining world before his eyes?
& pet blue jay, all of them squatting for years
in Nørrebro.

He'll write to me from there,
enclosing with one letter a poem
set in the environs of Cape Ann, where
Mahler's words first emerged, getting jagged,
granite stones of both Gloucester & Rockport
down on paper to float
across the ocean.

There's Walter Benjamin
with Bertolt Brecht in Dragør,
Denmark, the former down with nephritis,
while Brecht blames the illness on effects suffered
by Benjamin's reading
Dostoevsky's *Crime & Punishment*.
I love that.
That a book could be that powerful,
for good or ill.
Benjamin recovers fully
enough by September 28, 1934
to travel to the southernmost port
in Denmark, the town of Gedser
on the island of Falster.

::::

According to the *NYT* obituary,
Robert Hellman died exactly

thirty years ago this past
Saturday on a ferry
between Germany
& Denmark.
Is it any wonder, now,
the past few days his voice,
which so sonorously broke
the silence so long ago, making the world
resonate before me, animating the immediate,
vaulting
toward the unknown
future that is today?

Robert Hellman, 65, Is Dead; Was a Writer and Translator

Published: July 30, 1984

Robert Hellman, a writer and translator, died July 26 of a heart attack on a boat between Germany and Denmark, friends in New York reported. He was 65 years old and lived in Copenhagen.

Mr. Hellman had lived in Denmark since 1973. In 1975 he returned to the United States to be playwright-in-residence at the Guthrie Theater in Minneapolis for a year. There he wrote a play called ''Open Shut.'' He also wrote ''Kling,'' which was performed Off Broadway, at the Phoenix Theater, in 1964.

He and Richard O'Gorman translated ''Fabliaux, Ribald Tales From the Old French'' in 1965. Mr. Hellman had taught at several institutions, including the University of Iowa, City College and Juilliard School.

:::::

Attempting to recapture circumstances surrounding the last full day in Denmark at the Museum of Modern Art just outside København, the Louisiana, where Bent & I traipsed through the site-specific-open-air labyrinth, titled, *Self Passage*, with views of Sweden across Øresund Strait:

Tangential
to the core of our talk,
& for that matter, essential,
the image made out of a fragment
in a piece by Anselm Kiefer of a figure
entering either brothel or concentration camp.

At the same time,
associating it with the historical
insistence of the King of Denmark,
when the Nazis invaded, walking the streets
of his own country (in protest,
tramping, a bhikkhu
with mendicant
sensibility)
wearing
a bright,
five-
pointed
yellow
star.

::::

Took the ferry
out to Peaks Island
early yesterday morning
with two books in black
canvas bag: Eiland & Jennings,
Walter Benjamin: A Critical Life,
& Neruda's, **Stones of the Sky**.

Found a little cove
with goldmine
of volcanic
rock.
Black
stone

galore,
as if I hadn't ever noticed before the difference
between sands of
the mainland
& this island,
imagined I'd never see outside
Isla Negra or lakeside Antinana
with its *grapes of jasper, or rock honeycombs*
bored out by volcanoes or bad weather.

This score of jewels placed
on paper plate,
& photo sent
to Bent, who preferred "The masked marauder on the far right,"
that combination granite/diorite
one sees so often
in Gloucester
& Rockport,
the same stones
Hellman got down
as words on paper & floated
across the ocean.

:::::

Any reminiscence
of that long, four-month journey
back in 1974 ending up only as far as Veracruz,
Mitla, Oaxaca, Zihuatanejo, Mexico City often begins
with the recollection that we started out
thinking
we could make it
all the way to Isla Negra
to see the humble home of Pablo there.

But this time, instead of shrugging
in disappointment

about not getting there
I recall, instead,
that our young son-in-law,
Patrick Campbell, did make it
at age 18, & I wanted to hear more,
writing:

Dear Patrick,

Saturday I finished writing a "booklength" poem [114 pages] titled "Anatomy & Geography".

Yesterday I sent a proofed version to my friend, Ben Bollig, who teaches at Oxford University, & who has committed to writing a *Preface* for the book.

This Saturday he heads down to Chile to teach, give lectures, & present a gift to a 100-year-old Chilean poet, Nicanor Parra.

He plans to reread my manuscript on the flight down.

Now, I don't know exactly why I've gravitated to Pablo Neruda's work this week, but I just read a couple of pieces out loud to Kathleen from a small book titled, **Stones of the Sky**.

She asked a question about whether he was talking about Chile in the context of the work, & I said, "Ya, Isla Negra, where I headed, naively, in 1974. You'd have to be a millionaire to get there."

Then I recalled your story about going there, even entering Neruda's house, if I'm not mistaken. After a couple of drinks, will you try to sit down & write down EVERYTHING you remember about being there, especially the landscape & the light, the sea & of course ANYTHING Neruda.

ALSO, would you also kindly ask whoever you were with at the time to do the same thing, & share their experience with me?

Thanks so much!!!

Love, Bob

Patrick wrote back:
Hey Bob! Cool question!

As I read your inquiry I was immediately flooded by really great memories of Mr. Neruda's house that you so fondly admire. I remember being there with my uncle Clyde, whom I respect a ton!! Talk about a guy who knows everything about everything and can remember calculus class like it was yesterday. That's probably why I finished college. He didn't because of one thing or another and didn't finish. So I did so at the very least I could show that his influence was immense in my life. So even though I didn't want too, I finished, maybe even for him. He taught me baseball, how to ski, how to have a spirit of adventure. Little did I know he would also influence my appreciation for people and history later in life. Yet at the time I was pissed for having to give up my skiing time for some jackass poet. I'm an athlete damn it, why do I need culture. Ha, what an ignorant jackass I was.

So it was with great fortune I got the opportunity to end up at Neruda's house checking out the beach, a rugged one at best. Big black rock, rugged waves slamming the shoreline and a swimmer in the distance! Wow, how could someone swim in such rugged water. I watched him for a long time, thinking he would just drown. He/she didn't. What a bad ass I remember thinking. And what crazy bastard would live in this rugged ass beach! This ain't no Bahamas!

I remember going into his bedroom and thinking what a view! He would eyeglass the ocean often, checking to see if any treasure would show up. Later down below, a shed or another room, he stored bottles with different colors. He had quite a few of them. It was a humble place nothing too fancy, but I got a sense of contentment from it. I liked that. I like gathering info even though that I never met him, never read his work you admire, whom my uncle held with such awe, I got to experience a sense of contentment. A good view, hopefully a sexy Chilean lady in the bed with him, and an opportunity to check and see what the ocean would bring. What a mystery. Sometimes good sometimes bad I imagined, but nevertheless, some experiences bringing a man to a sense of contentment.

Here I was a complete stranger anxious to move on, but yet you would have me examine what I felt. I never thought going to his abode would mean anything considering I was only humoring my uncle, but yet as you have made me examine my memory somehow I felt that Neruda and I may have had something in common. Like a sense of adventure, a link to water, and enjoyment of a comfortable home topped off with good food and good drink. I'm not used to the ocean, but did feel a huge sense of being a little speck of sand when I saw how huge his backyard was. The damn ocean!

Now I didn't eat with him, but our driver took us down the road to eat at a restaurant off the ocean. Was it similar to the food he ate and the great wine he drank? If so, then him and I would get along great! I remember my uncle and I had to drag our driver in the restaurant to eat with us. We explained that we wouldn't gain the full experience if he was in the car while we ate. We wanted fellowship with a true hospitable Chilean. Turns out we were right. He was such a great guy, who just like me had ambitions of being someone some day, probably read Neruda's work as much as I did. Which is sad because you should have been on that trip instead of me Bob, but he had a sense of adventure. Life wasn't stuck for him. He wanted to afford a tiled roof with lots of land. I could respect that. He wasn't just an embassy driver. He had a plan. He was focused, driven if you will. So with the ocean air, great seafood, and awesome wine topped it all off! It was a really great high for me being 18 years old and miles away from the states.

Wow, haven't thought of that in a long time. Thanks Bob. Cheers! May you one day experience what I didn't understand at the time! Would I do it again if I knew I couldn't go skiing? Absolutely! I get the sense he was a badass in his own way and I respect that!

::::

Who's the writer here anyway!!?
No, the right man saw that house!!
Letters save lives.

::::

Spent yesterday, Monday morning, July 28, 2014,
at the local art college library, so inviting,

so enclosed & open at the same time,
conducive to writing, the first
thing I checked out were
discards for sale,
& who's waiting
there for me, but **Robert Motherwell
& Black,**
yes,
for a buck!

Talk about a goldmine
of volcanic stone, the first page
I turn to this morning, Tuesday, July 29,
contains his *Soot-Black Stone #3,* 1973, &
if that's not a cat,
ok, not a pipe,
but the image
of a black-cat
stone,
I don't know
what is.

[I had a difficult time finding, or even imagining beauty, that is, what *is.*]

Charged beyond belief at what else
this gem of a book may contain.
Damn, seriously = *Altamira #1,* 1975!
He's measuring the height of the ceiling
with five small horizontal lines + three larger,
jagged, (standing in for prehistoric time), vertical lines.

::::

This morning, too, I'm back briefly at the Louisiana
Museum of Modern Art just outside København
inside the Sculpture Garden with Bent, who
places my identification card, the Jack
of Spades, on a ledge of Noguchi's

1986 piece made of basalt,
Queen of Spades.
It's a joy to see
the two together,
as if an act
of illicit
Love.

Earlier that week, last August, 2013, I was momentarily
an uncitizen of the world, having misplaced
my passport under a pile of manuscript papers
we'd all been reading from the night before
on their Roskilde dining room table.

All I had in my wallet to identify
myself
was the Jack of Spades,
which Camelia claimed stands
for the image of troubled youth, an interpretation
that in many more cities of the world than Roskilde
has rung
true.

::::

Begin to worry I may not ever be able to pull myself away
from the pages of **Robert Motherwell & Black**!!

Look, the 2nd epigraph is from Rimbaud: *My hungers are the ends of black air.*

Look, the great poem by Lorca, (who's blacker than Lorca?):

A boy brought a white sheet
at five in the afternoon.
A frail lime ready prepared
at five in the afternoon.
The rest was death, and death alone

at five in the afternoon.
…The room was iridescent with agony
at five in the afternoon.
In the distance the gangrene now comes
at five in the afternoon.
Horn of the lily through green groins
at five in the afternoon.
The wounds were burning like suns
at five in the afternoon… -FGL

Comment by the artist himself in answer to interview question:
Q – Is your European bias due to the fact that you were so highly
influenced by the Europeans who came over in the 'forties, like Max
Ernst, say?
RM – No, it's because I like *quality*. It's as simple as that.

::::

No, I'll never get out of these pages,
nor may not
want to.

::::

Sun came out momentarily just now lifting me up out of those dark
pages, only
to make me recall
that image
by Harry Crosby,
whose work was included with my own
first published poems in pages of that small magazine
out of Gloucester, *Red Crow,*
1973.

Here it is:

```
black black black black black
black black black black black
black black black black black
black black black black black
black black  SUN black black
black black black black black
black black black black black
black black black black black
black black black black black
black black black black black
```

Harry Crosby
19 rue de Lille
Paris

Reminds me, too,
that Kathleen's Mother,
Nancy Leet Thompson,
was Motherwell's secretary
for many years, making me wish
she were here now to shed more light
on these brilliant dark pages, similar to the way
on Sunday we wished her father, L. Don Leet,
were with us on the beach at Peaks Island.
Former head of geology department
at Harvard, he could identify
that cache of pebbles
& stones gathered
onto a paper plate.

Lunch today may well be this
paper plate of stones,
as Olson quotes
Rimbaud: "I offer
in explanation, a quote:
si j'ai du goût, ce n'est guères
que pour la terre et les pierres."

::::

Let's just say I'm hungry.
To continue to wander.
I got my mile & a half in this morning.
Moved in & around Aalborg, Paris, Baja,
even bumped into Fernando Sanchez in Mexico
City, where he was working on a mural left behind
by David Siqueiros, who'd passed away six months earlier.

Purchased a small portfolio
of Sanchez's drawing, etchings,
notebook sketches.

I used one of the images to publish a broadside
with a piece written by Susan Wilkins.
Where is that?
Two versions:
first one
purple ink
on yellow stock.

Didn't like the result, so asked friend Dan Carr to print it with silver ink
on Arches black.
Oh, ya, that's Mexico.
Where are those drawings,
etchings, & notebook sketches
only now coming to mind from exactly forty years ago now, & jolted
into existence by the added
statement here by
Motherwell:

> All my life, I've been obsessed with death and was profoundly
> moved by the continual presence of sudden death in Mexico
> (I've never seen a race of people so heedless of life!) The
> presence everywhere of death iconography: coffins, black glass
> enclosed horse drawn hearses, sigao skulls, figures of death,
> corpses...

Makes me wonder what happened to that piece of obsidian
found down there in Otatitlán, where the Black Christ
housed in the yellow & black tiled church blesses
the formerly Aztec population.

Or,

the way Lorca uses the gypsy word "*duende*" apparently corresponds
in unusual poetic discourse to (more or less) "demonic". —RM

I have a photograph of Motherwell's lithograph I wanted
to purchase at the Susan Rothenberg Gallery
on Newbury Street in Boston.
Two reasons I didn't:
1.) cost $1,100.
2.) Title: *Gypsy Curse,*
but beautiful black ink on red paper!

PLEASURE OF FRAGMENTS

Similar to January, I'm in no hurry. Cold grey air, almost visible itself.
Breath inside of scarf, or out, free, accentuating deep realities of Northern
New England, cold truths in grey, layered clouds, rich, indomitable sea,
where the massive *Nordic Cosmos* lounges heavily with a full hold of oil.
Leave nonchalance along the waterfront, return home to an array of books.
Goya in no hurry. Black, in no hurry. A book on Motherwell purchased
years ago at a chain going out of business, something I could not otherwise
afford, became pages stored away for later use. Shimmering on the shelf
of one bookcase, asking to dovetail with numerous Goya tracts, against
the cold grey outside, the heat of black, so prominent in Goya, his own
house walls covered, in fact, in black. Motherwell's assistant claims he'd
mix two parts acrylic Mars-black with one of water so the painter could
hear paint splash, make black sounds of Lorca's *duende*, which Motherwell
interpreted as music. In solitude, then, wrenching language out of live
air, harsh contrasts between excruciating nonverbal seconds, pleasure of
fragments, sentences themselves.

SERIES OF ELEGIES

In the pitch black of close to three in the morning, when out of dreams I get up to read & write, she says to take the Mexican blanket at the foot of the bed, adding that she loves me, unraveling white wool of the Chiapan blanket protecting me in the middle of the night after dreaming of the flautist ready to play a series of Elegies, she said, the jazz audience applauding along with her tempo, rhythms for use, archetypal construct, model example for poetry & prose, she knew what she was doing by appearing before me, my head just under the microphone in awe & almost familiarity with the figure who now leads me back to the study, where at the opposite end of the house in a room with no heat, temperatures below freezing, Lorca's words piled high on the table, burn. Motherwell yearned for solace of paint in his *Lament for Lorca*, scorched black paint in which we smell ash in the air, or as Rafael Alberti wrote, "Motherwell's black/ profound compact entered into with night," which I found turning the page in the book next to the Goya left upside down on the table like lost pages of history in the night above the white Mexican blanket protecting me while the body reads & composes in pain & joy of solitude expressing utter respect for the most poetic of American painters. Smoke-filled pain to the extent that when I stood alone in New York before Anfam's placement of *Elegy to the Spanish Republic*, or in DC before *Reconciliation Elegy* both Goya & Lorca stood up to be heard in tones of joy & terror rising out of the black blood of night under the earth & ash-filled sky.

:::::

Let's let the heartfelt image
of Motherwell's *Elegy for Salvador Allende*
help hoist me up out of these pages like some *deus ex machina*:
collage made of acrylic & paper labels, all
75 X 70 inches of it
& still available
at Antoine Helwaser Gallery
on 79th Street = the sun seemed to move

across the July 29th sky, but it's really been me
& this paper plate of stones moved
across the sky & anchored here,
now, out of those pages
with black coffee
at the table
close to
the earth,
wandering,
writing all day.

:::::

Ok, I'm out, & although hoping to get a letter
from Ben Bollig in Chile, I get a brief note
from Richard Pierron in Nice, France.

He describes the accompanying photograph of an alcove/cave
in Nord Ouest Près de Borko, home of the Dogon in Mali.

Describes the cave this way:

Place of various cults. The excavation extends in a meander on a height
and width under 1 meter, below a cliff nearly 38 meters, arriving on a large
room containing bones of animals, small fatty sacrificial libations, feathers,
masks and other statues. Place of taboo. For only insiders. Elders have the
right to access. After many small sacrifices and checking of my approach
to the oracles, I had the chance to enter... A fabulous place and hidden,
forgotten treasures an area revered and respectful... –RP

Earlier in the day today I took a few moments & stood transfixed
by the blackness of our own Dogon granary door, thankful...

:::::

Notes save lives.

:::::

162

On Friday afternoon, the 25ᵗʰ, took a picnic down to what they call the foot
of Munjoy Hill at the edge of the sea, just up from the beach on a bench
next to a double-trunked tree. After lunch, moved up under shade
tree away from the hot July sun.

Didn't take long to recognize an estranged friend
identified by these serrated leaves
I was once so familiar with,
but Dutch elm disease
did a number on all
those ancient
Cape Ann
elms!!

Picked a leaf
for bookmark.
Anything can be
a bookmark, but an anvil.
Here,
it marks four
lines & a Roman Numeral
by Pablo Neruda:
> ### XXII
> I entered the amethyst grotto:
> I left my blood among purple thorns:
> I changed skin, wine, outlook:
> ever since, violets hurt me.

Not the only bookmark in his little book, **Stones of the Sky**,
there's a printout of a dream
from the same morning,
listen:

Dream 7/25/2014: We purchase a lamp. I ask the shopkeeper to place
a label in her handwriting above the bulb & shade to read: PARIS.

That way, when we get it home, the city contained in the word will be
illuminated above
the illumination.

PARIS & all
that entails:

Courbet's *L'Origine du Monde*; Village Voice Bookstore, (now, regrettably, closed), where I happened on Kristeva's **Desire in Language** in 1987, & sought out her **Crisis of the ~~European~~ Subject** in 2000; Caviar Kaspia at 17 Place de la Madeleine, where I saw the former Russian count with the young girl I thought at first his daughter, Champagne, Vodka, & weighty mound of beluga; Baudelaire's Hôtel de Lauzun on quai d'Anjou, Île Saint-Louis; Rimbaud's footprints on rue Monsieur le Prince, etc.

::::

Surprised in the pages of the same small book of poetry
of Neruda's late work by another bookmark, more
or less: a small pebble from the island beach
& paper plate of stones transported by ferry,
it must have migrated all on its own
marking the line, *the mounds of*
ultramarine stone, although
this one's as yellow,
& same size as
a blackbird's
eye.

::::

Maybe the pebble wanted
to *read* at the end of its destination
in migration as much as I, too, wanted
during my wandering on earth & across
the blank page?

Nevertheless,
this pebble brings
to mind the one Francis Ponge
conjured up in words in 1928.

To put it in present tense
Derrida says, "He is always at work."

I dig that!
Not having recalled a day
in the last 17,124 =
47 years,
that my organs,
those divinities,
as Kristeva calls them, have ignored,
(either individually, nor in choric tandem,
along with appendages,
fingers & toes, or larger
limbs, arms & legs,
let alone torso
with Solar Plexus
located behind stomach,
in front of aorta & crura of diaphragm),

the importance in the world of the realm of poetry.

Francis Ponge's pebble
brought to mind
by my own
migrating
from island sand
to paper plate to pages
of a book, how different
& alike are they?

One could begin elsewhere
for evidence
of difference
& alike
at the same time:

A stone as a surface of inscription and *effacement,*
such is the magic writing pad of whoever is Ponge.
It holds some surprises for us. —JD

To begin elsewhere in order
to get somewhere:
illogical
tactic.

Why not?
Ponge quotes
Rimbaud in *Introduction*
to The Pebble, written five
years <u>after</u> the poem in 1933:

"If I have any taste it's just
for earth and rock."

Thereby, beginning at the end.

His pebble is
immortal, existing
next to *Temples, Demi-Gods,*
Miracles, while mine is ephemeral,
at once, marking that Eternal Time, when
Freedom found us on the island beach one
Sunday morning.

Ponge's pebble, so abstract
as not so much to exist,
but to become
something
other,
the equally solid springboard
to conception.

My pebble, so concrete
& small as to have slipped
through my fingers finding its own
way into the pages of someone else's book.

Both stones are igneous
& of ink, thereby made
by fire & desire.

::::

Sun suddenly approves…

::::

On one of my walks today kept an eye out for signs.
Flora fauna waves currents geology celestial events wind
climate clouds tones others fences paths internal heartbeats breath.

Death tagged right along with me, & gratefully acknowledging
its presence, too, to a great degree, although not continually,
as if when reaching the height of the seawall, recognizing
down below some perfectly, purposely placed
foundation stone anchoring earth against sea
safely for decades, even centuries,
white granite linked
by hot magma
to green
diorite
both faces
of the Janus-head
smiling, one toward land,
the other ocean.

Red sails in distance.

The day became a gift
with seven crows flying east
across the Eastern Promenade.
Cardinal heard before seen, Hell,
skunk cabbage tried to hide stone tools
formerly in use, & took those rocks as sign
to put to good use here, to carve & etch at least
a date 7/31/2014, knowing I'd done the same thing
on this date 7/31 five years ago 2009, here:

NICHE SOURCE FORM

I.

When heat is earth's perspiration in this neck of the waters, visible to the naked eye, itself, devouring all it can, now that summer rolled in on all fours like some strange monster welcomed into the city to rid it of its year-long malaise. Goldfinches go crazy piercing the sultry air with erotic-geometric lines of flight. Catbirds scratch the same air with their call. A house wren lands on an oxidized iron rail, as if to shout, "I'm no sparrow!" Visible heat all the way out to the horizon across the water, across the field of vision, flush right up against the ledge, which is the edge of earth protecting anything inland, west. Ledge says caution. Ledge says before, & beyond, at the same Time. Says shelter ancestral niche source form secret hard angular indelible discreet fragmented impenetrable epic magma core.

II.

See how the wind picked up? Right up out of a hidden abyss? Monstrous fingers & forearms like Keith Jarrett inspired by some far-reaching, blood-let desire transformed into percussive sound upon leaves of trees, waves. Musical universe. True, once in tune with it. Sensation as latent sound become sound, or language, or as Kristeva theorizes, even color itself. Deep, deep green today, that wind picks up out of the black earth deep, deep green driving it heavenward, toward a blue lamentation. Now some cloud formation keel-steers itself connected to both sea & sky, a phenomenon not seen in all my years. All my years, all the moments in all those years. Virginia Woolf is exquisite comparing waves to broadcloth. Just the other day I saw a worn tear in my jeans compatible in its warp & weft weave to a text, itself.

Only thirty-four minutes left
in 7/31/2014, who knows how many
in the entire span of life, what with Death
accounted for tagging right along with me,
& gratefully acknowledged to a great degree,
not continually. Five white egrets on the Back Cove

abreast the coming storm, which I took
as good omen, as my own
will to overcome all
obstacles, & write
this minor tract
acknowledging
Death as one
to overcome.

Kenny Dorham over KCSM Radio in San Francisco on a trumpet
I'd recognize as that same accompanying Coltrane on the album
Coltrane Time, which I've walked to, & driven to, many times
before. Dorham, now, with exactly twenty-three minutes
left in the day, & month, on *Angel Eyes* from his album
This Is the Moment, 1958, marking the recording
debut of Cedar Walton, you know, the pianist
Frank O'Hara used to etch the time & date
of 12:20 the afternoon of July 17th, 1959,
when at the Ziegfeld Theatre he
sees a photo, & suddenly,
knows Lady Day
Died.

Signs
in flora
& fauna,
New England
aster, say, mullein
& staghorn sumac,
groundhog chomping
grass near our newly discovered
double-trunk elm, those crows & egrets
already mentioned, signs, even numbers
like 23 always reminding me of my brother
born on 1/23/1952, & the number 54 always
reminding me of the year Nanzu flew us to New York City,
saying on the 12th floor of the Taft Hotel,
after opening the secretary drawer for stationery,
"Bobby, you can do whatever you want," & where

we saw three double features, all war movies, a TV game
show called CONCENTRATION, & ate a slice
of apple pie at the AUTOMAT for a quarter.
It's now 12:01 AM
tomorrow.

::::

More or less imagining I'm done
for one day, less than fifteen
minutes later on the day
I just called tomorrow,
whatever that means,
reach across library
table for light
reading:
Blaise Cendrars, where the back of an envelope
& sloppy ink-strewn Post-it note hold words
of my own from who knows when:

>Out here for the second
>time today, the *Montagny*
>still docked across the
>bay. Why wouldn't I
>open one of the three books
>in my black canvas bag
>randomly to Blaise
>Cendrars', "A line that
>fades away / good-bye
>It's America…" Weeds
>grow out of the tops
>of pier poles, America
>forever returning to land
>& water
>
>close to silence,
>the waves, scuttling
>through abandoned

pier poles once the grain
warehouse of
Grand Trunk Railroad
where wheat landed
via rail from Canada
then fed the world
via Portland ships
all close to
silence
now.

12:27, 8/1/2014

The 1st begins
full of promise
simply from light
through kitchen bay
window, although not
long before the front page
attempts to contradict any such
optimism. I ignore it, turn online
to Venice Radio, where right now,
an hour later, Frederico Moreno Torroba's
(1891–1982) *Sonatina per chitarra Op. 52*
is playing, not in the low sun in front of the house,
but in the shade of the backroom,
where my library table
filled with this work's
sources greets me
intimately,
even

before turning the lamp on,
especially Ponge's **Things**, whose subtle cover
of carafe filled with red paint & aquamarine glass stopper
soothes the Soul in the half-light
until I turn on the study lamp
& open to the master's own
words:

*The most intelligent thing seems to me to be to re-examine one's biography
and to correct it while owning up to certain traits...*

*The poet should never offer an idea but a thing; i.e., even ideas he must present in
the pose of an object.*

*The poem is a thing of joy offered man, made and posed especially for him.
This intention must not be lacking in the poet.* Italics printed in Japan in 1971

Promise of the day continues as the 1st's light slowly rises
over this little cape's roof, & while I'm
not surprised
to find
the added phrase
in Ponge's last-page bio,
embracing it as a validation
of the value of a poet's work:
"Always in financial difficulties."

:::::

Workmen arrive in white van
at our neighbor's mammoth house
right next door hoisting ladders in noisy
racket of clanging steel attempting to counteract
(by crass American disregard for others' sensibilities,
even before 8:00am) the classical Mendelssohn *Concerto
per pianoforte e orchestra in re minore No 2. Op. 40* & my own
internal,
unflagging
optimism chiming in
as minor music all its own,
heightened now by that grand
American ongoing antagonism of utter
lack of any level of élan,
I'll turn to jazz
right soon,
already in tune

with that internal modal,
say Monk, say Mingus, Dolphy,
or Marilyn Crispell, & Cecil Taylor!!!!!

:::::

Here's how it happened on the second of August: she & I walking in the
quiet
air
are
interrupted
by a droll monotone
voice approaching behind
us, a male voice dominating
the dialogue & killing any sense
of our beloved silence,
so I stop. Let them
pass by without
a glance,
whereupon,
she draws my attention
to a Swallowtail Butterfly
lifting our spirits lightly on
the tapestry of its wings.

Since I already walked a few miles
on the treadmill, I let her go on
ahead, saying I'll meet her,
rendezvous, at our desire
under the elms,
however,
at the top granite step of my shortcut,
I disturb a small garter snake sunning itself
on the stone slithering away slowly into the foliage,
& taking my imagination with it, as if CHANCE were
leading me in a new direction.

Why I thought of Thoreau, I don't know, but I recall once having some
twelve volumes of his journal borrowed from Bowdoin College Library.

Now, the online index cites: *Snake, green*, so I follow up on a number of
pages: resting like a cold-blooded creature on his entry for August 1st
1860, he's looking out over land in his own neighborhood of Concord, a
tract called Conantum, in fact, a place named Miles meadow, & clues us
in, those of us in the future, reminding us:

"How much of beauty – of color, as well as form –
on which our eyes daily rest goes unperceived by us!"

There we have it,
the gist.

Swallowtail Butterfly lifting spirits
above the noise gently landing
back down on our beloved
silence.

Bulrushes, goldenrod, raspberries hidden in the thicket,
Things, as Ponge would say, color & form Thoreau,
both reminding me today to heighten senses, refuse
to allow beauty in the simplest things, (clover she
marveled over), to go unperceived.

People, sometimes, too.
No sooner had we rendezvoused
at the picnic table under the elms,
than three teenagers came up to us
with clipboards & inquisitive looks.

Yes, they could ask us a few questions about ecology,
but only a few, because you see, my wife works hard all week,
as do I, but in a different way, & she's taken Friday afternoons
off for the entire summer, & here we are on our vacation hours,
so shoot: Sure, we recycle in answer to the white girl's inquiry,
but wait, What's your name? I ask the silent young man
standing closest to me, Abbas, Ah, Abbas, & Fatima
& Isabel, but must tell the mackerel tale of the other
Abbas, who caught five fish, & held his hand up
to count them as if that hand were a wave
of Peace.

Yes, these young people, a gang
of future beauty approached us
with élan & courtesy & jotted
down our answers on
clipboard folders.
We all shook
hands,
twice.

Their innocent visages
gave off a visceral
energy comparable
to all the flora
& fauna that
fascinated
us for days
before.

The Class: Abbas, Fatima, Isabel,
teaching us well.
By example.

::::

Led by green snake
to beauty.

::::

Genet's *Maids* is at the Lincoln Center Festival, opening Wednesday.

There's that, & the constant Vortex, in which the night before
perusing shelves for some light reading before retiring,
(volumes unrelated to the current project), I choose
The Collected Poetry of Aimé Césaire.

Instead of randomly heading toward the poems
themselves, as I have every time previously,
gravitate toward Eshleman's *Introduction*.

It's not long before the Vortex
of allowing everything in
at the same time swirls
into gear, that funnel
where *what is* comes
down from the sky
through the utter
openness of
the head of
the poet
via pen
& keyboard.

Eshleman cites the importance of Rimbaud's choice of Africa (we should know
what he called all poets!), Cendrars' African legends, & Frobenius, who
in March 1911 searching for the creators of African glass, similar to
that found in sites with terracottas & bronzes in the Yoruba Holy
City of Ile-Ife, entered the craftsmen's quarter of Bida, Nigeria,
where Massaga tribesmen, working in a guild system, were
manufacturing the glass in two indigenous colors, yellow
& black, leading him to call the splendid Past, the poem
of related cultures.

Not long after, Eshleman adds Genet's *The Blacks* to his references,
a play in which before beginning it the playwright asks, "But what
exactly is a black? First of all,
what's his color?"

Eshleman refers to Césaire's own version of the Vortex
from his essay, "Poetry and Knowledge": "everything
that ever was, that is ever possible... all pasts, all
futures in all fluxes, all radiations," in brief,
"the cosmic totality".

::::

THE 'BLACK PAINTINGS'
OF ROBERT RAUSCHENBERG

(*Oh! palms and diamonds!*) —Rimbaud

Rimbaud claimed his own hunger equal to black air.

Thirst for a drop from fractured glass of the invisible. Litter crossing
parched ground. Flowers sprouting from unexpected fissures in the
ancient calendar wheel, slowing down in ratio to the world's pain. Bad
blood of the weakest sacrificed without reason, or to reason, dried, or
flowing. Under the sun of Harar burlap sacks of coffee worth more than
that of the body.
BLACKWORK: toil paid for in cash, the transaction going unrecorded,
not
taxed. Death disguised as fate only the book or work can outrun.

Aching scrotum hauling gravel.

Tequila, whiskey, black wine break open internal vessels of truth.
Cornucopian promise, empty or filled. Florida of *The Drunken Boat*.
Vomit in the limo. Nietzsche's preference for satyr over saint, clown over
saint. Terror & laughter.

Peace found: only at the uterine wall. *The sea of the vigil like... breasts.*
Woman's labor & man's. Desire on the lips. The utter teeming
fermentation,
gestation of Hell. Lake bed of cracked mud we all rose up from. Obsidian
scar. Come into existence, take birth; burst forth, spring up; crop up.
begin. again. Make fresh start bud germ (perils lust pearls last) egg
embryo rudiment.

Rimbaud creating alchemical gold & god.

Turn work to flesh. Up from the soot & rot, if need be, outrun fate, a breath
disperses the boundaries. Make coal shine. Ink up the palimpsest. Gash no

177

branches to mark return. Every word, he said, derange sense, set touch free. Strike invent steal fire, map as you go, continue in that frenzied state knowing the final destination is still in question.

VORTEX OF WRITING

Train Glasgow to Edinburgh. Same Mexicali to Guadalajara. Munich-Salzburg. Peroni Beer truck Rome to Genoa. Mail boat Rijeka to Split, bus Split to Belgrade, plane Belgrade to Venice. Barge Paris via Moret-sur-Loing to Sens. Drive all night from Memphis to Elk City, Oklahoma. In rental over high pass to Calistoga, or down Route I-5 out of Seattle with Mount Rainier forcing its way into corner of eye all the way to Olympia. Chauffer-driven van with assembled film crew all the way from Mexico City down to Veracruz. Even the inferno of Sunset Boulevard will well up with sixteen-year-old in the back seat, track marks visible on her arms. However late in early morning today, the deep desire for mechanical, physical, imaginal transport toward ecstasy, where travel & freedom (time & liberty as Apollinaire might say) merge into the vortex of writing. Walk down narrow rue Jacob, or Bertin Poirée by accident, or filled with purpose. Sentences in steps. Fragments up out of train tracks. Single words culled out of rancid diesel on anonymous Dublin Street. Shivering in a Glasgow café with luggage in storage at cheap hotel we can't get into for another five hours, happily embracing. Wishing I could envision a seat at the Maestranza arena in Seville, (similar to our box above the orchestra in the Parterre at the Met?), or at the bar at the Ritz in Madrid before standing in front of Goya's *Black Paintings* in the Prado. (Granted, I once turned the corner unprepared for Picasso's *Guernica* in New York's MOMA.) Once claimed to have left my past behind, but not today. Dive into Mediterranean in Nice to cure aftermath of sweet vermouth served at gallery opening the night before. Don't even mind university professors boring me stiff in Edinburgh, what with all the time in the world to let their babble fall on deaf ears. But listen to Axel in Bremen, or Manuel in Oaxaca, or Bent at the Louisiana Museum outside Copenhagen, & one knows why one roams & wanders on foot, or by train, or bus, boat, plane, truck. Proust via involuntary memory hearing tap on lip of teacup calling up hammer against locomotive wheel.

CYLINDRICAL VORTEX OPENS
TO ALLOW EVERYTHING IN

Crazed, difficult book, as strange as circumstances when I purchased it as one among two large paper bags I filled to the brim for $5.00 each at the bookstore (yet another one!) going out of business a few years ago. Yes, I felt guilty, but there I was in another happenstance of destiny with ten bucks in my pocket. Someone was going to buy these gems, not only the old, very used, very read copy of the final volume of Proust, but cookbooks & Baedekers. No poetry fit the bill. No one discards good poetry, so rare. (You never find a used Olson, a used Cavafy, a discarded Tranströmer!) But here this crazed, difficult book with the price of $3 marked on the ear of the title page in pencil, Roland Barthes's, **Writer Sollers**. So recently, when a new friend shared her thoughts about writing, I tried the book, yet again, having found it impenetrable in previous attempts to crack it open. Barthes uses Philippe Sollers' writing as an example of something new, a writing without audience in mind, a universal utterance without beginning, (think of Baudelaire's serpent cut & begun anywhere within his dream of poetic prose!), writing that *sets out* without destination, writing without a subject, but rather an overall *effect*, a *tone*, something reminiscent of Bach. If it emanates from anywhere, it emanates from a tension within the body. He talks a lot about the movement of language. Without saying so, an intimation of its relation to dance. He refers to a "moving, electrified screen," says, "memory will not stay still," & comes back round to say there is no new language, only how it is used, & that the ultimate pleasure is that of the sensual: Hegel's flight of the owl only at dusk; or Bataille's "bowl of milk" in *L'Histoire de l'Oeil*; & Marx's silhouette of a weaver; "the sensual is always readable." After discussing the process with my wife, I told her it reminded me of the *vortextual*, by which the upper reaches of the cylindrical vortex opens to allow everything in: conjecture, knowledge, memory, passion, history, impulse, music, while it all filters down through the vortex to the carving burning laser focus of the pen, or keyboard, at hand, at fingertip edge.

::::

179

At Rikers Island guards break
the already broken spirits
of a resoundingly
black populations'
already broken
spirits.

In 2013 inmates younger than 18-years-old
sustained 1,057 injuries in 565 reported
uses of force by correctional staff.
Overall population
at Rikers Island number
11, 000 prisoners, forty percent,
4,000, diagnosed with mental illness.
Of the 500 young men between the ages
16-18, 51 percent are diagnosed in this way.

::::

Gaza & Rikers & Abu Ghraib.
Gaza & Rikers & Abu Ghraib.
Gaza & Rikers & Abu Ghraib.

::::

Guards use radios,
batons, & broomsticks,
pepper spray, fists, knees,
& boots to beat & abuse defenseless
inmates most times outnumbered six to
one.

::::

Genet's *The Blacks* (*Les Nègres*) performed for the first time
on October 28, 1959 at the Thèatre de Lutèce in Paris.

First performed in United States on May 4, 1961 at St. Mark's
Playhouse in New York.

CAST:

Roscoe Lee Browne . . . . Archibald Absalom Wellington
James Earl Jones . . . . Deodatus Village
Cynthia Belgrave . . . . Adelaide Bobo
Louis Gossett . . . . Edgar Alas Newport News
Ethel Ayler . . . . Augusta Snow
Helen Martin . . . . Felicity Trollop Pardon
Cicely Tyson . . . . Stephanie Virtue Secret-rose Diop
Godfrey M. Cambridge . . . . Diouf
Lex Monson . . . . Missionary
Raymond St. Jacques . . . . Judge
Jay J. Riley . . . . Governor
Maya Angelou . . . . Queen
Charles Gordone . . . . Valet
Charles Campbell . . . . Drummer

THE SET: Black velvet curtains. In the middle of the stage, on the floor, a catafalque, covered with a white cloth. At the foot of the catafalque, a shoeshine box.

DIALOGUE: [*gist of 121 pages reduced to 2*]

THE VALET: Where are you going?

THE GOVERNOR: To stamp out the Blacks!

ARCHIBALD: Be quiet. (*To the audience*): This evening we shall perform for you. When my speech is over, everything here! — will take place in the world of reprobation. If we sever bonds, may a continent drift off & may Africa sink or fly away.

THE QUEEN: May it fly away — was that a metaphor?

ARCHIBALD: (*severely*): The tragedy will lie in the color black!

THE MISSIONARY: God is white.

THE VALET: You seem sure of yourself.

THE MISSIONARY: For two thousand years God has been white. He eats on a white tablecloth. He wipes his white mouth with a white napkin. He picks at white meat with a white fork. (*A pause.*) He watches snow fall.

BOBO: We know all about it. We're black, too! But in order to refer to ourselves, we don't adorn our metaphors with stars. Or grand nocturnal images. But with soot & blacking, with coal & tar.

VILLAGE: I remember how I suffered to see that tall, gleaming body walking in the rain. Her feet were getting soaked…

BOBO: Her black feet. *Black* feet!

VILLAGE: In the rain. Virtue was walking in the rain, looking for White customers, as you know. No, no, there'll be no love for us…

(He hesitates)

VIRTUE: You may speak. Every brothel has its negress.

THE JUDGE: The Queen is asleep. (With a finger to his lips) She's hatching. Hatching what? Celtic remains & the stained-glass windows of Chartres.

(Below, Village & Virtue, who have been talking voicelessly, now continue aloud.)

VILLAGE: Our color isn't a wine stain that blotches a face, our face isn't a jackal that devours those it looks at… (shouting) I'm handsome, you're beautiful, & we love each other! I'm strong! If anyone touches you…

VIRTUE: (thrilled): It would make me happy.

(Village is taken aback)

VILLAGE: I died in the hold of a slave ship.

(Virtue approaches him.)

SNOW: Swear! Just as others change their family or city or country or name, just as they change gods, swear that it never occurred to you to change color in order to attain her. But since you couldn't even dream of royal white, you dreamed of a green skin… You've still got it!

ARCHIBALD: I order you to be black to your very veins. Pump black blood through them. Let Africa circulate in them.

FELICITY: Dahomey! Dahomey! Gentlemen of Timbuctoo, come in, under your white parasols. Tribes covered with gold & mud, rise up from my body, emerge! Tribes of the Rain & Wind, forward! Enter on horseback. Gallop in! Blacks of the docks, of the factories, of the dives, of the Ford plant, of General motors…

BOBO: Greek tragedy, my dear, decorum. The ultimate gesture is performed off-stage.

DIOUF: (Slowly removing his mask) The light there is rather queer. I'm on high, & not on the ground. Am I perhaps experiencing the vision of God?

BOBO: Are you a white woman?

DIOUF: The first thing to tell you is that they lie or that they're mistaken. They're not white, but pink or yellowish.

BOBO: Then are you a pink woman?

DIOUF: I am.

BOBO: Are you proud?

DIOUF: Proud, no.

THE JUDGE: I'm not accusing *all* of Africa. That would be unjust ungentlemanly... No, one can't hold all of Africa responsible for the death of a white woman. Nevertheless, there's no denying that one of you is guilty, & we've made the journey for the purpose of bringing him to trial. But no corpse at all – why that could kill us.

ARCHIBALD: We're actors & organized an evening's entertainment for you. Unfortunately, we haven't found very much.

FELICITY: But everything is changing. Whatever is gentle & kind & good & tender will be black. Milk will be black, sugar, rice, doves, hope, will be black. So will opera to which we shall go, blacks that we are, in black Rolls Royces to hail black kings... —JEAN GENET

::::

I get a kick out of the answer both actresses playing *The Maids*, (which opened last night at the Lincoln Center Festival), give to the question: "The relationship to the sisters" (characters based on Christine & Léa Papin, who murdered their employer's wife & child in Le Mans, France in 1933) "is so fraught. Was it difficult to rehearse that, or were you able to put it all aside & go out for a drink afterward?"

CATE BLANCHETTE: We drank our way through it.

ISABELLE HUPPERT: No, no. I wanted to kill her. She was in great danger.

CATE BLANCHETTE: It was hard. It's the intensity of the play. It's such a labyrinth. There are times I felt like I was getting lost in it.

::::

On our second of three walks I saw a ferret cross the path from ocean rocks to clump of trees. It's the first time sighting a ferret there, although a fox balanced itself with amazing agility in that exact spot years ago.
This brave animal reminded me of the ermine I saw one
winter emerging from rocks on Brace Cove
sprinting to the inlet's edge.
Like a dream vision

quest, that image
remains etched
in memory.

Two days before the ferret
raced across the Eastern Trail,
spotted a tanker rolling into port,
got binoculars out of the car to catch
the name: *Silver Lining* with her Panama Flag
had been in St. John, New Brunswick the night before.
We caught her heading out just yesterday, & where today,
no kidding, she's resting, sprawled out for all to see
in Brooklyn, of all places.

VISION DESTINY

She asked that I pay extra attention out there on my walk without her,
report back sightings of any egrets or herons. Love the request, but not so
much the further ramification of eventual walks without her. Became as
primitive as I've ever been out there, ancient stones joining in the search,
the hunt, when suddenly a scree sound from above matched the shadow of
the osprey flow right over between the sun & me. A fledgling followed by
both parents. Taken as talisman. Believe it or not, now, the *Jagd (or Hunt)
Symphonie* by Leopold Mozart just came over the classical radio station.
I've no horses, nor horns, but caught the osprey for her, & in some sense
with the added musical coincidence, the vision that we'll walk together,
when the Time comes.

::::

It wasn't Coltrane,
whose *Live at Birdland*
& *Live in Paris* covers stare
upright on my desk right now
iconic as can be, but in the mix
on the disc for walking the treadmill,
who & what comes on but Jimi Hendrix,
Voodoo Child & *Hear My Train A Comin.*
Mountain comes down at the side of his hand,
& we know the engineer driving that train, don't
we, Mister Death?

Maggie Jones, *Northbound Blues,* 1925
Cow Cow Davenport, *Jim Crow Blues,* 1927
Leadbelly, *Scottsboro Boys,* 1938
Charles Mingus, *Wednesday Night Prayer Meeting,* 1960
John Coltrane, *Alabama,* 1963

Just listening to the Lamentation of the World
with a little help from the Blues & Jazz.

::::

This morning felt the need for new music
to tramp the treadmill, scanning cd rack
& settling on perhaps the oldest collection
I own, so old cover photo & inside liner notes
by Nat Hentoff are long gone: **WE INSIST!**
Max Roach's Freedom Now Suite.

Damn, I tramped good & hard to those breakthrough
tunes with Abbey Lincoln on vocal sounding out
that whip a cat o'nine tails so you could almost
feel 'em on someone else's back, cause it wouldn't
be anyone with white skin in those cottonfields &
though I've known many a mean foreman, would
never know the DRIVA' MAN on horseback, in fact
though, come to think of it right this moment, not

on the treadmill, where I pictured those foremen
as lesser threats than the DRIVA' MAN, I did work
right next to a guy was prison guard at Cummins
Unit, part of Arkansas Correctional Department,
who told me that he was part of the Hoe Squad,
that is, rode horseback with a rifle overseeing
chain gangs digging rows for the farm's produce,
which, no shit, did still include cotton. He added
that his favorite duty, however, was not overseeing
with rifle on horseback, but inside the facility
on Death Row, where he never did nothin' much.
There's a page you can check out online, where
they list the names on Death Row, & what color
they are, 18 black, 14 white, although we should
recall Jean Genet asking, "But what exactly is
a black? First of all, what's his color?" BTW,
today, they tally the 18 black & 14 white men
as their list of names on Death Row at 31.

WE INSIST!
1. DRIVA' MAN
2. FREEDOM DAY
3. TRIPTYCH: PRAYER / PROTEST / PEACE
4. ALL AFRICA
5. TEARS FOR JOHANNESBURG
      Max Roach & Oscar Brown Jr., 1960 [CANDID]

::::

If any correlation between seeing the ferret scurry across the path
& picking the season's first red raspberries out of thorn-filled
vines at cliff's edge, it's merely the sweetness of surprise.

Friday morning begins on a high note listening to Venice Radio across
the water & air waves, Fernando Sor 1778-1839 *Grand Sonata per
Chitarra* Op 22 (20:32).

Not long, however, before I'm reminded of the one place left out of my list of cities visited in 1967, alluding to London, Dover, Calais, Arras, Brussels, Rotterdam, Amsterdam, Hamburg, Bremen, København, Helsingør, Berlin, Stuttgart, Munich, Salzburg, Rijeka, Spilt, Belgrade, Venice, Rome, Capri, Genoa, Nice, Paris, Amiens, I fail to insert there between Stuttgart & Munich: Dachau.

I go there
today, because
that same year, Genet,
1967, is writing an essay
on Theater in which he envisions
future cities harnessing their own columbaria,
crematoriums, brick ovens, if you will, modeled
architecturally on Dachau.

We know ovens at Dachau erased names
& hid the dead, as Celan would say, in graves
dug into the sky. To look at where it is geographically,
or graphs showing the simple structure of this first concentration
camp itself, is to belie the utter incomprehensibility of its motivations
to the extent that upon entering the gate with the motto *Arbeit macht frei*,
one feels a certain amount of complicity in addition to grief &
lamentation.

Genet drew, on a separate page from the essay, "That Strange Word" his vision, albeit "clumsily" (page no longer exists) a schematic of how he thought a theater should appear. One wonders how different it may have looked from the blueprint of Dachau, I mean, if one wants catharsis from the acts of drama, then what more would one need than barracks & shower baths, infirmary & morgue?

According to Genet, "The inside of the oven & of the chimney can remain black with soot."

::::

Yes, on Wednesday
the 6th of August, we remember
Hiroshima, which remembrance stretches
a few days ahead to Nagasaki. Now they say
ISIS is burying women & children alive in the sand.
Man, one has to wonder about Man... wonder about Man.

::::

Would like to place an image here,
in lieu of Genet's lost drawing
the image of the Map
of the Original
Dachau
Camp,
as if to match
the image of Lamentation
contained in the sheet music
of Marilyn Crispell's composition,

Sound of the Downward.

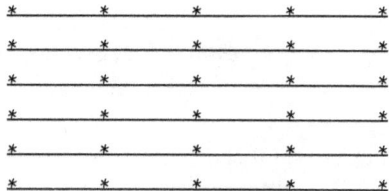

ONE WORD DREAM LIBRETTO

What aspects led to it, how exactly the dream occurred the way it did in terms of imagery, sequence, sound, dénouement, & ending will remain mysteries, but surely, isolation on the island the day before, & knowing nothing of where things were or where we were going, other than following the paved road as directed by the first people we asked after disembarking, until the fork a few miles later, all contributed to the scene, but could never explain it fully. When we sat on the wharf level with the glistening Atlantic, I told her it felt like a dream, & then an unspoken comparison to both heaven & death shot past me faster than language. (For aren't sex & death & heaven beyond language?) We lolled there in the middle of time, time as slow & weighty, as to no longer be time at all, but living only, breathing only, sensing Nature having something beyond history, beyond any possible prediction for the future. Rock cliffs, stands of pine indecipherable as the expanses of cloudless sky, & depth of ocean. We must have stopped trying to figure things out: that night music filtered throughout the dream, solo stringed instrument, notes spirited, not droll, not monotonous, almost jaunty in its rhythm, surely taken from some folk dance motif, when suddenly a lone word sounded from a male speaking voice: "Dachau............" Whereupon the music ceased immediately, & silence became as palpably extended as those hours spent on the shell-sand cove at the furthest end of the island.

::::

She takes Friday afternoon off, so we hoof it crosstown
from the International Ferry Terminal all the way
to the corner of State & Congress, where
our French bistro, Petite Jacqueline,
serves wine by the glass half-price
from 11:30 in the morning till 6:00 at night,
a kind of lengthened Happy Hour.

That gorgeous Rosé haze I walked around town in in Glasgow,
Olympia, now here in Portland on a Friday afternoon with her
at my side, what could be better?

Watch out now where the better
can sometimes pose as enemy
of the good,
but before
returning to the car
parked for free on Thames Street,
we head into Micucci's on India Street,
where we know we can find another luscious
organic Sicilian Rosé, when I'm surprised
to see one of my wine guys still working
on a Friday afternoon, Bob Cormier,
recently back from being feted,
wined & dined
at a vineyard
in Bordeaux.

Bob further elaborates
his own nights in Paris,
mimicking with a minor stagger
how he used the cell phone GPS to mark
his whereabouts in relation to the hotel after midnight
& an immense amount of wine.

He's bilingual, so gets around
France pretty easily.
I love hearing stories
about France,
& trading stories,
too, you know:

the train ride on our first trip together from Paris to Cahors,
then Carcassonne, Marseille, Nice, flying back to Paris,
another train immediately to Reims, where Kathleen interviewed
PR execs from Charles & Piper Heidsieck, as well as Veuve Clicquot,

& where back in Paris after midnight on the Pont des Arts
with a crescent moon balancing itself
atop the Eiffel Tower, drinking
a bottle of Grande Dame
given to us there
in Reims.

So,
with two bottles
of organic Rosé in hand,
along with cans of Portuguese
sardines, we're paying the cashier,
when Bob Cormier shows us how well
he heard the train from Paris to Cahors story
buying us a bottle of what is known as the black wine of France:
Le Malbec du Clos Triguedina vin de pays du Comte Tolosan.

Produced by the award-winning Jean-Luc Baldes, winner of the Best
Estate & Winemaker in Southwest France, *Le Malbec du Clos Triguedina*
is a rich, ripe & fruity wine bursting with red & blackberry flavors. Red
Cahors wine, ALC 12.5% by Vol. Puy-L'Eveque, France

The gift of a bottle of the black wine of France.
There's a song inside that line written by Bob Cormier,
whose last name is the same as my first childhood friend
living across from us at the corner of Union & Bartlett in Beverly,
Frankie Cormier, whose older sister, Carmen babysat, lovely Carmen,
whom I kissed under the tent made of chairs & blankets.
Gift of a bottle of the black wine of France.
If I can't sing it, dance to it. For the gift
of a bottle of the black wine of France,
Merci, Monsieur Cormier!!!

::::

WITHIN THE VORTEXTUAL WORLD I TRAVEL

The vortextual world. That's where I live, swirling vortextual world, chaotic in its orderliness, everything happening at once. Autumn forced honeysuckle back to allow single branch of the season's last raspberries to rise above where they hid for months. Knew that hiding place, waiting their arrival, unexpected, right on Time. Picked eight berries. Cupped right-handed all the way back to car parked on Thames Street. She ate with joy within reach of my vicarious pleasure. On my makeshift desk she'd placed the letter I recognized immediately as that from Bill Heyen in Brockport, NY. Silent, there, I recalled how previous letters sound when mail carrier slips them through the letter slot in our front door. Extra vibration, low register, left-hand tone from far end of piano, accompanied by steel brush across brass cymbal as it slides across hardwood floor, music to my ears. Lived so long with empty mailboxes. He'll enclose a pocket poem, or pig note dug up from the underground of language, & no mere truffle, laminated in plastic as it is, giving it that added longevity, so that when opened becomes music to my eyes long blinded by darkness of empty mailboxes. I'll read the fine script, savoring each word & gist of his latest communiqué. Then get back to the rest of the work strewn across desk, which this week finds me gravitating toward three Polish poets. I don't know why, until I ask myself, "Why?" Well, answer is, a Pole's language is one of the three Lechitic languages characterized by lack of transition, which must be why I've gravitated toward Milosz, Herbert, & Zagajewski.

I define it as laconic speech, straight to the point with that slight, innate bend toward oblique irony. Hitting the mark. Fast. Marksmen, then? Fast, sometimes as fast as automatic weapon's fire, unassailable. Staccato. Blade in line; parry; disengagement. That's not all the vortextual world held in store for me this week. Walking, at one point, although society says I'm a certain age, glance left toward sea, turn right toward ledge said, "I am one & two & eleven & seven & seventeen & twenty-seven, & nine & fifty-nine, oh ya, I'm all those recounted earmarks." Making Barthes's notion the life of the mind is desire more than idea make sense. Yes, the Goya project is

winding down, however, a book recently given to me by Geoff Gronlund
contains an interesting essay by critic Barbara Rose, whose interview with
Rauschenberg I recall prompted the statement that his *hand is one step
ahead of his head reaching for contact*. What Rose gets from Goya is that
for the first Time, then, Truth is Ugly, linking Goya's Time to our own.
Black is the color of his & our Time. As of just late last night, I'm going to
the inaugural exhibit & opening of the Clyfford Still Museum in Denver
in November, thanks again to Geoff Gronlund footing the bill + personal
invitation from curator of the show, David Anfam, where within the
vortexual world I travel, I'll keep eyes & ears open to the vibration of the
color black as backdrop & foreground of, if not Beauty, Truth & Brutality.

That last & final word there,
above, how *Brutality*
as word, concept, act
rolled so easily
off my tongue,
as if I know
only that
one thing,
& how,
in knowing
that,
from an early age,
recognizing it as a sort
of governing force of the universe
one can open doors & texts & others
(friends & enemies?) peer into
areas as obscure as poetry,
truth, beauty, art, sex,
(love, even?), skin,
Solar Plexus
located behind stomach in front
of aorta & crura of diaphragm.
Rose of the Soul.

::::

I knew a 'Rich Man' once,
who said he could afford
to ignore the rest of the world.

::::

Everything swirls around Paris today like traffic circling
the Arc de Triomphe, we chose to climb stairs
to the top, kids in tow.

Beautiful CHANCE
accidents like picking up
Bill Evans' *The Paris Concert*
recorded at L'Espace Cardin on
November 26th, 1979 on which one hears
intense involvement of the audience, enthusiastic,
but restrained, respectful applause, or silence, listening.

Headphones on
on treadmill before
9:00 a.m. dentist appointment.

Speed belt up a few notches, but not
to match rhythm of Bill's starkly elusive
work on the Denny Zeitlin tune, *Quiet Now*.

Mastered, fine tuned over the years, jazz history
tells us he included it, along with *I Do It for Your Love*,
All Mine (Minha), & *My Romance* in many live performances.

Paris: we're on Île Saint-Louis, camped out
in front of Hôtel de Lauzun
in homage to Baudelaire,
who rented rooms
upstairs, & wrote
the first of his
Fleurs du Mal,

in true
coincidental
fashion,
which he'd deem
a correspondence,
out from under Pont au Change
used as arch roof by the young clochard
spotting us on the bench, eyes glued to her
& me, in my best American stance of violence,
at times in life unavoidable, or worse, inherent,
although still seated in as subtly insouciant a posture
as possible, body language doing all the work, as color
van Gogh said would do for the painter of the future,
without giving him a second look, brandish little steel
blade of Swiss Army knife against the sun,
as if to show the unshaved young man
in dirty rags his own face from that
distance away, & in an
instantaneousness,
never really witnessed
in America itself, this Frenchman
understands, & turns back toward his humble
hovel, offering me a sigh of relief, & lasting jolt
of guilt.

::::

Love when Henry Miller points out
English critics complained that all his writing
addressed only one subject: himself.

Yes, he gladly admits millions of words spent that way.
Reminds us of quitting his job at Western Union, becoming
a librarian & bookseller, (what a ticket chopper is I may never know,
but one of the few jobs I haven't had), ranch hand, & after "a hundred
other equally important things (spiritually speaking)... landed in
Paris..."

Rimbaud worked in a box
factory in London;
for beer money
gave German
lessons
to the landlord's son
in Charleville; but willing not to work,
as well, (*Work, now? Never, never. I'm on strike.*)
found his way to rue Bonaparte, knocking on the door
to the Librarie Artistique, where he got the address
of André Gill on Boulevard d'Enfer,
whereupon the political cartoonist
gave him a ten-franc note & told
him to go home to mother:
Rimbaud did not go home,
but slept on coal barges
& outscrapped dogs
for food.

No wonder in *Bad Blood* we find, "I am a brute…
I am a beast, a black."

Paris swirling around
like traffic circling the Arc de Triomphe,
or funnel of upper reaches where cylindrical
vortex opens to allow everything in: conjecture,
knowledge, memory, passion, history, impulse, music,
while it all filters down through entire vortex to carving,
burning laser focus of pen, or keyboard, at hand, at fingertip
edge,

or when I witnessed Brassaï, legendary friend of Henry Miller,
transport Paris to Cambridge in order to give a slide lecture
on the brilliant black & white photographs contained
in his book, ***Paris by Night***.

Memphis, Chattanooga, Nashville, Chickamauga. Past snowy fields of cotton…
alligators yawning in the mud… the last apricot is rotting on the lawn…the
moon is full, the ditch is deep, the earth is black, black, black.
　—Henry Miller, **Sexus**

Loosestrife labeled
an invasive species, however,
when that flock of white moths
hovered around the minor stand
of stalks sucking up nectar, they
seemed right at home = white &
purple, colors of Eleusis.

In this morning's dream we dove
into an intrauterinely warm, aqua water
so brilliant & saline, we swam = I invited her
to swim with me in the intrauterinely warm, aqua water,
but that was not enough for me, needing more. I was just
about to take off her bikini bottom, I wanted more than water,
when tragically,
I woke up.

::::

Told the duplicitous couple become a bunch
of detractors in last night's dream, a day away
from the intrauterine swim, that I could read
what was on their minds, in fact, that's exactly
what I wanted to do: scribble what they thought
in ballpoint right across their foreheads.

::::

Fresh air, the real sea, on our walk we spotted three osprey high in the sky,
which meant the juvenile finally grew up & out of the nest the pair built
near the ferry terminal gantry, fresh air, the real sea, & three osprey
spotted cruciform-style high in their ever-widening gyre.

No surprise either that the first tune at home coming
in on Jazz Radio out of San Francisco was *All Blues*.
Hell, if that isn't a mid-August tune nothing
is, & as I look it up, now, the album itself,
Kind of Blue, was released exactly 55
years ago today: August 17th, 1959!

The deejay explained his choice a bit further, reminding us
that it was the birthday of the great jazz genius, Bill Evans.

He, the deejay, began to impress me with the scope of his jazz expertise.
Had an in-depth story to accompany each tune, I mean it became obvious
he was an impresario. KCSM has a massive library. Truly eclectic, I've heard
a lot of new music formerly unknown to me,
& surprising how often they select work from the height
of the period I'm most interested in, late fifties, the entire sixties decade,
you know, Coltrane, Mingus, Monk, Sarah Vaughn, slipping Bird in now &
again,
Dizzy, Raahsan Roland Kirk, Cannonball Adderly, & Mal Waldron,
whose birthday the deejay, Sonny Buxton, pointed out
was the same as Evans's.

You know Waldron, the pianist who came to Frank O'Hara's mind
immediately
upon seeing Billie Holiday's photo in the *New York Post*
on a day when the poet was deciding between Verlaine
& "*Les Nègres* of Genet."

Bill Evans has been as much a jazz hero of mine,
as Monk, Miles, Coltrane. There's a tune I wanted
to remind Sonny Buxton of just in case it hid undetected
in their vast store of music there at the station, because
the song is not listed with Evans's name on the title of the disk.

Lord knows how long I've owned it.

As I look it over now I'd say I got it in DC
during the last of my four years working there

twenty years ago. Must have been intrigued
back then regarding the coincidence
of the recording made in Ljubljana,
Yugoslavia, in 1972, five years
after finding myself stranded
in those godforsaken towns,
Rijeka, Ljubljana, Belgrade,
although I did love Split.

Simply called *Live at the Festival*,
there's only one tune with Bill Evans on it.
But it's over 15 minutes long, & you get to hear
Bill's voice on the introduction of *Nardis* written by Miles.

Sonny was unaware of the record,
which didn't surprise me, but I found out
later: he once owned two Jazz Clubs in the Bay Area,
Milestones & Jazz at Pearl's; taught Jazz History at the university;
played drums with Billy Strayhorn, & football for the Oakland Raiders.

Hell, that 1972 Ljubljana Festival tune
must be one of the few jazz facts
Sonny Buxton didn't know.

Jazz History says Miles gave Evans no credit for his collaboration
composing *Blue in Green* & *Sketches of Spain*, standard practice
for band leaders back then, including Bird. On our walk this
afternoon, Kathleen points out how her vision is drawn
to the deepest of greens on leaves of trees at the base
of Munjoy Hill, judging equal, depths of shadows,

[A mid-August day
here on the eighteenth
alright, I just want
to acknowledge her
contribution to this
month's most
irrepressible
aesthetic.]

shadows,
which to my eye
were nothing but richest
black, although with the revelation
regarding Evans's collaboration, my imagination
longed to infuse them all with a tinge
of blue.

(Is such phenomena
of *Blue in Green* shadows
any different than my dream
of intrauterinely, warm aqua water?)

Didn't happen right then,
but does now in memory,
a day later, knowing, too,
there was no written score
to Evans's *Peace Piece,*
but stayed on in the studio
after the session for *Everybody
Digs Bill Evans,* & created
Peace Piece in the most
improvisational of jazz
mastery & fashion.

::::

In last night's dream, I stood
on one of those long fiberglass boards
some people just stand on on calm water
& use a single oar to row. I stood inches away
from the front tip, not hanging ten, I'm not that good,
even in a dream, but tall & confident with no anxiety
about maintaining balance.

Modus operandi was a long, slender branch of a tree,
which instead of paddling, pole-vaulted against

the ocean bottom, passing a number
of swimmers, including
a young blonde in blue
swimsuit, who then
by-passed me with
a pair of fins on.

That all seemed preparation
for the waiting room in the doctor's
office just a few hours later, when after
taking at least three wrong turns in the car,
& two more on the wrong floors & turns off
the elevator down the corridor, I still arrived
a half-hour early. That's an old man talking ever
I heard one. But I came prepared with reading glasses
in black canvas bag & a copy of the previous manuscript
in this sequence contained in one of those great Bob Slate
thesis binders, as well as the earlier reference **Motherwell & Black**.

Because the dream continued to carry my high spirits along,
you know, newfound ability to balance & pole the longboard.
I wanted to check Motherwell's, *Beside the Sea* series, seeming
to recall the image of a figure riding black spatters as sea spray
clinging to surfboard.

Probably hard for any reader, here,
to believe these sequences of coincidence,
but maybe body & spirit *can* collaborate
to produce consistent acts of poetry, in spite
of wrong turns:

I opened the book to Figure 20, *Beside the Sea No. 24*, 1962, in Joy
in the waiting room of doctor's office, of all places,
to witness fellow dream surfers frolicking in waves
& sea spray made of black oil paint
on Strathmore 5 ply rag paper.

::::

Remain within the confines
of my mendicant sensibility.
Yet complain in a minor key,
"I hate my poverty," not a cent
in my pockets, the rain dripping
through the backroom ceiling,
flood in the cellar reaching all
the way to asbestos flooring we
don't have dough enough to
remove, to remove, remove to,
that's what I'd like to do, while
those deep green leaves & black
shadows haunt my days & nights
with blue only as a mood seeping
in in a minor key audible enough
for her, to her, to ask, "Why?"

Empty pockets with no change
even for a 3-Franc glass of wine,
say, in Cahors, the black wine
of France in a Blue Mood.

   Yesterday, tomorrow, black & green,
you haunt my laurel wreathe...
       —**Federico García Lorca**, *Three Portraits with Shading: Bacchus*

::::

Even ran out of black pepper
for three days, how bad is that?

Imagining how it was once worth
sailing around the world for...

::::

Even Lorca's *duende* hid from me for
a few days running, as well it should,
as well it does with its black sounds
underground.

Instead, I found a book bought the first day in New York
for the exhibit opening: *Abstract Expressionism, A World Elsewhere*,
curated by friend, David Anfam, in September 2008,
Lorca's, **Poet in New York**, accompanied me around
the streets, around the gallery, around the world
elsewhere:

SPENT SOME TIME WITH LORCA IN NEW YORK

Spent some Time with Lorca in New York, & glad I did, because I, too,
wanted a fresh angle on America's city. Spent some Time with Lorca in
New York, noticing who exits the Escalades, & who freights the garbage
& heavy boxes down grates of sidewalk dumbwaiters. Spent some Time
with Lorca in New York uncovering Dutch power structure in faces of
individuals' smiles of pride under blonde hair, above stiff, grey suits, while
opposite, the obviously downtrodden glower, continuing to make you
wonder if justice is possible, or that a man of color could ever become
president in this Godforsaken country, as the Spanish poet wrote, "a
world shameless & cruel enough to divide people by color when in fact
color is the sign of God's artistic genius." Spent some Time with Lorca
attending the *Abstract Expressionism: A World Elsewhere* exhibit, curated by
my friend, compassionate genius, incomparable critic, David Anfam, who
reiterates the importance of revolt, fresh perspective, genuine sincerity of
artistic endeavor way too soon sucked up, formalized, & used by the power
structure, so that when I stood at an angle, as oblique & marginal, as out
of the way as I could, absorbing the lines & forms & colors, juxtapositions,
flow, lacunae, majesty, & detail of one particular painting, Motherwell's,
Elegy to the Spanish Republic, the later, equally political variant of which,
Reconciliation Elegy, I visited on a daily basis working for four years at the

National Gallery, where upstairs in a plaster, windowless cave David slaved for ten years over the **Rothko Catalogue Raisonné**, it paid to have spent some Time with Lorca in New York, because slowly from all the way across the room I suspected that Goya, Picasso, & Lorca lurked on the surface & at the depths of the massive rectangles & ovoids, linear pillars & ellipses, when all of a sudden the *Elegy* took voice in the form of visual chorus, sung, whispered, & screamed, Goya's black-lace mantillas, Picasso's Guernican heads, arms, & torsos asunder, Lorca's plaintive song of struggle, pain, & blood soared across the gallery room, the cry, cry of injustice continuing unabated skyscraper top down to underground homeless since the Time Lorca spent in New York.

::::

Lorca in letters home to Grenada:

"… an exquisitely fine woman, full of the deep, moving melancholy that all blacks have…
At the last party I was the only white…
The blacks sang and danced…
The blacks are an extremely kind people…
At the party there was a black woman who was, without exaggeration, the loveliest, most beautiful woman I have ever seen in my life. It would be impossible to imagine more perfect features, or a more perfect body…
I have also begun to write, and think what I'm writing is good. They are typically American poems, and almost all of them have to do with the blacks.
I think I will return to Spain with at least two books…"

::::

The mask. Look how the mask
comes from Africa to New York.

They are gone, the pepper trees…
          —**Federico García Lorca**, *Dance of Death*

::::

Last week it was with a certain amount of trepidation,
I took down from the shelf of books held in reserve
to support this project, (after all, Kristeva reassures,
"Love has no need for fiction,") + the fact novels
are a genre I put little stock in any longer, unless
Hemingway, Dostoevsky, Miller, Duras, but
James Baldwin's, *Another Country*,
called out louder than the quieter
Derrida, Deleuze, Benjamin, etc.,
& proved to be the right choice
to speed read halfway through
in two days, then plod
slowly in & around
the labyrinthine
timeline of his
Book II
in the same volume.

Worth the effort to see
how far ahead of his Time
Baldwin is by allowing traumatic
wounds of his black body juxtapose
that of white New York City power structure,
fold into biracial couples & bisexual liaisons, characters
of mix & unmatch, where another country is the map
of different color skin.

Jazz club where young sax kid is from nowhere
other than "Jersey City or Syracuse," but plays MAD
in pauper's rags with only twenty years rough experience
enough to blow roof off top of skulls of those in the audience,
or more specifically juxtapose, soon after, the way chief protagonist,
Rufus Scott, makes love with a weapon to a pure product of America gone
crazy in Kentucky proving that Love is also another unknown country like peasant
houses shrunk to empty hovels by the cathedral at Chartres.

Ay, Harlem! … your grand king a prisoner in the uniform of a doorman.
      —Federico Garcia Lorca, *The King of Harlem*

::::

According to the playlist to KCSM Radio out
of San Francisco they played *Odwalla Theme*
by The Art Ensemble of Chicago five tunes ago,
which I missed while on the phone, but that group
is the reason I wanted to come back to this writing
business, since for two days running the soundtrack
to walking the treadmill has been their *Full Force*.

OK, so I should know it pretty well by now, right?

10-second lacuna of silence early on,

as if mimicking some long-distant dawn before man,
slowly, ever so slowly the sound of conch shell gives
way to whistles & bike horns, marrying jungle to city,
& I'm jostled on my walk, you know, eyes closed &
shades on per usual, the jungle is just outside Veracruz
for me with a little bit of Africa tossed in & built round
the yellow & black tiled temple holding the Black
Christ made of ebony, & the city is Chicago, or Glasgow,
or San Francisco, or New York, Boston, Memphis,
on *Magg Zelma*, all twenty minutes of it on the treadmill
in & out of jungle become city, where Gervasio climbed
that palm tree in Cosamaloapan, remember? Such skill,
second nature, two legs like two more hands & arms: that
Gervasio? Joseph Jarman wrote *Old Time Southside Street
Dance*, so I participate, dancing sidewise to the hard-to-find
rhythm, but it's there alright in between chords, subtle, abstract,
& I'm sauntering into that grocery store in Memphis, the only
white man in the building learning what that's like. Lester Bowie
on trumpet. That's Lester Bowie on trumpet, period, nuff said.

       In the darkness the world begins to be reborn,
I'm walking in a newborn world, where the magma still
flows hot my igneous rock on paper plate my dawns &
celestial twilight, where the surface of the earth is equal

to the brilliance of a distant star & a car fender brushes
by a vulnerable body. The voice you'll hear is one out
of the wilderness, Malachi Favors Maghostus, yes,
the human voice without articulation never meant
so much. Roscoe Miller on conga & glockenspiel,
gongs & piccolo, soprano, alto, tenor, baritone, &
bass saxophones without a minor hint of cacophony
is no easy trick, you Famoudou Don Moye crack
that tympani, tip those bongos, caress your chimes,
clap wood blocks, blow that beginning of the world
conch shell. Soon open my eyes, while all this Time
my Solar Plexus behind stomach, in front of aorta
& crura of diaphragm leads the way.

::::

In last night's dream we were aboard ship & the stars
in the sky were so voluminous
as to equal the light of the cloudless
blue sky she & I stared supine
at the day before trying
to feel earth turning
                on its axis,
which
we did.

Aboard ship
provisions arrived
for a long journey: boxes
containing a massive tome I imagined
at first a dictionary, but obvious now, the huge
Morris' **Human Anatomy**, Tenth Edition, printed
in 1946, the year I was born, borrowed from Bowdoin's
Science Library two days ago.

Among the many boxes a small travel writing desk.
The stars though, we couldn't get over the stars, as if they
were destination & destiny at the same time, you know, anatomy
& geography, at the same time, because these navigational stars pointed
the direction, & were already part of the internal body, say the sympathetic
chain plexuses, including celiac, or Solar Plexus, part of the sympathetic trunk
connected to specific parts of the brain.

According to Morris' **Human Anatomy**, Tenth Edition:

"The method of gross dissection is inadequate to analyze these plexuses
and their connections. Also, because of the intermingling fibers from various
sources in the plexuses, the functional connections of many parts of the visceral
system were impossible to establish until special methods of experimentation
were devised."

::::

BY CHANCE, solely,
I picked it up, the cd was stray,
in a place all by itself, not with Jazz,
Blues, Rock, Classical = *John Cage: Works
for Percussion*, solely by chance, I say, & for three
days running walked on the treadmill listening hard,
not easy to music written from 1939-1943, a few years
before I was born, & coinciding with some terrible history.

First thing one glimpses,
when listening, eyes closed,
shades & headphones on, is
that Silence is the foundation
from which all his music
emanates, rises up, or digs
down: Zen Zero as open,
full, & empty at the same Time.

First track, *Second Construction*, emits

10 full seconds of Silence one

can *hear* listening close.

I walk blindly, eyes closed, on treadmill three days running with this music +
noise & Silences, almost an echo, or forebear of the Art Ensemble
of Chicago's *Magg Zelma*, where now their bicycle horn
& whistles turn into Cagean car brake drums
& tin cans, the Ensemble's tympani
into Quatuor Hêlios's steel
thunder sheets,
at the same
Time
sharing that awakening to earth sea sky call to the unseen god, the conch shell.

I walk to Rotterdam to talk with Dutch mates about desire
in writing, where everything is newly constructed after
heavy German bombing devastated the entire
waterfront, over onto Stuttgart to talk
with Mrs. Tauber & her older sister,
both in their nineties, sharing their
meager food transformed into
banquet: one egg, half
tomato, & black
coffee,
now military
percussion sounds
its alarum, 1940, after all,
mixed with bells & flags of Nepal,
where the first people, the Bön played
skull drums & blew thigh bone trumpets.

Suddenly, I slide across in direct line of latitude
(26 degrees) from Nepal to Okinawa,
where my father transports troops
as radio man on Liberty Ship
S.S. Jean Lafitte & hears
in nightmares for years

after the War sounds
of Japanese
attacks.

The steel thunder sheets
Quatuor Hêlios uses to
great effect in all three
Constructions, dated
1939, 1940, 1941,
respectively,
call up
the image
of the plane
I saw at the National
Gallery of Art, the vehicle
Anselm Kiefer titled *Angel
of History*, this construction made of lead
with wings carrying burned books made of lead
facing a companion painting on the wall called *Zim Zum*,
a phrase from the Kabbalah meaning "contraction," or "drawing
of breath" in order to make a place for creation, this desolation
of a landing field for his destructive lead *Angel of History*
& military terror forcing me during my three day
march (Cage could hear with his feet) to recall
the awfully terrifying script Marguerite Duras
created for the film *Hiroshima Mon Amour*,
dialogue & narrative for the strangest
of couples, Her, from Nevers,
& Him, Hiroshima.

After my geographical heart trekked to Rotterdam,
Nepal, etc., ending up, somehow, in Hiroshima,
I purposefully gravitated toward his quieter
four-part *Amores*, in which the composer
attempts to link the "erotic and the tranquil,"
to the two-part *She is Asleep*, in which, finally,
a human voice emerges.

John Cage told his teacher Arnold Schönberg,
that he had no sense for, nor desire to include harmony
in his compositions, but it's there, in the voice
of Martine Viard, as if it were Her in Duras'
Mon Amour, that the first hints
of harmony ascend without
words, but humming
consonants, mouthing
vowels, birdsong say,
nature's primitive, corporeal, dream-time catharsis.

::::

8/28/14 A leaf
               fell
                     outside
our bedroom window,
                       or was it
                           merely
                               a shaft
                                   of light?

Well, I know
that was an acorn
just drummed three
percussive notes upon
the backroom roof.

Leaf, or light,
their silent
movement,
accompanied by
the same tree's
percussive fruit
producing a minor
Cagean dynamic.

RAUSCHENBERG'S 'WHITE PAINTINGS'

Schönberg deathly afraid of thirteen. Fear contributing to the creation of great music. At the start of one of my many odd jobs, the manager of a small restaurant let me stay at her apartment until I could find my own place. She called from work one day to ask that I go down to her cellar, get a bottle of 1896 *Madeira*, bring it into the dining room that evening.

Going down those stairs, for the first time, I realized someone else was there. A young blond man, I assumed the one who'd quit the job made room for me, hunched over a stack of blank music sheets dipping an old pen into an inkwell, & without the slightest disarray, or sign of blotting, placed notes within linear stanzas. Other sheets spread out neatly to dry. A good bottle of wine aerating on the table.

Undeterred, neither of us exchanged a word.

I retrieved the dusty *Malmsey* or *Rainwater,* more likely *Bual,* & as I walked upstairs, I wondered how much fear he had, if any, that those potential sounds might not reach the light of day.

John Cage feared exclusivity. Turned crisis inside out, allowing everything in. Composing 4'33" in response to *The White Paintings,* he constructed silence, & made breath the ultimate musical phrase.

Writing another piece, *In the Name of the Holocaust,* the musician's forearm slams across an atonal field of black & white keys sounding a death knell.

Prophetically, in 1942, years before many chanced to fear its actuality.

:::::

My second walk yesterday,
the one after listening to the music
of Cage on the treadmill through headphones
for the fourth day running, I made it down to the waterfront,
where the seawall is built up by large indigenous stones, erratics,
not quarried, but left by that glacier millennia ago, the one the birch
trees continue to wave goodbye to, to one that carved the channel between
all the Calendar Islands in Casco Bay.

I centered my attention on one in particular
under the fine 90 degree August sun.
He consisted of pure black granite
outlined by white quartz. One
of his relations stands out
halfway up the highest
peak of my East End
cliff path, both fine
hieratic heads
as ever seen.
I wanted in
wandering
a dialogue
but not
a word
was
heard.

The event didn't disappoint,
but quite the contrary, the silence
between us there yesterday still resonates
here today with my paper plate
of stones found weeks ago
on the island beach next
to me on the desk
chiming in.

Olson tells Creeley the anecdote of the Black Mountain student who
told John Cage he wanted to go to Japan to study calligraphy,
whereupon Cage answers with a question, "why go there?
we are Japanese here."

I went there [here], too, on the treadmill with Basho on the Back Shore
of Gloucester with Joseph Schuyler taking photographs of rocks. =

Next day, went round asking for *Shinobu-mojizuri* rock, reaching
Shinobu village. At a hamlet just the other side of the mountain the rock,
half-buried in earth.
Some village children tagged along & explained.
In olden times, they said, it used to be on top of the mountain,
but villagers tired of people passing through tearing out their green grain
to try(?) on rock bowled it over into valley face now hidden.
Might well have been so. —Basho

BY CHANCE
I CHOSE
to listen to *Guillaume Apollinaire*
& the Musique de Erik Satie through
headphones on the treadmill yesterday
waiting a good 63 minutes & 25 seconds
in order to hear the actual voice of Apollinaire
reading *Le Pont Mirabeau*, sweating profusely
listening to the voice of a god, I gladly, madly
listened intently throughout this compact disc
recorded at 54 rue Saint-Lazare – 75009 Paris,
overhearing, eavesdropping, one might say, on
the poems read aloud by various other voices, picking
up phrases from the French here & there & digging most
especially a piece previously unfamiliar with = *IL Y A* from
Calligrams goes:

> *There's a ship that has sailed away with my love...*
> *There's an enemy submarine with designs on my love...*
> *There's a foot soldier passing by who is blinded by the asphyxiating gas*
> *There's everything we have slashed to pieces in the gutlike trenches of*
> > *Nietzsche Goethe and Cologne...*

... reminding me that one critic of Cage's work alludes to the
military origins of musical percussion, oh yes, military origins of
musical percussion reminding me that Cage's father, John Milton
Cage, Sr., was an inventor, propulsion technology & in 1942
began work for the Naval Department on radar.

War
is what
I wanted to address
back there listening to Cage
from 1939-1943, & now, say,
opening the *Times* on a daily basis
to Syria Gaza Libya
Nigeria Congo Ukraine
Horrors of War,
Lorca, & Apollinaire
writing *IL Y A* from the trenches,
> *There's a foot soldier passing who is blinded by asphyxiating gas...*

ISIS Iraq Mozul
is really Nineveh,
where ancient art is
outlawed & destroyed
in the name of War.
Afghanistan Kashmir
Mali Mozambique
Texas Missouri
Sudan Yemen
Pakistan Central
African Republic
the world-wide
geography
of War.

War on Earth: *The Territorial Imperative* by Robert Ardrey: ***A Personal
Inquiry into the Animal Origins of Property and Nations*** =

*In our terrifying laboratory, the Second World War, we watch the repeated
spectacle of predatory powers, directing the most sophisticated war machines
which the mind had yet devised, colliding blindly again and again with energies
galvanized and organized by an animal instinct the existence of which would
have been denied by the most learned minds of the time. I have said enough
about the Japanese and Pearl Harbor. A less-remembered episode in southern
Europe is equally revealing...*

Taken by surprise,
when earlier in the day
at the farmers market we chose
five stalks of gladioli, white, only
to find at the end of the day, after long,
indolent hours stretched out gazing at the sea,
a flock of ten (counted them) egrets assembled just
as languorous in a pool on the salt marsh at Back Cove.

Reminding me, then, that I once saw three of them land at once
over there, as if those six legs were a toss of the I-Ching, or reference
to Olson's poem, "A Toss, for John Cage", *E, arbitrary sounds, and F–fur,*
say, / or a finger drawn across a surface, any of the small cries / which need
amplification for us to hear...

On June 15th, 1952, a month before he wrote the poem for Cage,
Olson writes to Creeley concerning his approach to method, or Way:

"...method is not the path but it is the way the path is known..."

"... one can grant hits from chance,
in fact I take it that the John Cage school
of music-making — the music of changes— is just
this automatism, and that Boulez means to cover it
with this alternative to the arbitrary (Cage even backs his
composing by unpredictability up to the use of the method established
in the I-Ching (Book of Changes) for the obtaining of oracles, that of tossing
3 coins 6 times!"

Not by chance
drawn to the music
of Pierre Boulez, no,
but as soon as the Apollinaire
& Erik Satie cd landed in my hand,
I knew I'd want to listen as immediately
as possible to *Le Marteau sans Maitre*, Boulez'
homage to the work of René Char, translated as *The Hammer*
without a Master. I used this music back in 1973 as background
to the composition of a fairly long series, & potentially bad poem

called, *West Gloucester, Winter Sun*, published in Thorpe Feidt's *Red Crow*.

One finds clear evidence to the relevance of this music
here in the words of Char, who traces the origin
of his series of poems under the rubric
The Hammer without a Master
to the reality of the years
1937-1944, when during
those years the only
solace for this
resistance
fighter
was the flow
of the River Sorgue,
a body of water, he says,
baptized this work during that
timeframe we're only too familiar
with in the previous work of Cage, a Time
when Char saw firsthand *the allegory of war beginning*
to take on concrete existence… the hallucinating experience
of man riveted to evil, of man massacred & still victorious.

How often I listened to this music on vinyl
in the early years as a poet, & now, again,
the cd through Bose headphones, rather than
huge 901 speakers in the early 70's, yet now
no less intriguing, mystifying, & appropriate
here to link Cage's percussion & the Art Ensemble's
traffic noise, as against the lilt of Apollinaire's
voice carrying us back to 1912 before the horrors
of World War I & World War II, ever-growing list
of apocalyptic conflicts.

::::

On my second walk today the *Dear Dancer*
with her high mast & double-sail rigging dared,
with a crew of eight, to challenge the dense white
fog, which I saw as pretty brave for a pretty name.
The vessel paralleled my own gait, no faster than that
at all. It was as if I were on the water, her dancing partner.
Ha, that'll be the day. Then this fool came out of the sumac
smoking & saying goodbye to Brownie, "See you, later, Brownie,"
with an added guffaw at the jaw bordering on the idiocy I see written
on the faces of five-star American generals in the Pentagon + getting a whiff
of cigarette smoke, another one of my major nemeses. So I picked up the pace,
in fact, started jogging, which is unlike me, even though I got the treadmill up to
43 earlier in the morning, hightailing it really, & not bad for a guy ready
to turn 68 in a month. Judged which way wind blew & chose a path
I knew away from land at the edge of stone & sea, stones so fine
I began to see the path crossed with the corporal as something
of a sign & blessing to get down here, where
I'd seen another Dancer with her Birdman,
& although I couldn't pinpoint
that exact location, I found solace
& solitude there next the granite wall
like a Cagean wall of silence + small pit
of fragments worn beyond current use as tools.
Wasn't long though before the fool reappeared:

"Hi, ya. Don't kill yourself on the rocks." Hm, what does one say
to that? "Been coming here for 30 years." Pause. "You must
know the environment pretty well then, huh?" "Ya." "Born
in Portland?" "Millinocket, can't get there from here.
My father's president of a big company in Colorado,
but still can't program a VCR. Old school, love
that." "What's your first name?" "Jeffrey."
"Robert. What's the book?" "Asimov's
Foundation, I read it a couple times
before, but recently picked it up
again."

I don't need any more
science or science fiction
than what props up
before me in real
life on a daily
basis, but
did say
that I
liked
rereading things.
He agreed. I said nothing.

"Found yourself a good spot.
I gotta find one, too." "OK, Jeffrey,"
signing off with the same *tone* my wife
once dismissed a haughty waitress in Carcassonne,
saying, "*À bientôt*," with an added wave of her hand.

He did, too, about 20 feet away, acting as major imposition
on my solitude, but I'm used to incorporating random
interruptions into writing, & wouldn't have had this
mad, tragic scenario to jot down in a notebook
a few minutes later without him.

::::

As anyone
who knows me
knows I prefer moment
to monument, or memory.
However, those white bookends
of last Saturday, morning gladioli,
& twilit egrets lounging by the salt-marsh
pool seem to trump any present second, or
better yet, call forth extended images as strong
as the high wind all Labor Day weekend animating
the Soul of every object top cloud & sky down to flower,
weed, & gash of rock. White bookends, morning gladioli, &
twilit egrets lounging by the salt-marsh pool to trump the present

second, or better yet, call forth images animating the Soul of every
object top cloud & sky down to flower, weed & gash of rock…

On my *first* walk today,
before both mentioned above,
I defaulted to listening to that old standby,
Coltrane Time, where Cecil Taylor opens up so
perfectly on this with extremely fine dissonance throughout.
Listened to the whole album walking the treadmill this morning.
Kenny Dorham wasn't pleased with <u>Cecil stealing the show</u>, especially
on a tune the former composed!! In fact, the album was reissued in 1962
by Blue Note under this title, while previously recorded in 1959
under Taylor's leadership titled *Stereo Drive*.

My friend, Marilyn Crispell, acolyte of Taylor,
(both originally with the New England Conservatory),
cut her chops on Cecil's fast-paced, percussive, muscular,
almost deconstructive approach to avant-garde, free jazz.

She shared the stage with Taylor
at the 17th annual International Festival
of New Music in Quebec in 2000.
Twenty years earlier I saw her perform
Taylor's compositions flawlessly in Boston
in a tight, sleeveless & backless black dress,
slaying the ivories & the audience.

ROUNDING THE CORNER

Peripatetic I called myself, when she called me at home to make sure I got
there all right, what with my continued refusal to buy into the American
second-car in the driveway syndrome, refusing insurance for any other
vehicle other than my body, & even that is only catastrophic. Otherwise,
I'm free. To roam. Scope things out. Check damage from the recent storm,
which Captain Dunbar tells me carried eighty-one-mile-an-hour winds
across the harbor to Cape Elizabeth. Plenty of trees down, where one can

peek under root boles for complexities & old stones. In my trek through town I stopped off at Micucci's for some cheap, but good Italian wine. Anna was hanging just about everything she could out of her halter top as cashier near the back door. The equivalent of four bottles of wine for under $15. Further on I stopped into Rabelais, the new bookstore on Middle Street, where Samantha & Don Lindgren have been open for exactly a week. My purchase of a first edition from 1960 of *Gastronomic Tour de France* went a long way toward bringing back memories of Nice in '67 & Cannes in '94. Told them so in just so many long-winded words! Don knows the meaning of "trivium," Samantha has a face filled with grace. The bus on Elm was filled with the usual suspects, along with a couple of young women who could have been in the dream last night I told Kathleen concerned "my Niçoise entourage," a half dozen women from Sweden, Germany, France, & the States. It was all good in the dream, & perhaps because of that, on the bus, as well. Got out early, trekking a few extra blocks to the house, where I opened the wine, put on *Shifting Down*, that brilliant collaboration between Cecil Taylor, Coltrane, & Kenny Dorham. That's me, very peripatetic, no car, shifting down, no brakes, rounding the corner home.

::::

On my third walk last night the Osprey hovered
just above our heads with all its sharp angles enveloped
& soothed by the easy flow of effortless, low-level movement.
A large flock of cormorants floated & dove, at first seeming to fish,
but there were no fish. I've seen them gather in large numbers before
readying for migration, once in October in Scituate Harbor, but here we're
further north, so perhaps a September preparation is in order. I know they arrive
here chevron after chevron in April, just as they had in Massachusetts. Migration,
that drive of combinatory forces of anatomy & geography she & I have mustered
together so often before: Salem to DC; DC to Winchester; Winchester to Scituate;
Scituate to Portland; & even now, investing in legal removal of those asbestos
tiles, we're making preparations to sell this little Maine Cape & head down
to Florida in April, just the reverse of the ancient cormorant, but no less
in need to gather ourselves together anatomically & geographically
for the journey ahead. The journey ahead has a fine ring to it,
while I think I'll take the ease in flight of the Osprey &
muscular discipline in preparation for leaving by
the large flock of cormorants on my third
walk yesterday as omens, or at least
Signs.

:::::

In the dream last night a petite woman, very lithe
descends from above as close to me as could be without
covering me with her limbs & torso, she seemed suspended
there, but then logic intervenes in the dream, & of course,
she is balancing on her right hand & arm while holding a small,
round beanbag, then moves along the floor in dance, now she looks
at me, turns around & looks at me, petite, somehow Italian, God, how
the real world flows into the unconscious like watery imagery, drop by
drop, this young woman in her black leotard is an amalgamation of the black
spider staring up at me from the bottom of the stone pit yesterday as I crouched
down examining the shards; she's the name of the yacht that braved dense white
fog, *Dear Dancer*, here *Dream Dancer*; she's Anna Cavina, whom I alluded to
to Kathleen quite recently when we added salt from Bologna to the yellow
farmers market tomato bought for a buck last Saturday. Anna taught
at the University of Bologna, the oldest continuously run university
in the world, founded in 1088. Anna Cavina forever diminutive
& young, as Senior Fellow at The Center for Advanced Study
in the Visual Arts, on her last day there over lunch gave
me Italo Calvino's **Invisible Cities** (dedicated, signed
in extremely fine script with added words in Italian
I can't for the life of me make out) as parting gift.

:::::

When Christine Montross was a medical student
she was so fascinated with cadavers, autopsy,
cadavers, anatomy that she went to Padua
to see the oldest permanent Anatomical
Theatre, the Palazzo Bo. She observed
the close quarters there where crowds
of standing students might faint over
the railing. Bologna's Theatre, built
a half-century later than Padua's,
erected in 1637 is larger, less
constricting & dramatic.

What I love most, however,
about Dr. Montross's research
into anatomy & geography is not
the dissection process of the cadaver,
but her description of live Italian students
she found celebrating graduation on her first
day there at the Università degli Studi di Padova.

She describes a young woman right out of the Marina
Abramović School of Performance standing on a bench
just inside the gate of the school courtyard wearing nothing
but white briefs & black bra drinking from a bottle of Champagne,
reading aloud from the text on a poster she created for the occasion,
while fellow students break eggs over her head, rub butter all over her
body, drop fusilli down her drawers, & string sausages around her limbs.

She laughs.
She's alive, a far
cry from the nameless
cadavers she & fellow classmates
were intimate with during previous
semesters. Welcome anytime to my dream
world in the future *Monica, Dottore Filosofia,*
as once the spider, the yacht, & Anna Cavina combined
to become Dream Dancer
in black leotard
carrying soft
beanbag.

One could say I've turned Solitude
into Carnival, meaning I can hear from no one
for days on end, & yet through unconscious mechanisms
dreams are peopled with dancers, jazz accompanies me, tramp
streets carrying my own cadaver this anatomy, that geography Berlin Paris Mexico City
ecstasy rebellion derangement wine abstinence tramp bare ground stones erratic rebirth work
trance ever-changing chance play convergent hungry noise jazz tearing the mask locating
Soul there behind stomach in front of aorta & crura of diaphragm Freedom I want to say,
"Ah, Freedom" as breath raises Soul from diaphragm shadows of cadavers carried
by living anatomy carnival suffering Solitude peopled in dream streets tramp

in bad shoes old boots my color my car black & white Truth elusive senses
alive to light dark corporeal drive meat of anatomy that sympathetic chain
of ganglia running from celiac plexus or Solar all the way to brain
Carnival of Solitude music of Coltrane Cage Crispell
long lost voice of Apollinaire echoing off walls
of silence in Lexington, Kentucky visceral
cadaver inside live anatomy I carry tramp
streets tramp Carnival tramp Solitude
tramp rebel power trespass a poet
can't trespass Freedom to tramp
boundaryless tattoo & traumas
as passport bizarre licentious
wild alone dream peopled
spontaneous forbidden
fruit of truth elusive
body tramp cadaver
excess Carnival
dance streets
Freedom.

Did you know an egret's wing & a white
gladiolus blossom are practically translucent?
I saw the bird above me against the sky,
the sky seen through an egret's wing,
the bay window visible through
the flower both reminding
one of that woman so
long ago whose
skin so white
I imagined
looking
inside.

I recall mentioning the Feminine in public, in writing, seeking
the Feminine, & paused a second, a mere half-second later
answering the as yet unstated query, for the pause meant,
"What do YOU mean by the Feminine?" & what rose
up immediately is, "Voice of Silence, image of
the Hidden, embodiment of Beauty,

signature of Peace, source of
Love, etc." convincing
myself that perhaps
I could feel free
to address It.

:::::

Got out here
early in order
to catch the sun
on water,
which I'd done
hundreds of times
before in hundreds
of different locales,
but that's not all
I was after.

I suppose
I was looking
for a sign,
or direction,
& as I walked past
the rows of goldenrod,
mullein, New England aster,
a lone, blue chickweed blossom,
beach rose gone to orange hips,
encroaching sumac with their staghorns
straining deep red in competition
with just as phallic bulrushes,
it wasn't until I spotted
the bittersweet turning
its variegated colors
behind a chain-link
fence bordering
the sea,
that the Feminine
began to speak,

reminding me
of Sappho's
nickname
for Eros
as the *bittersweet*
& a dream from long ago
reappeared here: I was riding
a bicycle, when all of a sudden
one lens of my glasses filled up
with honey, the other
mustard, & two
ladybugs
(I was between women in love & life),
swam
in between
the condiments
& my dream eyes.

This bittersweet behind
the fence, talked,
or at least
showed
me
the way down
past an empty bottle
of Gregory's 5 Hurricane Malt,
past a rusty engine block = talk about
what one has to do to get away from the filth
of the Masculine? out beyond onto a row of large
stones I'd never once traversed, when most looked
back up at me in welcome, & urged me on to this very
edge of sun on water,
where the waves swirl
around mouths of stones,
& one can hear an ancient language
much more raw & primitive than mine
or yours, rugged & deep-throated, reaching
at times high-pitched singing, Kristeva's *chora*
inside the vessels formed by this assemblage,

this properly built-up reach of boulders
all talking, or singing in welcome
& praise of the tactile, sensuous
Nature of the Feminine.

Four days running I walk the treadmill listening
to the artistry of Marilyn Crispell on piano,
which exquisite sound on 3-cd *Complicite*
was recorded live in May of 2000
at 17th annual International
Festival of New Music
in Victoriaville, Quebec.

First, on *Prayer*
I walk with her in
Inman, in Porter, in Central, in Harvard Square,
Cambridge, then along the sand at Nauset Beach
with a cheap bottle of Korbel so-called champagne,
then attend a gig at Sandy's in Beverly, where Illinois Jacquet
insinuates that Sandy Berman had something to do with rival club
owner Lenny Sogoloff's Lennie's on the Turnpike recently burning down.

Her Silence quiets the Soul.
It's risky. I mean she's on the same
stage that May night as her mentor,
Cecil Taylor, included on this album,
where in a review Bill Bennett says
that *no one has better understood*
the percussive soul of the piano
than Taylor, & his ability to create
& reprise moving inner voices in
the textural & harmonic density
of his performance is unique.
At the same time Bennett says,
Marilyn Crispell charts a course
for her audience that is more
clearly defined than those of her
compeers here… Crispell pursues
a more affective muse than Taylor,

with spaces in her playing… that take
us from a meditative opening state
to one of ecstatic optimism…

Marilyn's left hand reaches bass level of piano equal to that of Reggie Workman,
with whom she's worked, or the right hand reaching the high screech
of Anthony Braxton with whom she's played & recorded. Hell,
Crispell takes me to the high thousand-foot cliffs of an eleven-
kilometer walk near Conduché to Cabrerets & the Grotte
du Pech-Merle on *Voice from the Past*, & where did this
image come from while on *Storyteller*, but of me
holding in my arms on board his last ferry ride,
the head & shoulders of Robert Hellman
struck down dead at 65 by
a heart attack?

I'm in Paris, of course,
on her *Paris*, or Olympia, Washington
in *So Far, So Near*. Constitution Ave. in DC
on *Conception Vessel / Circle Dance* with Gary
Peacock on double bass & Paul Motian on drums.

Have to admit
that male *Pietà*
that arose while
listening to *Harmonic*
Line was a bit disconcerting.
Disconcerting seems the perfect
word of improvisational interruption
that causes the jolt of recognition, my friend
Robert Hellman, now nothing but dust & spirit
& memory of his voice on Mahler's, *Songs of a Wayfarer*,
all those teachable moments, he as storyteller, conveyed
without the pedagogic pain the academic carries round
in his doctor's bag. Tell me the one again, Robert,
of you & Olson out there on Cranberry Island
in Maine. Robert, please reintroduce me
to Joe & Rose Dunn before you read
your work & Pound's & Olson's

at Charles Street Meeting House.
How many beers did we drink
at Harvard Gardens in Scollay
Square? Irby was there along
with Lansing & possibly
Thorpe Feidt?

I told her about the bit
of disconcerting concern
I had about the male *Pietà*
emerging out of Crispell's music
while walking fast on the treadmill
all the way to some place on the water
between Denmark & Germany, Hellman,
more or less dying in my arms after being
taken down from the cross of just over 65 years
of living.

But then, again, I'm driven
forward & back in both directions
by notification that Richard Schechner is
back at it at eighty-years-old combining his
view of the erotic world between Pauline Réage's
Story of O & Shakespeare's **Hamlet**.

Of course, Ophelia is the one resurrected
here, not the male protagonist. In fact,
if actresses on stage in rehearsal
don't kiss well enough
Schechner insists they do it again
with more intimacy, nothing faked.

Asked if he might be accused
of being a dirty old man, he admits,
he's old, but wouldn't think of actually
touching one of these young women, although
he will look at their Beauty, that's part of eroticizing
the theatre, just as he had back then in his earliest

experimental work, *Dionysus in 69*, where
in the book, photographs of the original
production show a male *Pietà*.

Dionysus in 69
frontal nudity, audience
fondling, Schechner abandoning
his role as critic for New Orleans based
Tulane Drama Review for New York Happenings,
Grotowski's Poor Theatre, & his own Performance Group,
where in 1968 in Soho's off-off Broadway Performance Garage,
men in jockstraps form the floor of womb. This birth ritual. Where
girls spread legs next men's necks, a roof to the imagined building's structure.
Females' self-contained ecstasy. Movements that reenact,
(Olson's *dromenon*) birth-giving rhythm.

Stefan Brecht's take away = *be sexually open*
& you will be sexually free; realize yourself
as a physical being among physical beings
& you your mind will be free; allow the erotic
its unbounded access to your sociability;
don't be afraid to be queer & you won't be…

Dionysus in 69 based on my favorite play of all time: Euripides' *Bacchae*.
Saw the Francois Rochaix version at ART in Cambridge in 1998,
but missed this avant-garde update exactly thirty years earlier.

Schechner traces sources for the avant-garde, including: *the esoteric*
& highly influential theories of John Cage- based on his devotion
both to 'present-centeredness' Zen Buddhism & to chance /indeterminacy
as the overriding process of (musical) creation-the very act of dis-interested
looking (at what? at anything/everything) creates art.

Imagining O opens tomorrow night at Kasser Theater = Want to go!!!!!!!
So Bad!!!!!!!! Want to wander there, where the audience will merge
with cast, spill onto lawns & balconies like water & oil in motion
like the mix of the **Story of O** & **Hamlet**, dressing rooms
bathrooms O over to Ophelia brought up out of her
watery grave *O tending the fire O in her black*

dress O goes over to Anne-Marie grabs both
her nether lips thinking this is how they lift
fish in the market by the gills SO I put on
Lady Essence's Rap Album the one she
traded with me for my book. Lady
is Sarah Violette from Harbor
Fish O SO I walk & wander
with Lady Essence's Rap
in my ears on her album
The Root of It, sings
on the tune
The Worst,
that if she
finds her
girl with
a man
she'll
probably tear
his arms off, Ya,
Sarah, Queen of Maenads,
tear that bastard's arms limb
from limb O naked *O will get*
dressed will fasten her stockings
to the four garter-belt snaps in front
& on both sides, then the girl will lace
her up as tight as possible waist & belly
pressed inward by the presence of the stays
that descend in front almost to the pubis left free,
as did her hips, corset shorter behind leaving her rear
completely free,
O & Ophelia
rises up resurrected
speaking her mind
rather than
her lines.

It happens that.
It happens that this
phrase, *it happens that,*

came to me on my first walk
today as something other than cliché
to marvel at CHANCE CIRCUMSTANCES
of day's events, where after R & J Enterprises', Wayne,
Ismael, & Joaquin, legally cleaned out the cellar of asbestos
tiles, I took down fragile ceiling tiles in goggles, mask,
& hood, sweating profusely all the wine from night
before like Dionysus himself, Dean of Lesley
College, Shawn McNiff, once called me,
"Robert, you look like Dionysus in all
that hair!" he exclaimed before asking
me to read there back in 1979. Ya,
with the poison gone in both cases,
drove up to the local art college
library for look-see at what
might be deacquisitioned
& on sale as the previous
Motherwell & Black
was for a buck.

Sure enough,
The Quest for Longitude,
unopened, brand-new, really,
of no interest to anyone else there
is there on the sparse sale rack with little
yellow dot standing in for the price of three dollars.

I buy it.
Kathleen paid
me $60 for tearing down
all the ragged stray ancient as old
as the house itself ceiling tiles. The intro
to the book says it fairly concludes a symposium
of 500 people in Cambridge, Massachusetts,
with the famous physicist, Philip Morrison, standing
up before the final talk, pulling out a small "black box"
& announcing:

"Latitude: North 42, 22.456', Longitude: West 071, 06, 904,"

in order
to inform
the convocation
of their exact location,
or where they all *actually* were.

No sooner does that CHANCE CIRCUMSTANCE
                         occur in the context of a very Beat
man, who sweated
            hard last night's wine
                like Dionysus reveling
                      in DANCE,
but out of the corner
           of my eye I catch
                the color & gender of this young person
getting up from a computer desk,
                black & female, I gather,
                      & register the difference, after all
I'm not here to ogle the young
                would-be artists,
                  but astounded to find what
she's left behind
      still
        reenacting
           on the screen
                in black & white
              on YouTube, a fragment of a Maya Deren film black
              Haitian swirls
        in DANCE
&
TRANCE
      the white chicken
              upon which so much depends
                      in the Haitian *Divine*
Horsemen Fragmentos video
              left behind for me by CHANCE

CIRCUMSTANCES
&
the young shining
black-skinned art
student extraordinaire
presented, no less,
by Jerzy Grotowski
in 1997 at a conference at the Collège de France
in Paris.

... also came here to find what they have on Anselm Kiefer,
you know, nothing like Bowdoin Art Library, these kids
don't care so much about what art is as making it
themselves, which of course is a big problem,
but not one addressed here, where
what I care about is what art is
& making it at the same time
according to rules
of   CHANCE

like opening the Kiefer Catalogue there
from the Stedelijk Museum, Amsterdam,
Bilder 1986-1980 (don't ask about chronological
reversal) randomly turning to page 66, figure 23, titled
Ausgiessung, 1984-85:

*emulsie olievenf acrylverf Kunsthars/doek – met assemblage van varenhalmen
lodern object* = emulsion oil acrylic phenolic resin/canvas – with
assemblages: fern stalks lead object 330 X 555 cm

Louisiana Museum of Modern Art, Humlebaek (Denmark): Partial Gift
from the New Carlsberg Foundation.

Of course, I have in my black
canvas bag all the paraphernalia
from the Prado that Bent Sørensen sent
& arrived the day before before I had a CHANCE
to thank him for the treasure trove, which came as substitute

for my getting there to Madrid, the Prado gathered & assembled
in floor plans & postcards, sent here, just as he enabled me to spend
one grand day in life there at the Louisiana Museum of Modern Art,
Humlebaek (Denmark) standing together before Anselm Kiefer's
majestic *Ausgiessung*
in awe.

Latitude: North 42, 22.456', Longitude: West 071, 06, 904

That's the exact
(corporeal) approximation
in Cambridge, Inman, Harvard,
Central Squares you'd find Marilyn
& me tramping around in in 1979, or
when Shawn McNiff called me Dionysus
& asked me to read at Lesley College before
all the young coeds, including Pamela Brighton,
which coordinates are important to me today when
Marilyn's cds arrive: *For Coltrane* & *Live in Berlin*.

Put them on one at a time
into the Bose radio on kitchen
bay window while reading **Dionysus in 69**,
which also arrived at the local branch library
on Stevens Ave via interlibrary loan.

Read the text.
Don't gawk at photographs.
Read Schechner's & cast members
text, don't gawk at photographs,
while listening to Marilyn on
Dear Lord, or *For Anthony Braxton*
on *Live in Berlin*, black Haitian dancers
from leftover YouTube video by young art
student extraordinaire rises up before my eyes
inside my ears in Berlin, where Dionysus chants
in the Performance Garage where once
was a dirty old garbage truck & no
electricity, Schechner & his crew

washed & cleaned the dirty
old garage transforming
slowly surely into real
space for ecstatic
performance of
unutterable
words
&
postmodern
prayers the skin
the largest organ displayed
in all its glory like a primitive
unashamed god, *Dionysus in 69,*
the year I saw Miles at Lennie's & dropped
Sunshine Acid during a three-day snowstorm
dropping 45 inches of snow, 1969, or when standing
in front of the Old South Meeting House in Boston, vowing
not to, under any CIRCUMSTANCES,
go to Vietnam.

A dead fly
on the inside
flyleaf of my
Penguin copy
of ***The Bacchae***.

So open
up William Arrowsmith's
University of Chicago version,
which Schechner preferred for his
adaptation, to where the Messenger tells
the story of how Pentheus desired to watch
the orgies performed by Maenads, wanting a better
view like a high seat in 1969 at the Performance Garage,
so Dionysus forced a tall mountain fir down to the ground & placed
Pentheus there for him, not to see, but for the Maenads to see the one who'd
mocked his rituals like the way Creeley said "To mock a poet is death, to marry
a poet is death, to be a poet is death," Dionysus says, "Women, I bring you
the man who has mocked at you & me & at our holy mysteries. Take

vengeance upon him." Whereupon the girls clawed at the root
like Sarah does on her rap album, *The Root of It*, or as
Marilyn's African roots on *Burundi*, live in Berlin
in 1982, trunk & branches of the tree, circled
by maenads upon which the highest branch
Pentheus in his terror sat & they brought
the tree down with a thousand angry
hands…

"One tore an arm off…"
like Sarah will, if she finds her
girl with a man, "ribs were clawed
clean" like ivories under Marilyn's fingers.

Euripides says the Bacchae hoard, "played
ball with scraps of Pentheus' body,"
as all the naked women must have
done at the Performance Garage
in New York City in 1969.

The live body.
The live body & cadaver
have a lot in common. To carry
death along with one is what Freud
says we do in the difficult text of **Beyond
the Pleasure Principle**, which if you were to
read it, so scientifically complex a series of concepts,
hypotheses, theories, one recalls exactly where one was
reading on the deck of that apartment in Manchester, Massachusetts
feeling one's own death so strong a drive & force within one one can't
ever forget it.

Live body & cadaver, ribs clawed clean
under which the Solar Plexus string of nerves
located behind stomach in front of aorta & crura
of diaphragm breathes a sigh of cathartic relief after
reading Euripides' **Bacchae** or Schechner's **Dionysus
in 1969**.

Days of the vortex, when everything falls into place.
Days of the vortex, when everything falls into place.
Days of the vortex, when everything falls into place.

::::

We were stressed out from pressure on both sides of the house,
one neighbor's tree limb crashing down on the chain-link & stockade
fences, & on the other side neighbors renovating addition to already large
Victorian till middle-o-the night with hammer blows & electric saws,
we were livid & in no mood for anything this side of good =
took a walk around campus of the local university
up on Stevens Avenue & stumbled upon an unknown
labyrinth, the University of New England Labyrinth
into which we entered in a new-found healing joy
we wound round smiling walking the womb-like
structure: reborn, shedding anger thinking of the thread
woven by Ariadne, bride of Dionysus, located outside the Art Gallery.
UNE states: *Labyrinths are found across the globe, existing on all*
continents, but Antarctica. The earliest labyrinth dates
back to 2500 BCE. Labyrinth patterns embody
universal archetypes that span all cultures
& traditions. We found our way into
the labyrinth into ourselves. Into
& out of the labyrinth, into
& out of ourselves.

The next day, 9/11/2014, spent walking
listening to Crispell's *Live in Berlin*, where
I walk past Brandenburg Gate, tree growing out
of upper right-hand corner there in 1967, & in 1982
at *Quartier Latin* Marilyn shatters ivory keys on *ABC*
[*for Anthony Braxton*], *Chant*, & *Burundi* on Black Saint
records, Billy Bang on violin, John Batch drums, Peter Kowald bass.

In the car on my way to the waterfront in the rain
on 9/11 Crispell renders as fine a version
of Coltrane's *Dear Lord* as anyone's
heard, eyes well up.

::::

There's a stray
copy of a page
from a notebook
somehow surfaced
in middle of writing
desk, contents taken while
reading Cixous' **Three Steps on the Ladder of Writing**
& Mary Ann Caws' "Robert Motherwell: Working through the Night."

The page underlines "The Story of the Black Id,"
a retelling of a story by Poe about a kind man
who adopts a Black Cat, & that Cat loves
him to his own Death. Black
Cat's Death is the act
of the man's Black
Id. That's a fascinating
phrase, the Black Id.
The Black Id.
There's a deep
secret hidden in that phrase.
A liberating secret.
I believe if I chanted that phrase
long & quiet enough to myself, The Black Id,
The Black Id,
Black Id,
Id,
I'd
find
a liberating sense of Freedom.

The Cat is resurrected as a Black Spot,
which the man, again, tries to blot out.
I prefer the Black Spot to the Black Cat,
but Love Hélène Cixous' use of the phrase
The Black Id, the center of Poe's & our own
Soul.

In the same notebook from 1997 Mary Ann Caws
says that Motherwell views the depth black
gives other colors borders on miraculous.

Suggests taking a look at one of Goya's
last great still lifes, that heap of fish
with glints of silver, reading into it
richness & tragedy, life consuming
& ongoing & ended, what is to be
said & silenced: "We will not last."

Lorca's *duende* & Mothewell's *Night Music*,
everything that has black sounds… hearing
Dear Lord on 9/11/2014.

Among nine postcards + floor plan of the Prado
arrived here a couple of days ago
from Bent Sørensen is Goya's
Pero Semihundido.

One of the *Black Paintings* from the walls of Quinta del Sordo,
this one portrays the stray as abject, lost, yet visionary.
I see this animal simply stopped in his wandering
gait between one adobe railing & larger ochre
wall. The Black Dog sees the Image of God.
A frightening vision. Goya can leave no
wall alone. God is there, but like most
of us, this animal doesn't know
what to make of It. The Image
is not stagnant. It moves,
but does not speak.
Nonetheless,

Goya's Dog
verges on
Belief.

The Black Id.
The Black Id.
The Black Id.
The Black Id.
The Black Id.

Blood of Love.
Blood of Love.
Blood of Love.
Blood of Love.
Blood of Love.

TIME'S PULSE

What Motherwell says about preferring earlier versions of *Elegy to the Spanish Republic* intrigues me no end in the sense that the dust of a Madrid sidewalk, or blood turned black on the sand of the arena, (man's or animal's), prison bars with flakes of rust, these remnants of the finished version's glossed abstractions, are similar to notes drawn on the blank page in Time's pulse & charge, in pure corporeality.

Another of nine postcards from the Prado
is the *Butterfly Bull* Goya drew in black
lithographic crayon in old age in Bordeaux
picturing this animal, most rooted in the earth,
hooves ascending, cock dangling, exasperated,
helpless in the sky. *Butterfly Bull* with wings
has lost his haughty air.

WHEN I WENT TO SPAIN
I RODE THE CORNADA, GORE OF THE BULL

Those mornings one turns a corner, sudden surprise, not the corner made of brick with foundation stone underneath, granite curbstone adjacent, not even out for a walk, yet, but internal corner, where the jolt of Hemingway saying the odor of courage *is the smell of smoked leather*, & the image brought up is that of the matador who exhibits both instinct & courage through the left hand holding *muleta* low to the ground, & therefore the attention of bull's head & horns in order to rise high above it with sword through aorta for a clean kill, (not the coward who makes a mere show for the crowd), but the great left hand he says a great killer in the arena needs, along with honor & style & luck, which my own old man valued, & mentioned so often, the great left hand of his favorite boxer, Sugar Ray Robinson, glove in the face of every opponent keeping them at bay, or that of his favorite pianist, Erroll Garner, plunking down freewheeling bass lines unheard before with strong, improvisational left hand. So there I was this morning turning the corner internally via the strange passage of *corrida* in Madrid toward Madison Square & Carnegie Hall right up to where I am now, of course, as reluctant as any humble man to voice assurance of courage, that foolishness, but noting lineage inherent in the image of the old man, who had both fine left hand in the ring aboard ship in the Navy for five years during the war, as well on the piano his father taught him, standing, this Time with dirt shovel over shoulder waiting for the rat I told him ran & hid under the back stairs. Eight-years old, standing behind him. Patient. Time e-x-c-e-e-d-i-n-g-l-y long. Somehow he sensed which side the rodent, big as any seen before, or since, would dash, which when it did swung the shovel landing square on its head, breaking it in two, sharp steel spade + splintered half-handle flying up from the ground five-feet high in the air exactly parallel to the entire carcass of the rat. As clean a kill as could be made in this deadly American sport of daily life.

Dirt of arena.
Plant that animal
back down there.

Hooves dug into sand.
Ready for the fight Lorca
says the torero will throw
his heart (muleta) over the neck
of the bull with a caress.

The battle struggle dance in the dirt.
Bellow of the bull resounding against
the equally black sound of "the beheaded,
Dionysian scream of Silvario's siguiriya."

I think of the two-stringed instrument called a *rutilo*
the overseer played for us on the plantation outside Veracruz,
Mexico, the only country Lorca said, "could take my country's hand."

AT THE CENTER OF ART

It may well be the center of all art. Its eventual, unspeakable mark. Certainly courage is not conscious, learned, nor necessarily, given. Inherited? Perhaps, but blood is not always that quick, & something on the order of picador's thrust, *banderillero's* barb, or finally matador's sword, offer evidence of scar & wound called courage. It's all unconscious, & beyond anyone's claim. After all, few can capture it: for example, the upraised right hand of the man before the firing squad in Goya's *The Third of May*, or Hemingway's purely visceral understanding that, "the bravery of the bull is the primal root of the whole Spanish bullfight."

THE DISASTERS OF WAR

Terror goes a long way, spawning trauma at the depths of living. However, transformed in that dark undercurrent, in dire circumstances, at the bitter end of a long ordeal, the whole enterprise can turn around, reverse the fear. Two examples come to mind from *The Disasters of War*, which didn't see the light of day for thirty-five years after Goya passed away. In *What Courage!* a young woman climbs over battlefield dead to light the cannon against relentless onslaught. In *They Do Not Want To*, an old woman's dagger is the exclamation driving home the point written quietly in pencil at margin's edge. Perhaps it's just that man has to earn courage, woman's is innate.

The Black Id.
The Black Id.
The Black Id.
The Black Id.
The Black Id.

Blood of Love.
Blood of Love.
Blood of Love.
Blood of Love.
Blood of Love.

Words in Language of Love leading to Dénouement
& Climax of the Play today: Mons Bellybutton
Bulbs of the vestibule Chanel # 5 Pink pearl
Do not disturb sign Corset Rear window
Breasts College try Geneva Street
Dance Virginia Dead Soldiers
Long braid of blond hair
Tailfeathers Vulva
Mouth cleansed
6:37
On top Of
Cock Time
Skin Breath

Light Cold
Quiet
Sigh

:::::

My Soul once floated in a dream down the aisle of a bus
front to back between the eyes of our youngest daughter
& me as a Rose pressed inside two panes of glass, Eros,
my Soul, located as a mass of sympathetic nerves behind
stomach in front of aorta & crura of diaphragm, an unheard
sigh.

:::::

SO, I hear Schechner's *Imagining O* opened
right on Time for me here as I round
the corner for the final stretch of
this alchemical experiment,
this Dionysian series
of bursts & plosives.
Who said she was
a tongue? Read
that somewhere
works for me.
Ophelia & O,
right on Time
out of Time
the caress
of muleta
across
neck

of the black bull in the arena, Schechner threatens
the audience that if he hears a peep of a cellphone he'll
destroy it & throw the culprit out of Alexander Kasser Theater,
then directs the audience, that's right, you attend you volunteer

for the army of the theater, & may find yourself in the erotic space
of the Balthus Room, (recall Anna Cavina knowing him in Rome,
& referring to him as, "*Baltooooz*"?) where Calista Small reads from
Réage's **O**, while backstage Gabriela Moreno (why am I not there?)
acts resurrected Ophelia on screen, in fact, there's a chorus of Ophelias,
a chorus of Ophelias could chant, a chorus of Ophelias like I could
The Black Id, these Ophelias dressed in white & undressed
in flesh just as I could shout *Baltooooz*! at the sound of
Anna Cavina's footsteps walking down the main hall
of the National Gallery of Art to ask me for a book
for her research into the **Geometries of Silence**.

Quiet, no shouting! No cell phones, the way
Schechner & I like our performances,
ordered & chaotic at the same Time.

(I'm not there at the Kasser Theater,
but have been
to Elsinore.)

Bernardo: Who's there?
Ghost: Mark me.
Hamlet: I will.
Ophelia: You are naught.
              I will mark
                    the play.

&, daily,
when the girl
who was in the music
room had been untied, O
would replace her until the bell
rang for dinner.

FIN.

Why I'm flashing to that night
at the jazz club at 13 rue Saint-Benoît,
Club Saint-Germain, where Django played, & Miles

& Bud, did too, & where I saw Harold Singer from Chicago
play, the night I met Marguerite Duras, & she gave me the secret
of the Black Block that is already there as a paragraph that must be
broken down, sculpted, I'm not exactly sure, but the erotic will quite often
take me there to rue Saint-Benoît, where she wore that tiny black dress
& we drank three bottles of Muscadet, or perhaps less often to her
work published by friend & mentor, Barney Rosset:

The Man Sitting in the Corridor:

She's wearing a light-colored dress, made of light-colored silk,
with a revealing tear in front. Under the silk the body is naked.
It might be a white dress, perhaps. Washed-out, old.

I can see the man weeping as he lies on the woman. I can see
nothing of her but stillness. I couldn't say, I don't know
anything. I don't know whether she's asleep.

::::

They're fixing three of my teeth at once
at the dentist with Time in between to read.
Happen to have Duras' **Writing** in my black canvas
bag & Post-it note passages where she talks about solitude
& alcohol, Rome's geography, fountains, & clay, & that clay
reminds me of the most brief, obscure dream from the night before,

>   but in order to address that one
>   has to address the dream from the night before that,
>   when my anonymous friends said they were going for a walk,
>   but would be back in a half-hour, so immediately
>   after seeing them head down the road I began
>   to paint myself.

What the Hell?
Paint the naked body
in a myriad of colors Kristeva
in her "Giotto's Joy" essay, says
escapes the mind's censorship. Ah,

247

now we're talking: the body becoming a work
of art with color in abstract forms covering the very organs
she & Arendt claim our Divinities, quickly, as in Action Painting
the dream found me instantly naked without bothering to undress, paint
from the tops of toes & feet all the way past shins & thigh outlining in reds
& purples, yellows & greens, browns & orange, the torso, obviously heart,
where the Solar Plexus extends the sympathetic nerve cluster all the way
to brain, although I stop just below the neck like most tattoo artists, &
witness anonymous friends returning during their allotted sojourn
away, this Time the dream allows me to get dressed socks shoes
pants shirt jacket, leaving them no evidence that my body has
turned into a Work of Art.

That said,
the next night
I dream that clay
I possess, that clay
my ancestral body once
was, is ready to be thrown
onto a revolving potters wheel,
no kidding, & shaped with fingers &
hands into what, when I awake, I imagine
would have been the amphora, or vessel Kristeva
says is the womb-like, <u>preverbal</u> form of the *chora*.

As had happened months ago,
when my life turned into poetry,
now my unconscious desires that
my anatomy become a work of art?

Huh!

I could compare this Time in the course of writing
that perhaps as Lautréamont wrote in **The Chants of Maldoror**:

"It is time to curb my inspiration and to pause a while
along the way, as when one looks at a woman's vagina.
It is good to inspect the course already run, & then, limbs
rested, to dart forward with an impetuous bound."

(Which I do.
Take Time to proof
Book I of this project,
& make a list of works
in order of reference, adding
five slow pages to the manuscript.)

The night of the pause
from the course of this writing,
the caesura away from "inspiration,"
who shows up in the dream, but a writhing
Jean Harlow, wanting to go only so far.

The women of my dreams, for the most part
don't have recognizable faces, rarely
names, let alone movie stars.
That never happened before.

I once stood in Paris for a long Time before
Courbet's *L'Origine du Monde*, just as Duras
has the male character of **The Man in the Corridor**
stare at the female character:

"Eyes still shut, she lets go of the dress and stretches
her arms along her sides in line with her hips, and alters
the parting of her legs so that they're angled towards him
and he can see even more of her. So that only he can see her
torn-apart sex as fully as it can be seen…"

Or, say, right out of the film, *Red Dust* of my Jean Harlow dream.

::::

Times an error can change one's direction

for the better.
          Used a quote from memory of Kristeva's
          from her study of Proust as an epigraph
          to the prose poem, "Time has a Way,"
becoming unsure of "Love has no need for fiction."
          So searched through most of the notebooks
          in my archive, finally finding it
          there more correctly:
          "Indeed, love knows nothing of fiction."

Leafing through so many notebooks,
highlights jotted down in serious hours
of research & study.

The Equinox came
& went last night at 10:29,
but this morning
          on my walk I took note that the stones
                    knew quite well the change of seasons,
                                        turning my way
                                             in silent
acknowledgement.
Kristeva points to the importance of stones
to Proust, stumbling upon one
that triggers involuntary
memory connected between
the Guermantes' library stone
& that of the Baptistry
in Venice.
She points out that altars
in the Middle East were
made of deliberately chosen, unhewn stones.

There's a Joy
in rereading
these lines
of hers,
where she takes note that Proust,
in contact with the 'living stone"

becomes a living stone, a "stream of light"
a participant in the sacred,
in "transubstantiation."

　　　　　Here's how she sees it:
　　　　　　　　　"Proust… maps
　　　　　　　　　out a psychic & transpsychic universe
　　　　　　　　　that is extremely complex,
　　　　　　　　　a seductive place,
　　　　　　　　　a source
　　　　　　　　　of communion & sacredness
for those who love to read.

Stones told me this morning
that autumn had begun.

　　　　　　　　　::::

I get high.
"I'm a Tantrist,"
said, Charles Olson,
& wrote, more than once.

Elsewhere Olson sums up his view:
"The Animate is the aboriginal instance of activity…"

Nails it there, as if it were the briefest manifesto of perception.

The Animate surrounds me on these treks sun on water doves fluttering
stones loaning their massive weight & ancient memory to internal electricity
of Solar Plexus sympathetic nerves running from the center of one's being to top
of skull staghorn has turned brilliant red vibrating there in the new season's first
hours bend & bow of Queen Ann's Lace at the slightest hint of wind bison
I make out at the far end of the cliff Fish Point not named for no reason
& East End Beach today where Atlantic water probably as warm
as the year's going to get held the naked little black girl in
the palms of their waves, & there, at the other end
of the strand, about as far as one can go along
the very bottom reaches of the foundation
of Munjoy Hill, an ecstatic stand

of moraine locusts against
the edge of the entire
continent, just five
trees, but three
double-trunked,
so sturdy,
whose
bark
grows
thick
as height
doesn't, but top
branches duck down
under wind, against waves,
roots move further into unfathomable
terrain.

Just opened another notebook
in which Kristeva in her previously
mentioned essay, "Giotto's Joy,"
quotes Matisse: "Ultimately, there
is only a tactile vitality comparable
to the vibration of the violin or voice."

Three out of five days I listen to Bach's *Cello Suites, Nos. 1-6,*
played by Pablo Casals, at the same time reading the work
of Roland Barthes, which on all counts offered a lot
of Lautréamontean pleasure: pleasure of the text
is the unveiling of the sex, but since we
cannot hurry the exposure the rhythm
of getting there gives satisfaction.

On this, the sixth day
of alternately, & at
the same Time
listening to
Bach
& reading
Barthes,

that non-
anachronistic,
vortextual
attempt
at method
leading
to nothing
but pleasure,
Casals plays,
Komm, süsser Tod,

intuitive foreknowledge
of Freud's own **Beyond**,

while Barthes claims Casals
once remarked that rhythm is all
in the ***delay***.

::::

On our first day in Nice, France,
twenty-five years after
my own month-long
stay <u>outside</u> there,
on the beach,
in the hills,
<u>not once in a hotel room</u>, we crossed
yet another since-then, built-up obstacle, almost
a highway, trying to get down to the old port,
wearied by the maze of unfamiliarity,
we stopped in at what we came
to call the "Arab bar."

This place,
welcoming us
with its three walls
after crossing the open-air
threshold called the front door,
tossed a subtle, exotic caul over us.

Smiles & nods,
no language *per se* =
the plate of Niçoise olives
arrives before we order. How is it
that this initial event became the most
lasting memory?

When Barthes found himself
half-asleep on the banquette of the bar/*boîte*
in Tangier, he found the same absence of the other
civilization he'd left behind, & which we just traversed
with difficulty to land here in this oasis. No one
wanted anything more of him, or of us.

A Good Thing.

There, he distinguishes between
the "beheld" & the "heard" body.
I'm wondering if one gets to a point
in life, where instead of the binary
between sex & death, one can ease
into the realm of breath & death?

That would be a far cry from the trek
throughout so much the current text,
where so much was *heard*.

First, internally?

How does one listen
that closely to silences
of organs, other than that
one seems to key in upon pulse
of the blood itself coursing; charge
of nerves at center of the Body turned
Soul; sympathetic string of plexuses reaching
from lower torso to the brain; a system that even
knives, hammers, & scalpels of gross anatomy can't
explain?

::::

The image of the Carlo Crivelli's *Pietà*,
originally in Venice from 1476, now at the Met,
comes into view before my visual, (as opposed to aural)
imagination, focusing in on the open chest wound in the shape
of a mouth desiring
to speak.

Portland, 1:45 a.m. 9/30/2014

::::

WORKS CITED IN ORDER OF REFERENCE, BOOK II

Apollinaire, Guillaume, "Poem Read at André Salmon's Wedding" *Alcools.* Trans. Anne Hyde Greet (Berkeley, CA: University of California Press) 1965.

Mahler, Gustav, "Songs of a Wayfarer" Bavarian Radio Symphony Orchestra, (Hamburg: Polydor International) 1964.

Eiland, Howard and Jennings, Michael W. *Walter Benjamin: A Critical Life* (Cambridge, MA: Belknap Press) 2014.

Neruda, Pablo, *Stones of the Sky.* Trans. James Nolan (Port Townsend, WA: Copper Canyon Press) 1970.

Terenzio, Stephanie, *Robert Motherwell & Black* (Storrs, CT: The William Benton Museum of Art) 1980.

Crosby, Harry, "Black Sun" *Red Crow*: Gloucester, MA, 1973.

Olson, Charles, "The Kingfishers" *The Collected Poems of Charles Olson, Excluding the Maximus Poems* (Berkeley: University of California Press) 1987.

Ponge, Francis,. "The Pebble" *Things.* Trans. Cid Corman (New York: Grossman Publishers) 1971.

Derrida, Jacques, *Signéponge/Signsponge.* Trans. Richard Rand (New York: Columbia University Press) 1984.

Coltrane, John, *Coltrane Time.* Blue Note, 1991.

Dorham, Kenny, "Angel Eyes" *This is the Moment.* Riverside, 1958.

O'Hara, Frank, "The Day Lady Died" *The Collected Poems of Frank O'Hara* (New York: Knopf) 1979.

Cendrars, Blaise, "A Line" *Blaise Cendrars: Complete Poems*. Trans. Ron Padgett. Berkeley: University of California Press) 1992.

Thoreau, Henry David, *The Journal of Henry David Thoreau, Vol. XIV* http://www.walden.org/documents/file/Library/Thoreau/writings/Writings1906/20Journal14/Chapter%201.pdf

Césaire, Aimé, *The Collected Poetry*. Trans. Clayton Eshleman and Annette Smith (Berkeley: University of California Press) 1983.

Eshleman, Clayton, Introduction to Aimé Césaire's *The Collected Poetry*.

Genet, Jean, *The Blacks: A Clown Show*. Trans. Bernard Frechtman (New York: Grove Press) 1966.

Barthes, Roland, *Writer Sollers*. Trans. Philip Thody (Minneapolis: The University of Minnesota Press) 1987.

Baudelaire, Charles, Letter to Arsène Houssaye in *The Prose Poems*. Trans. Rosemary Lloyd (Oxford, UK: Oxford University Press) 1991.

Bataille, Georges, *L'Histoire de l'Oeil*. Trans. Joachim Neugroschal (New York: Urizen Books) 1977.

Winerip, Michael and Schwartz, Michael, "Rikers: Where Mental Illness Meets Brutality in Jail" *NYTimes*, July 14, 2014.

Soloski, Alexis, "Sadistic Fantasy in a Fun House Mirror" *NYTimes*, July 31, 2014.

Roach, Max, *We Insist*. Candid, 1960.

Arkansas Department of Correction: Death Row. http://adc.arkansas.gov/inmates/Pages/deathRow.aspx

Genet, Jean, "That Strange Word ..." *Fragments of the Artwork.* Trans. Charlotte Mandell (Stanford, CA Stanford University Press) 2003.

Map of Original Dachau Camp, http://www.scrapbookpages.com/DachauScrapbook/DachauCampMap.html

Barthes, Roland, *Roland Barthes by Roland Barthes.* Trans. Richard Howard (New York: Hill and Wang) 1977.

Rose, Barbara, "Goya Then, Goya Now" *Goya The Disasters of War and Selected Prints from the Collection of the Arthur Ross Foundation* (New York: The Spanish Institute) 1984.

Evans, Bill, *The Paris Concert,* Elektra, 1983.

Baudelaire, Charles, *Fleurs du Mal.* Trans. Richard Howard (Boston: David R. Godine) 1982.

Miller, Henry, "My Life as an Echo" *Stand Still Like the Hummingbird* (New York: New Directions) 1963.

Robb, Graham, *Rimbaud: A Biography* (New York: W. W. Norton) 2000.

Rimbaud, Arthur,. "Bad Blood" *Rimbaud: Complete Works, Selected Letters.* Trans. Wallace Fowlie (Chicago: The University of Chicago) 2005.

Brassaï, *Paris by Night* (New York: Pantheon) 1987.

Miller, Henry, *Sexus* (New York: Grove Press) 1965.

Davis, Miles, *Kind of Blue,* Columbia Records, 1959.

Evans, Bill, "Nardis" *Live at The Festival,* Radio Ljubljana, 1972.

Evans, Bill, "Peace Piece" *Everybody Digs Bill Evans,* Riverside, 1959.

Lorca, Federico García, *Collected Poems,* various translators (New York: Farrar, Straus and Giroux) 2002.

Anfam, David, *Abstract Expressionism, A World Elsewhere* (New York: Haunch of Venison) 2008.

Lorca, Federico García, *Poet in New York*. Trans. Greg Simon and Steven F. White (New York: Farrar, Straus and Giroux) 1998.

Baldwin, James, *Another Country* (New York: The Dial Press) 1962.

Art Ensemble of Chicago, *Full Force*, ECM, 1980.

Morris, Henry, Sir, *Human Anatomy* (Philadelphia: The Blakiston Company) 1946.

Cage, John. *Works for Percussion performed by Quatuor Hêlios*. Wergo, 1991.

Duras, Marguerite. *Hiroshima Mon Amour*, dir. Alain Resnais. Argos Films-Como Films, 1959.

Olson, Charles, *Charles Olson & Robert Creeley: The Complete Correspondence, Vol. 9* (Santa Rosa, CA: Black Sparrow Press) 1990.

Bashō, *Back Roads to Far Towns*. Trans. Cid Corman and Kamaike Susumu. New York: Grossman Publishers, 1968.

Apollinaire, Guillaume, [poetry], *Guillaume Apollinaire & the Musique de Erik Satie*, various performers. Paris: Adès Disques, 1968.

Apollinaire, Guillaume, *Calligrams*. Trans. Anne Hyde Greet (Berkeley: University of California Press) 1980.

Ardrey, Robert, *The Territorial Imperative* (New York: Athenaeum) 1966.

Olson, Charles, "A Toss for John Cage" The Collected Poems. Berkeley: U CA) 1987.

Olson, Charles, *Charles Olson & Robert Creeley: The Complete Correspondence, Vol. 10* (Santa Rosa, CA: Black Sparrow Press) 1996.

Boulez, Pierre. *Le Marteau sans Maitre,* various performers. Paris: Adès Disques, 1964.

Char, René, *The Hammer with No Master, Preface to the 2nd edition, Poems of René Char.* Trans. Mary Ann Caws (Princeton, NJ: Princeton University Press) 1976.

Calvino, Italo, *Invisible Cities.* Trans. William Weaver (New York: Harcourt Brace) 1974.

Montross, Christine, *Body of Work* (New York: The Penguin Press) 2007.

Crispell, Marilyn, *Complicite,* Les Disques VICTO, 2001.

Bennet, Bill, "Paul Plumly/John Oswald/Marilyn Crispell/Cecil Taylor, Complicite, *Jazz Times,* March, 2002.

Crispell, Marilyn, *Voice from the Past with Gary Peacock and Paul Motian on Amaryllis,* ECM Records, 2001.

Crispell, Marilyn, *Harmonic Line with Mark Helias and Paul Motian on Storyteller,* ECM Records, 2004.

Réage, Pauline, *Story of O* (New York: Ballantine Books) 1965.

Soloski, Alexis, "Still Dealing in Intimacy After All These Years" *NYTimes,* September 2, 2014.

Schechner, Richard, *Dionysus in 69* (New York: Farrar, Straus and Giroux) 1970.

Brecht, Stefan, *Review of Dionysus in 69, various performers, TDR, Vol. 13, No. 3,* Spring, 1969.

Schechner, Richard, "The Conservative Avant-Garde" *New Literary History, Vol. 41,* 2010.

Violette, Sarah, *Essence: The Root of It,* EssenceHipHop, 2014.

The Quest for Longitude, Ed. William J. H. Andrews (Cambridge, MA: Longitude Symposium, Harvard University) 1993.

Deren, Maya, *Divine Horsemen: The Living Gods of Haiti, 1953.* http://www.youtube.com/watch?v=Kx6SDc6MfAQ

Kiefer, Anselm, *Anselm Kiefer: Bilder 1986-1980* (Amsterdam: Stedelijk Museum) 1986.

Crispell, Marilyn, *For Coltrane,* Leo Records, 1993.

Crispell, Marilyn, *Live in Berlin,* Black Saint, 2009.

Euripides, *The Bacchae and Other Plays.* Trans Philip Vellacott (London: Penguin), 1954.

Euripides, *Euripides V, "The Bacchae."* Trans. William Arrowsmith (Chicago: The University of Chicago Press) 1959.

Freud, Sigmund, *Beyond the Pleasure Principle* (New York: W. W. Norton) 1989.

Cixous, Hélène, *Three Steps on the Ladder of Writing.* Trans, Sarah Caldwell and Susan Sellers (New York: Columbia University Press) 1993.

Caws, Mary Ann, "Robert Motherwell: Working through the Night" *Robert Motherwell on Paper* (New York: Abrams) 1997.

Lorca, Federico García, *In Search of Duende.* Trans. Christopher Maurer (New York: New Directions)1998.

Hemingway, Ernest, *Death in the Afternoon* (New York: Charles Scribner's Sons) 1932.

Collins-Hughes, Laura, "Ophelia and Friends, Dominated but in Control" *NYTimes,* September 12, 2014.

Cavina, Anna, *Geometries of Silence* (New York: Columbia University Press) 2004.

Duras, Marguerite, *The Man Sitting in the Corridor.* Trans. Barbara Bray (New York: Fox Rock) 2000.

Duras, Marguerite, *Writing.* Trans. Mark Polizzotti (Cambridge, MA: Lumen Editions) 1998.

Kristeva, Julia, "Giotto's Joy," in *Desire in Language.* Trans. Leon S. Roudiez (New York: Columbia University Press) 1980.

Lautréamont, *The Chants of Maldoror* in Kristeva's *The Sense & Non-Sense of Revolt.* Trans. Jeanine Herman (New York: Columbia University) 2000.

Kristeva, Julia, *Time & Sense: Proust & the Experience of Literature.* Trans. Ross Guberman (New York: Columbia University Press) 1996.

Barthes, Roland, *Roland Barthes by Roland Barthes.* Trans. Richard Howard (New York: Hill and Wang) 1977.

ANATOMY &
GEOGRAPHY

BOOK III

"And so I walked
thinking as I did so, I come from the last walking period of man,
                                                    homeward,
happy and renewed..."

—Charles Olson, *His health, his poetry and his love
all in one*

PREFACE TO BOOK III

"my own life become a poem…"
—*Anatomy & Geography*, Book III

Book III brings to a close one of the most original and ambitious poetic projects of our time. If one had wondered which direction the American long poem would take after Olson's *Maximus*, one need look no further than Robert Gibbons' masterful *Anatomy & Geography*. Like the *Maximus Poems* and William Carlos Williams' *Paterson*, which inspired Olson, each in turn inspired by Pound's *Cantos, Anatomy & Geography* is among other things a poem of place—of many places, in fact: places geographically locatable and described in the way that only a person who has immersed himself in their history and traversed them on foot can know them. For Gibbons, along with being a poet, who has schooled himself in the text of life as well as in the life of texts, is, above all a "stroller, walker, flâneur," as he compares himself to Baudelaire in the streets of Paris, which Gibbons has also walked with equal openness and studied determination, just as Thoreau walked the Concord woods, the dunes and beaches of Cape Cod or the wilderness of Maine. Indeed, as in the beginning of Book III, Gibbons walks the streets of Denver as another great American walker, Jack Kerouac lived and knew them: the bars, the flop-houses, wine stores and basement apartments where he, Allen Ginsberg and Neal Cassidy talked non-stop from night through dawn accompanied by the jazz that also inspired the conception and writing of *Anatomy & Geography*, while entering the poem's deepest rhythms.

The gorgeous shade of Kerouac, "Memory Babe," as his high school friends named him, haunts Gibbons' time in Denver "in grave shadows of Kerouac and Cassidy," as it is suffused throughout the poem itself. Kerouac and his own master Proust, whom Kerouac read in French, just as he composed some of the earliest drafts of his own road narrative in *Joual*, the French Canadian dialect he continually spoke and thought in, inspire

265

Gibbons' project of recollection, in which memory and dream, in concert with what is thought, felt, seen, heard and read, combine in epiphanic ways to inform his "own life become a poem." Appropriating "Ponge, Davenport, Apollinaire, Derrida, Barthes, Kristeva, Richard Schechner, & even synthesizing Genet's play *The Blacks*," is equally integral to Gibbons' process.

But it is not merely memory that drives and infuses the poem, or Gibbons' extensive reading ("lug a library with me wherever I go"), it is also, as Gibbons makes clear: "the same subjects that have obsessed me all along: body, walking, trauma, poverty, stones, sex, death, Holocaust, performance, CHANCE, color, jazz, black, classical, spontaneity, silence, language, letters, perception out of more than the eye, but organs, nerves, plexuses like the Solar located behind stomach in front of aorta & crura of diaphragm."

So, in effect body subsumes place; body becomes place as every facet of the phenomenological is experienced through the body. Place then is organic, just as Williams contended that Paterson was both city and man, and Olson experienced Gloucester not merely as Polis but also as the joint creation of geological upheaval and "Earth mass mother milk cow body."

Nevertheless, place in Book III, as in the entire poem, is concrete, whether it be Portland's Munjoy Hill, what Gibbons saw each day when he took the ferry from Scituate and walked from Boston's waterfront to work at Northeastern University—that lone apple on a single tree on Gainsborough Street picked for his wife's pie with the help of two "acrobats"— Pete's Café on Colfax Boulevard in Denver, walking into which was like entering the world of *On the Road* circa 1947. Describing his approach, Gibbons writes, "I saw [the poem] originally as an 'alchemical experiment,' which method of walking, reading, & complete openness to chance & coincidence led to an almost daily writing experience."

"No ideas in favor of experience," Gibbons asserts, just as Williams contended "no ideas but in things." For this is, above all, a poem of facticity, of what Joyce called "quiddity." Yet for all its incorporation of the writers, thinkers and visual artists who inspired it, the poem could not have been written without Gibbons' keen understanding of what Olson called "the proprioceptive." "This is a study of the body," Gibbons affirms, "organ by organ, where the skin is largest of all, & the place where sensuousness begins." And yet at its core, at the place where the poet arrives, or returns to, after the six-month journey of composition, the poet's 68 years of living, the "54 jobs" he held, the deep contemplation of the inexplicable evil and inhumanity of the Holocaust, there is "no room for coddling, taking things for granted, or sing-song spoon-fed Pablum masquerading as poetry & art," he concludes. "Resolved to Solitude," Gibbons says, "I spend all my Time alone or with stones." Or as he begins Book I: "All that walking/only to return/to alone."

This extraordinary American poem, for all the incandescence of its language and the poet's wide reading that informs it— the sense of lived life on street, in dream and in study—was written with deep humility, and it is with that same humility that it must be entered by the reader.

—Peter Anastas, Gloucester, MA USA, February 3, 2015

ANATOMY & GEOGRAPHY BOOK III

How many cities have revealed themselves to me
in the marches I undertook in pursuit of books!
—Walter Benjamin, *Unpacking My Library*

Painting, like poetry, selects from the universe
whatever it considers most suitable for its
purposes.
—Francisco Goya, *Prospectus for Caprichos*

Today, I stepped inside of Time,
as if it were a woman, & she was kind.

Down in my own foreign cave bunker with a last
sip of cold coffee, few nuts & dried apricots, I passed
Colfax Boulevard earlier this morning. Yesterday entered
through doors of Pete's Café there on the same road, another
world, circa 1947, where they were happy to have two new customers
rather than just the regulars, among them, Gary, whom I asked
to take a photo of, happy to do so, though he couldn't
abandon an ounce of cascading years' sadness
& blues, but just stared back as forlorn as
forlorn can be, while Joline told us she
was the last of thirteen kids, parents
running out of names + the added
saints' names her siblings got,
no, no saint's name added
to Joline.

On the way out here spotted the guy in the seat
next to me writing in his journal. Keld Sorensen
arrived in the States at nine-years-old way back when,
from Copenhagen, no less, where last year Bent Sørensen
crawled through in his car pointing out the statue of a trumpeter
in front of City Hall, saying the sound of the horn can be heard blowing

if the statue ever sees a virgin crossing the street, but no one's heard it yet!

Incredible script,
a work of art in its own right,
Keld says there are no ideas captured
in his pages, simply experiences of where he's been
like the days & nights up in Nova Scotia & New Brunswick,
& a few in Portland before heading back home to Redding, California.

No ideas
in favor of experiences
a true method for me, too,
I told him, using the daily log
kept between November 24th, 2007-
November 24th, 2009 as an example,
sharing the link to the archive with Keld.

On the 2nd leg of this journey,
after perceiving good omen
in the coincidance, that neologism
coined by Geoff Gronlund for just
such eternal events as the compound
Sørensens, I open to Kerouac's essay
on his bus trip west, where after he sleeps
through the Sacramento Valley, the first place
he sees is Keld's Redding, no kidding, *with its white
bunch-grass hills behind empty streets.* So I know.
Know this Denver journey holds promise,
while Pete's Café waits on East Colfax,
my daughter trying to find info on
the internet = tell her she won't
find any 'cause it's the kind

of place that doesn't exist
until you put one foot
over the threshold,
see Joline & Gary
& legless ones
in wheelchairs.

::::

In many ways this is a study of the body, organ by organ,
where the skin is largest of all, & the place where sensuousness
begins. Of course, too, this central nervous system become refrain,
Solar Plexus behind stomach, in front of aorta, & crura of diaphragm.
Take the heart, for example, how much we know about its mechanics,
yet at times so little about its emotional ramifications in terms of Love,
say, or grief, or music of lamentation. Sure, I'm interested in the function
of the heart, both mechanical & emotional, although not sure I'd be curious
enough to approach the science as Leonardo, who, in order to understand *pulse*,
strapped a live pig to a board, & using a drill like that used in Tuscany
for making a bunghole in a wine cask, drove into the beating heart
measuring the systole pushing blood into the aorta, no, not that
curious, but glad there are others willing to pierce the body
in their own way in order to know its inner workings.

For example mother gets the battery in her pacemaker changed
in two days, & my daughter found out on my birthday
two days ago by cutting into the pink frosting of the cake
what gender the heart beating inside her at four & a half months is =
It's a girl, her Beatific tears so exquisite a response to her sister,
who ordered the cake kept secret.

Parasympathetic fibers in the vagus & sympathetic nerves
control the beautiful rhythm of the heart.

::::

271

Caught the moon
just short of full setting
West-Northwest over the mountains
here in Denver in the otherwise pitch-black
sky before 4:00 in the morning.

Back to sleep, dreamt I saw David Anfam
sitting across the hall in what seemed like a conference,
or congregation, because we were all seated in church pews.
Then spotted Bill Heyen, & wanted to introduce the two, which
I gladly did, letting Bill know David was "the great Rothko scholar,"
& knowing David knew Bill's credentials as a fine poet, having written
of him often.

Continue my walking practice here in Colorado,
where there are many more creeks to cross than
what I'm used to back home along the coast.
That ancient willow dug in there in the center
of the creek at the corner of Wadsworth & W. 20th
Avenues is a beauty benefitting from constant
flow of water to the extent that all eight trunks hug
the mud, a tree in love with mud, leaves shimmering
in glee. That's me, too. A different species, granted,
but in love with mud of words & images that form
a confluence of text from constant flow of language.
In love with that setting full moon in the middle of last
night, & I suppose love could be applied to those two
guys who appeared in the dream, part of my fellow
congregation of writers, David & Bill, introduced
to one another in a vivid dream after catching the full
moon set West-Northwest, now, become this muddy
text. Down there in that creek, as well as the others
I've become familiar with, projecting Paleolithic images
onto stones dug in the mud, call them up from anonymous,
watery graves. My reading's the same way. Lug a library
with me wherever I go. Here, the massive collected prose
of Zbigniew Herbert, where he's inside the cave at Lascaux
speculating about Cro-Magnon man's "gutteral rites" before
the hunt. The ease with which color enters our Souls (Rothko

knew); "Black, brown, ochre, vermillion, crimson, mallow,
and limestone white," no wonder how quickly Herbert goes
from such subtle colors to the "warmth of Modigliani's women."

::::

Hell with television here in Denver,
drape map of Colorado across screen: watch
Black Hawk sidle up next to Carson City; Golden
not that far from Blue-eyed Buffalo Bill's grave; Trinidad
& Boncarbo down here right next to keyboard; Colorado Springs
& Fort Collins both the equidistant wings carrying Denver further West
on a daily basis; Fairplay, Leadville, Climax, we have to move here;
as expansive as the state is, all we plan to do today is check out
Tattered Cover Bookstore on Colfax for a copy of Stegner's,
The Spectator Bird, which Keld Sorensen was reading
on the plane, check out wine at Argonaut on Colfax,
which David Anfam told me I couldn't know
Denver without stepping into that place,
tipping point, he said, for his own
move to Denver, then check out
Solera, Spanish restaurant
further down on Colfax
with rave reviews,
run no less, by
chef owner
"Goose"
Sorensen!

::::

Met with Senior Curator, David Anfam, at Clyfford Still Museum yesterday,
where he took me round the newly mounted show opening tomorrow.

Excellent, of course, showing how Still's manual labor
as riveter for ships in Oakland at the beginning of WWII
transitioned his craft from realist draughtsmanship into more
cerebral abstract planes, very first room revealing that stunning,
if not immediate manifestation.

Went to dinner at Euclid Hall for marrow & foie gras, sharing a bottle
of the black wine of France, Cahors.
Talked a lot about possible move
to Denver next April.
Also reminisced about our time together
at the National Gallery of Art,
wondering which one of us have made
more enemies over the years, claiming the prize
myself based on Manuel Ávila Camacho's now famous advice:

> "Robert, if anyone ever betrays you,
> even in the slightest way, cut them
> out of your life,"

his fingers mimicking scissors across the high mountain air of Oaxaca!

:::::

In the dream last night I sold a small book for a hundred bucks
to a Mafia Don, don't ask. It may have been my copy
of Olson's *'West'*, or the original Hemingway
In Our Time published by William Bird's
Three Mountains Press, Paris, 1924,
30 pages limited to 170 copies
with an added 50 for review,
becoming well-known
in close literary
circles. Both
great books.

Dream may have stemmed
from the fact that I brought along two copies
of *The Degas* to give to Anfam over dinner the other night.

Praising physical aspects of the book
created by Mark Olson in less than a dozen pages +
frontispiece of one of Degas' three portraits
of his cousin Estelle Musson,

David read it immediately,
commenting page-by-page.

Honored to watch him be unable
to put it down, he said,
reading it was part
of our dinner
conversation.

Even silence between us
was palpably enjoyable
over the black wine
of France, Cahors,
something akin
to the quiet
of the blind
first-cousin,
Estelle,
arranging the bouquet
of flowers pictured in the frontispiece
from the New Orleans Museum of Art.

Here just outside Denver on my second walk today
I talked to stones bordering # 5020 Cody Street,
volcanic tufa with one eye, & what could be
the same basalt used by Noguchi to sculpt
the *Great Rock of Inner Seeking* I used to
visit & caress so often on my lunch hour
away from the library at the National
Gallery of Art for years.

They seem to understand my silent, internal
language. Took note of black locust
in the yard next door. Praised
an aspen quaking
in the wind.

On the first walk today one-year-old
Grandson, Levi, already

exhibited his own
fascination with
leaves & trees
& birds,
pointing out
every one, giving
me a renewed sense
of his neighborhood, land,
& expansive Southwest geography
from an enthusiastic tour guide, if not
precocious aesthetician.

::::

Full moon came & went in the middle of the week out here
in Denver like the gorgeous Amish girls wearing long
skirts & black silk caps in our motel dining room.

::::

Wake up at least sensing
it's going to be a kind
kind of a Friday with the good dreams
of the night before soaring over the mountains
& disappearing into the unwritten history
of the unconscious like the moon I caught
nearly full, ninety-nine percent full,
& the gorgeous young Amish girls
turning every head their way
like this full moon they called
another Blood Moon.

Those lost, good dreams falling away
into unwritten history of the unconscious
without regret, so much like the early morning
four o'clock moon caught setting over
the Rocky Mountains, & vanishing
Amish girls to God-knows-where
in their slender skirts & black silk caps

above eyes that dare not look up other than
in submission to man & God, this music sailing
over airwaves from Venice Classic Radio boding well
the Friday just ahead with Bach's *Harpsichord Concerto No. 2 in E Major*,
which I listen to intently in quiet joy,
then call up original sheet music
composed in his hand...

reading it simply as marks & signs
of joy heralding appreciation for life
the moment the day ahead, look, there,
on the first of sixteen pages of the original
sheet music, the title scrawled in magnificent
script in pen & ink giving one an inkling
as to how the rest of one's own day
may unfold, followed immediately
after by the added caution of
Mahler's *Symphony No. 5.*

These are sites I dig
heading up or down
the longest urban street
in America, Colfax Avenue:
the little blonde black girl
pushing baby stroller past
White Swan Motel, dressed
in visible black bra under
white halter-top accompanied
by her slender lover you knows
done Time, or a bit further down
the Mexican family of five heading
down the unnamed alley between Knox
& King.

Colfax isn't Seventh Avenue
in LA by any means, but cultural
gravity yanks the down-&-out
here in struggling fashion where
The Pit Stop waits with welcome

open arms & Bar X Motel constant
Vacancy signs. Kathleen spotted
a family of four get off the bus
with all their belongings on their
backs, felt their sense of desperation,
offered up a prayer. I swear the guy
waving bouquets of flowers for sale
at passing cars (who'll pull over
right there on Colfax anyway?)
waved the same bouquet on my
way back to Cody Street after
finding Stegner's **Spectator Bird,**
& a used copy of **Herself Beheld**
by Jenijoy La Belle at Tattered Cover.

Much rather see sites on Colfax
than window shop upscale stores
strung out along Pearl Street in
Boulder, & surely preferable to
rubbing elbows with the One
Percent in Vail or Aspen.

There's a white rose leaning over the table
as if to kiss me, leftover as it is from our
 22nd anniversary more than a week ago,
& still going strong upon our safe return
tonight from Denver ten to midnight only
to find three bottles of wine left by daughter
Avry, who spent a night here with girlfriend
in wedding party gathering on what happened
to be the day after our anniversary & day of my
68th birthday. Opened the expensive Muga Rioja
immediately, took broccoli soup out of freezer.
Had the Muga once before, but couldn't afford it
again, just stare at it on the shelf, then turn away.
Spent our last night in Denver last night at Solera
on Colfax. Essentially that's what one does as soon
as one returns from a voyage of any length, begin to
review, recollect, reassemble, scotch together events,

when here the day after the night of our return, staying
up all hours till 3:00 in the morning sort of extending
the journey in time with wine, I still get up at 7:00 with
her, & go immediately back to the very beginning when
the first observation I make in Denver other than the magnificent
impression the mountains make with their not-so-distant
cousin clouds is that at the corner of Colfax & Colorado
Boulevard the Royal Palace Hotel is closed for Good, so
try to look up when that event occurred & stumble on perhaps
the very last review of the establishment before its demise via
Trip Adviser online: "Snow in the room and gun shots"

"You could see light in the room and there was snow on the floor me and
my family left after we got are refund I had to call the police to get us the
refund and there was hookers at the curb and they check these by the hour
there was meth cooked In the tub at some point and a guy sleeping in the
tub we walked out and there was gun shots we called the police and got in
are car and floored it"
Stayed February 2014 Was this review helpful? Yes 1 Ask Christian S
about Royal Palace Motel

::::

GOLDEN, COLORADO

Get out here, you're struck by space.
Just off the plane, mountains & clouds equal
a married couple, genders obvious & pure.
I know Colfax Ave. from previous visits to Denver.
Right now I'm at the beginning end of the road
in Golden, Colorado,
where the street began as Native American trading route,
becoming Heritage Road,
then Colfax, & I-40.
When I lifted the shades

of the hotel room window this morning
to this classic American plateau
almost near at hand,
all I could imagine were first peoples
standing at the edge
overlooking the vast plain
north. Forget that clichéd
image of men on horseback,
these were on foot, trekking,
migrating, wandering, totally inside
the space I said now strikes us.
They were part of it. Internalized it?
That's in the near distance, but right here
practically knocking on the window,
(& would tap perhaps if there were the slightest wind against it)
the first lodgepole pine I've ever seen.
It's strange & handsome at the same time.
I imagine hands in the pine-needled
branches to this tree without limbs,
if you can fathom that?
No, no limbs to the lodgepole pine,
so it became standard materiel for shelter
uses of the tipi. This is no history
lesson, however.
It's just that signs
like mountains & clouds
are forever turning up to validate
a writer's quest, then new ones like the first real plateau
one's seen, along with first lodgepole pine.

Yesterday, in the first hours on the ground here,
getting off at exit 262A from I-70 West,
there at the bottom juncture
straddling Colfax Ave.
at Golden,
a bearded guy
about thirty,
kind of smiling,
I don't now if he was busking,

or merely panhandling, when we took the corner
too fast to make out the difference, but I know he knew
what he was doing, when he wrote on the piece of cardboard
in large letters **ON THE ROAD**, & lower, ***need provisions***.

No hobo, clothes too clean.
Maybe today's performance artist,
taking bus out here from Denver, who,
if we tossed him a dollar, we might overhear,
Go moan for man.

::::

"And that thoroughfare, born beneath the mountainous mountains of
rocky peaks so high, seeing as it shall victual to prospectors, explorers, and
men of chance, and whereas said men, in their sparse moments of recess
and requiescence, require relief of an immediate and carnal conformation,
let Colfax Way be a den of avarice, a cauldron of covetousness, a peccadillo
wharf in a sea-storm of morality. Let not a man walk Colfax Way and
wonder, 'Where shall I deposit my virility this eve, where may I encounter
mine intoxicant?' for he shall find all he seeks on Colfax." —Schuyler
Colfax, Vice President under Grant, from his 1878 autobiography, ***Cursed
Rickets***

::::

HARD LOST WAY IN, EASY WICKED WAY OUT

I.

Heard plenty of tales, folk getting lost, turning
new territory to their advantage.
We did our best to do just that in the immediate
outskirts of Denver,
where housing & apartment complexes
are such the same
they could be that circle The Beltway was in DC we found ourselves on
so often in order to get anywhere,
but here it's Wheat Ridge, Applewood, Golden,
where we stayed, to Arvarda,
where family & wedding was,
trekking between the two.

Stops along the way wouldn't add up,
as if streets were oranges & pears to
the constant architecture's Samo-Samo.

It wasn't till after the wedding I thought I could manage the labyrinth
on my own way to Denver. Wanted Colfax Ave. all the way in,
which *Playboy* once called the wickedest street in America,
but no, I was advised the preferable route
would be **I-70 East**.

No, again, the highway-powers-that-be decide
Saturday's a good day for roadwork
off Pecos St., & important enough
to block off **I-70 East**, entirely.

Detour led down Pecos,
where I assumed **I-76 East** would get me to the capital,
& Clyfford Still Museum, after brunch at Rioja on Larimer.

II.

Hell, no.
No signs to Denver along the way,
& no sign of Denver's buildings against the horizon.

Just didn't feel like turning around.
Pushed that rental car well past a 100 mph near Hudson.

Got off at I think it was a toll road called **420**,
where they photographed license plate & may
cause National to forward us the bill of $1.25.

Saw trucker at the side of the road checking his front end.

Pulled over,
told him we'd been lost five times in three days,
& here I was again.

No, he said, you're good, keep going on **76**.

Believe he had a French-Canadian accent,
& wished I'd asked, but I began
to get in a hurry, if not anxious.

Speed limit on **I-76** is 75 MPH, inviting
higher speeds, & although
I'd already felt simpático
with Neal Cassady,
when the rental easily passed 100,
I kept it just below that until Keenesburg.

Saw signs for gas station & lone motel.

Asked two guys pumping tanks if **I-76 East**
would get me to "Denva",
which accent they caught in unison,
& thought as loco as traveling
in the wrong direction,

"West,"
they chimed in at the same time
with that total cowboy lack of empathy
I was glad to experience,
'cause here they are
telling the hard Truth,
& there I, knowing I'd fly past
100 MPH in grave shadows of Kerouac
& Cassady the whole way back.

Surely find Denver's skyline with mountains behind,
where Jack contemplated building a cabin,
& washing face fresh
every morning in
cold water.

III.

95 was as high as I got
at around the same place close
to Hudson hoping a few high rises
in a distant city might shine glass & steel
against larger mountains behind it.

A lot of Kerouac's **Original Scroll On the Road**
concerns his own getting lost,
so I had that as precedent
to accompany Cassady's high speed,
although men & women
knowing what they're doing these days
have GPS visuals & vocals
keeping them on the straight & narrow.

What kept lodging in my mind was the incredible
vegetation at the side of the road,
when asking the French Canadian trucker
which way Denver was,
with sagebrush & other marginal flora
I'm unfamiliar with contrasting

lack of any vegetation
in remote confines of Keenesburg.
There were many rows of lush green corn in between.

I carried two images of Rembrandt
in my black canvas bag on the way
to the Still Museum, knowing I can
always trust him: in painter's smock,
in Vienna, when financial troubles started,
& later *Self-Portrait with Two Circles*,
images of man-made perfection equaling
a heaven he may have had doubts about.

IV.

Grown to love Denver after these three late-in-life visits.

Only had to ask once, maybe twice for help retracing my bearings.

Got on Colfax as fast as possible, where I bought some music for the rental,
Sweet Black Angel & *Loving Cup* by the Stones
weren't quite Jack's Bird & Dexter Gordon,
but I had those Jazz great ones' work
back home, & simply wanted to
Rock & Roll my way into town.

Parked at the side of the road at Glenarm,
ordered a Guinness at Earl's
on 16th Street Mall,
needing their facilities.

Cowgirls all came out of the woodwork,
no kidding from twelve to six===ty === horses
make cowgirls, don't they?

At Rioja, ordered the by-now usual pork belly
in garbanzo bean sauce after a beer
from Barcelona I hope to repeat
right there in that city in coming years +
as the dish arrived a glass of heavy Rioja, what else?

Bartender, Nico, from Martinique,
so I told him about the girl met in Paris
also from there, conjecturing
she could have come all the way down
from Gauguin's lineage.

Asked Nico for change of a few quarters
to park outside the Still, whereupon he gave me a handful
of 12, & with that fine offering found a space perpendicular
to the walkway in.

Now, there was almost as much obligation
in my Soul
to go see this artwork
as to attend the wedding,
which word is so close to that Portuguese
I learned this week for *thanks* = *obrigado*,
when upon return from Denver via La Guardia,
that nightmare, a notebook
from Porto & Bent
in Denmark
had fallen through
front door letterdrop
for my possibly expressing
something there here in the future.

V.

Now, again, the *obrigado* is both
to David Anfam,
who first invited me out here
for the inaugural show at CSM,
& Bent Sørensen, who thought enough
of my jottings & scraps
to want to see
more from me during his stay
at the Psy-Art Convention in Porto
for him to find that notebook, & send it
along when he got back home.

Anfam curates this
newest Clyfford Still
show: *Memory, Myth, & Magic.*

I began looking at Still's old *Self-Portrait at Age 18*,
true as Rembrandt, & then diesel-engine-run-series
of yellow rail cars blasting horizontally
across canvas against
later vertical abstractions, but close
to the realism of both **BNSF** same-color-yellow trains
I wouldn't have seen accompanying me
along **I-76**, along with black tanks hauling oil,
if I'd gone the right way
from the get-go.

Stood in front of *1944-N –No. 1 (PH-235)* 1944,
Geoff Gronlund & I chose for cover of
Olson-Still: Crossroad,
noticing minute, white dabs & brushstrokes
purposefully placed on massive
black canvas, as if some artist-god
arranged stars in the firmament.

To keep it real, took Colfax Ave. all the way home,
passing Mesa Motel first,
then Blue Sky Motel,
the White Swan,
G&G Guns,
All Vehicle Repair,
Homestead Motel,
Trailsend Motel,
Mountain Pawn,
Golden Hours Motel,
I-40 Motel,
A&D Motel,
& the Stowaway.

It was the right way to get home,
as opposed

to the lost way
in, although as always,
the hard, lost way in was at least
as good an experience as the easy,
wicked way out.

::::

That's another thing: I've never really learned to travel light.

Maybe, someday, when retiring from writing, & don't need
that accompaniment of books, lugging a miniature library
along with me wherever I go, you know, that shelf of books
Manuel Ávila Camacho took note of in the $40-a-month
shack back in 1974, or Paris in '87 discovering Julia Kristeva
at the Village Voice Bookstore on rue Princesse in the form
of **Desire in Language**, or lugging that & four more of hers
for her to sign, when we met in Cambridge last October, or
Hell, even all the tomes I toted 'cross the sea to Denmark,
when I spread them all out on Bent & Camelia's dining room
table to the extent that my passport got buried under all those
words & covers & my only identification for that day was the
Jack of Spades.

Which brings up another recollection of this most recent trip,
when I parked the car at the corner of Larimer & 15th Streets
in order to get a glass of wine at Cru to bide time before meeting
Anfam there at the Still mounting his newest exhibit: There in
the gutter facing, staring straight up at me, as if she were veritably
alive, shimmering under a slight haze of city dust, but animated
as a sign can be = the **8 of Spades**. The **8 of Spades** glistening
under the dust of the gutter, speaking to me, really, granted in
hushed tones, I picked her up, dusted her off, placed her in my
new Brooks Brothers sport jacket (half-price at the outlet in
Freeport just for this occasion) & headed over to Cru to sip
French red Burgundy until David was ready to see me at 5:00
at the museum.

Before going on here about the meaning of the playing card,
I want to mention the miniature library assembled,
lugged, added to on this particular trip:

Leonardo Da Vinci: The Anatomist by J. Playfair McMurrich, 1930;
The Collected Prose: 1948-1998 by Zbigniew Herbert, 2010;
Good Blonde & Others, Jack Kerouac, 1993;
The Subterraneans, Kerouac, 1958,
which was pretty weird in its own right in that
at the last moment tossed it into my satchel,
but realized from the sales receipt still
used as bookmark,
that I bought it right there
in Lakewood, off Colfax,
where we stayed with our daughter
purchasing it July 19th, 2013, during
the time our daughter got married,
probably thinking I'd use it
toward the Keynote address
in Aalborg, but never got to it,
wasn't part of the list of sources
for *Kerouac & the Ecstatic Act of Writing*,
didn't contribute to covering lost passport
making me exiled uncitizen of the world
for a day, when my only identification
was the Jack of Spades, which
Camelia, as reader of cards
interpreted as "Troubled Youth," nailing
my traumas to the wall,
table & pages.

The Subterraneans now contains
the **8 of Spades** as bookmark marking:

> Quick to plunge, bite, put the light out, hide my face in shame,
> make love to her tremendously because of lack of love for a year
> almost and the need pushing me down - our little agreements
> in the dark, the really should-not-be-tolds- for it was she who
> later said, 'Men are crazy, they want the essence, the woman is

the essence, there it is right there in their hands but they rush off
erecting big abstract constructions.

Practicalities by Marguerite Duras, 1987,
containing her essay, "The Black Block,"
which she explained to me one night
at the jazz club on rue Saint Benoît
that very same year, the Black Block
of text that must be broken down, a matter
of muscularity, she said, perhaps like Noguchi's,
Great Rock of Inner Seeking sculpted out of Black Basalt?

Then, of course,
I had to track down the book
Keld Sorensen read on the plane
from Portland to Newark & eventually Redding,
(which Kerouac alludes to in "The Great Western Bus Ride"
in *Good Blonde*),

Wallace Stegner's National Book Award Winner, *The Spectator Bird*;
& finally, stumble on a used copy of *Herself Beheld*
in which Jenijoy La Belle examines fictional
women's relationship with the mirror
image, quoting D. H. Lawrence,
among many other writers,
from *Women in Love*:

> It's all that Lady of Shalott business,' [Birkin] said, in his strong
> abstract voice, 'You've got that mirror, your own fixed will, your
> immortal understanding, your own tight conscious world, and
> there is nothing beyond it. There, in the mirror, you must have
> everything.

Bringing me back, now, here,
to quite the opposite of Hermione
Roddice's tight conscious world to this one,
which I view as truly *mystical*, again, as opposed
to Jenijoy La Belle's assertion of the mirror image for a woman
being *mystifying*, no, it's mystical here, when a few days later,

after dusting off shimmering, glistening, animated
8 of Spades, speaking in hushed tones,
I write Camelia there in Scandinavia
reminding her of the interpretation
of the **Jack**, & ask if there is
some meaning to the **8**,
& she writes back:

Hi, Robert,
All the **8**s are associated with thoughts, ideas, plans, imagination,
gathering to talk about money, love, war, work. So the **8 of Swords** would
be negative thoughts, bad ideas, disastrous plans, wrong crowd.

Good luck,
Camelia

Hmmm.

::::

Now,
we're here
to visit our daughter,
pregnant again at age 35,
+ one-year-old-son, Levi Marcus,
& his father, Patrick Campbell.

Wondering what the **8 of Swords**
looks like, this negative image portrayed
in Camelia's words, a phrase, just now
reminding me of a prose poem from
my first book, **Streets for Two Dancers**,
so long ago, back then ten years ago,
titled "Dream Naked," the third & last
paragraph seems appropriate to quote
right here:

She appeared the morning of the seventeenth of January,
Two Thousand, presenting two identical swords, red
scabbards, gold hilts. One hers, the other soon mine.
She pointed to framed paintings, photos on the wall,
"Do you have the image of the mountain?" "Yes, " I
answered, "internally." We kissed, ceremoniously. She
commented that I remained distant. It wasn't until I woke
that I saw words in swords.

According to Brigit Esselmont,
The Eight of Swords shows a woman tied up,
blindfolded, and surrounded by swords that act
as a kind of prison or enclosure. It appears that
there is no possibility of escape. She appears isolated
and alone as she stands in the midst of a barren, watery
wasteland far from the town in the distance. The sky is grey
and cloudy, indicating despair and a lack of hope. The woman's feet
do not touch the water, indicating that the feeling of being restricted
in the Eight of Swords is based on an intellectual assessment
of the situation and not an emotional one. There is a path
cleared before her, so there is actually a way out of this
situation but the blindfolds prevent the woman
from seeing her way out. —BE

Amazingly, & mystically for me, this interpretation
of the image & meaning of the Eight of Swords
(equivalent of the **8 of Spades**) describes our
daughter, Thea, to a '**T**'! So that on our last
full day there on Cody Street, we presented
our findings, including the card itself,
dusted off & animated in shimmering
Black & White, Camelia's caring
interpretation sent from Sweden,
where she & Bent are taking
Time off, + Brigit's
description of
the image.

Kathleen & I can only hope that the bindings
can be loosened by Patrick, the blindfold
removed by our daughter herself, &
those Swords turned into Words
of Love.

::::

On our first full day back in Portland, I'm digging
our own trees as if the black locust
in the neighbor's yard, back on Cody,
or the eight-trunked willow, whose roots must
lift the parking lot up, outside the wine store I walked to
every day, a few inches higher,
or even better yet, the foot-&-half-foot-tall locust
I meant to mention, growing out of a crack
in the cement sidewalk, validating
the fact that nature will continue
in her own unpredictable way
long after us = these oaks
here across the street
have turned a burnt-red
in the short period of time we were away,
the maples practically candy-colored,
& on our waterfront walk,
both stands of white birch still waving
anxiously goodbye to the glacier
remote millennia ago.

Also stood in a long line at grocery store
in order to replenish a few essentials,
when I noticed the guy in front of me waiting,
quite patiently behind a number of others
with just *The New York Times*.

Now, this guy looked about my age, tall,
grey, slim, & I admired the way he took the biding
of his time in an existential fashion, right out of Sartre
& the sixties, straddling ***Being & Nothingness***, until

he got to the cash register counter itself,
& out from the folded newspaper
comes this lone, large, russet potato.

I'm serious. I mean for me it was suddenly akin to
the weirdness I came to expect on Colfax Avenue.
My admiration didn't diminish, in fact, increased, saying,
"That's quite the purchase you got going there."

He smiled. Ya, he knew it was sixties-weird, too,
almost slyly, a wily old fox of a guy.
Through his grin he acknowledged
my observation with a certain
amount of humility & intelligence,
if not genius, I don't know, but after all,
the paper costs a lot by my terms,
not sure about his wherewithal,
he responded:

"Ya, I'm going to put some green chili on it
& read the paper."

There you go. That's as philosophical
a take on life as I've heard maybe even since
the sixties: bake a potato, add green chili,
& read the paper. Told him
I thought the print
version of the *New York Times*
was a work of art, & he agreed. Told him
I was writing a long poem called "Anatomy & Geography"
& that I was going to have to include him
& his purchase of newspaper
& lone potato.

LANGUAGE, THAT'S IT!

A kind of gravitational pull to land's end on either coast, when today I begin tracking Kerouac via journals, letters, & checking in on a few things others have to say, even play an excerpt of his reading *The Railroad Earth, Part I*, (which I also carry a copy of in my black canvas bag, included in a Penguin version of the ***New American Story***, edited by Don Allen & Robert Creeley, bought long, long ago, figuring I must have spent a pittance for it way back when, what with the back cover saying it cost 40p in England, a $1.35 in Australia & New Zealand, a $1.65 in Canada, & just under one rand in South Africa, but when checking for an American price, there is none on the cover, but look at that: twenty bucks written in pencil on the frontispiece! I must have been crazy back then for *The Railroad Earth*!). So why should I be surprised after heading out on my own daily trek to find myself stride for stride following the hobo walking the tracks hugging the coast. I keep an eye on him & on the cirrus clouds. He's authentic all right, waterproof backpack, & another snug-handled bag with what I assume are bottles for cash, hoping at least one is filled with beer or wine, or even whiskey, cause it's cold out here, & he's out here for a reason, those bottles directly connected to the reason he leans his head this way & that, looking, looking, maybe for that treasure of a stray wallet someone flush & stupid & inattentive left like the Time in Europe I found two wallets in my 3-month trek, each with cash, on the side of the Autobahn, or on the bus in Nice, oh, man, watching this guy's *modus operandi* I realize how little difference there is between us, the finest fine line, & when he turns back toward me to check, I see the wizened face of desperation, but not despair, & I realize right there & then, that by the end of most every day, I've found what I've been looking for, because I do not know what it is I'm looking for, but if it shudders subtly or ecstatically into language, that's it!

::::

I brought a stone home from the front yard of my daughter
& her husband's house there on Cody Street, which I'd need
Levi's Great-Grandfather, Don Leet, former Head of the Geology

Department at Harvard to know exactly what kind it is,
yellow & jagged, flecks of gold strewn here & there.

I project a certain Pleistocene physiognomy onto it,
cousin as it is to those larger stones bordering the yard
& street I held daily conversations with, the lava rock,
the basalt, & some kind of oval red stone rolled up & out
of the Grand Canyon itself.

This stone's on my writing desk reminding me of my time
there, good times with our daughter & grandson,
& my newest drinking buddy
son-in-law, Patrick,
who generously gave me a parting gift of wine.

Go ahead, retrace the steps in my oeuvre & see how
often its pages allude to the value of the rare gift
of wine just like the one Geoff & Angelina sent me
off with the day before leaving for Colorado, or

this one from Patrick: Domaine Laroque Imported by
Aquitaine Wine Berkeley, CA, 2012 I.G.P. Cité de Carcassonne.

(Been there, agog at the sailor
& his junkie whore on barstools,
while we waited on the laundry)

100% Cabernet Franc
(told Tom at Trader Joe's on Colorado
off Colfax just two days earlier it was my favorite grape,
but rare to find it in any other form than low percentage added to a blend)
back label reads:

> Domaine Laroque [la Roke] which means "the rock"
> is located in the hills of the famous ancient fortified city
> of Carcassonne in southern France. This 100-hectare estate
> has been making wine since the 6th century and derives its name
> from the stone age menhirs found in the vineyards. Today, the young,
> dynamic Albert Sarail and his family own the estate and are making

an easy-to-drink wine that combines the structure, minerality, and dusty rose characteristics of Cabernet Franc with the lively, fruitiness of wines from the south of France.

Domaine Laroque is a medium-bodied, fresh and fruity wine, with flavors of red berry fruits and vanilla. Enjoy it alone or paired with Mediterranean cuisine, pasta, lamb, chicken, pizzas and hamburgers. 13% alcohol.

A Jean-Christophe Calvet USA Exclusive Wine.

Needless to say, when Kathleen & I returned
to the motel from Solera on Colfax our last night there
in Denver, & opened the 100% cabernet franc wine
from Carcassonne we were as near to heaven
as we've been in quite a while, staying up late talking
between sips,
reminiscing about the trip,
which there & then, journey's event
had already turned
into some
kind
of deeply-etched, fond Memory.

::::

Believe Bent Sørensen nailed it,
when he wrote a few days ago saying
this project is no web of connections, but
a maelstrom. That suits the swirling demands
of the vortextual, at the same time corporeal nature
of the visceral, linguistic, hurtling, emptying force, Death
Drive.

Combining anatomy & geography,
as I am now pulled down
above a map of Argentina tracing steps
Ben Bollig trekked
on his recent trip journey voyage reading tour,
listen, as he tells us of landing in Buenos Aires

where he covers so much ground on foot in order, yes,
to expand his already vast cache of books
by Argentine poets.

Takes off for Puerto Madryn, (look at Madryn
hugging Golfo Nuevo = it's winter down there,
this is poetry business, not
some summer
junket)!

I'm following him
vicariously via atlas.
A book launch of his
newest essays in Spanish,
Activismo Poetico (update
& overlap of his earlier *Modern
Argentine Poetry*) at a bookstore in nearby
Gaimon with his poet friend, Cristian Aliaga,
who introduces him, & leads the lively discussion.

Meanwhile Barthes chimes in:

> The Text is not a co-existence of meanings but a passage, an
> overcrossing; thus it answers not to an interpretation, even
> a liberal one, but to an explosion, a dissemination.

Kerouac moans guiltily about taking advantage
of Mardou (Alene Lee) identifying her with
Baudelaire's mistress, Jeanne Duval.

Both Kerouac & Lee agreeing
they would have preferred a happy man
to the sad poems he left them,
so Baudelaire imagines
creating pure Romance out of pain
of his relationship, where he weeps
& confesses his faults
just as Kerouac shared
his should-not-be-tolds,

Baudelaire wants to create an atmosphere
of *great days* & Barthes writes
that the Text flows from:
"lights, colors, vegetation, heat, air, slender explosions of noises,
scant cries of birds, children's voices from over the other side,
passages, gestures, clothes of inhabitants near or far away."

Returning me to the atlas over which I presently hover,
where Ben trucks on with Aliaga to the South Atlantic
town of Comodoro Rivadavia balancing
on the Golfo San Jorge
for another talk.
These guys have guts
driving the 400 kilometers
in one day in winter,
this being the business of poetry,
not North American poetry, at that, with its prizes
& chairs & stars,
but Argentine with cardboard,
dirt roads, & risk of Death.

They'll eventually drive
seven hours to Aliaga's hometown,
Lago Puelo, not on this atlas, but I find
it online, & hear from the geography mapped
there the struggle of both poet & critic in the tone
of their masterful language, desiring to travel with them,
which in some ways I have.

:::::

In the middle of the night,
3:30 in the morning, in fact,
stumble on something written
on this date exactly five years ago,
on October 18th, 2009. Taken from a dream
that night, it reads: "Every step you take adds
goodness to the earth."

::::

She gets on the road early
to visit her older sister down
in Massachusetts, leaving me here
to my lonesome. So what comes over
the airwaves out of San Francisco, but
T-Bone Walker's version of *Goin' to Chicago*.

Forcing me to think of both cities at once
like Kerouac over there in the former city
of his **Subterraneans** fiction missing Mardou's
little brown body on the bed in the slums
of Telegraph Hill, or even more so
in the vortextual maelstrom
of the utter anatomical edge
of being alone,

that lack of the geographic here
in a Portland kitchen,
more like him in Denver,
(Jack's still so alive)
in the Scroll Version of **On the Road** wishing
he could head out West to California &
at the same time back East to New York,
unsettled as he is there
in Colorado with his plans
for sharing a house with mother & sister
& brother-in-law going awry.

I told her yesterday that,
no, it didn't seem like these ten years
in Maine have fled too quickly,

that living in the midst of Time,
the moment eternal/internal,
where nerves of the Sympathetic Plexus

emerge to carry one via rite of passage
of the instant of vision,
say, those egrets we made a destination of

standing on stones in the Back Cove
drying out from the torrential rain
of the night before so much so

Egyptian hieratic heads,
or their clear reflections
etched in shallow water

as much hieroglyphic image
sign & language at the same Time.

Not T-Bone Walker any longer, now,
Barthes, again, saying "Beethoven was the first man of music to be free."
"Ah, Freedom," as I sighed

a sigh of relief there
on the campus with the hills in the distance
haunting & visible above the red ground of Napa, California,

where I was settled in the anatomy
of my skin, & geography
lent it longitude & latitude

to the sense of that Freedom
in travel enough to jot down one's every move
in a notebook one doesn't need any longer to consult,

because the act of writing it down
etches it there
in the cerebral cortex,

& fingers as well, eyes
& olfactory system, dust on boots tramping
vineyards with John Muir's great-grandson,

Michael Hanna, Pinot Noir in hand
no less, one of the ultimate confluences
of earth & body,

spirit & matter,
walking & talking.

(OK, just opened the notebook to find the names of)
Bret & Robert de Leuze,
who spent two & a half hours showing me around
their magnificent winery,
ZD, where they made the only Napa wine I know of produced in Solera
fashion, the Spanish method using the oldest reserve wines
blended with the newest, called Abacus.

They opened a bottle & shared it in the boardroom,
memory so intense,
that when I saw a bottle at the airport bar,
Vino Volo, last Sunday in Newark,
I asked the bartender for a look-see,
able to tell him I'd had it before,
his telling us people there actually spring the $599 for it.

Think I'll start my morning
with a cup of $4.99 Sainte-Croix Syrah-Merlot
Vin de Pays D'Oc, 2012, leftover,
saucer covering cup from late last night,
not a fruit fly in sight.

Wait a minute, while jotting down that last line morning
turned to noon.

::::

The reader, should there be one, might judge the leap
from T-Bone to Beethoven, Kerouac to Barthes as harsh?

Not to me.

(I have to read this, too, you know, derive some pleasure
of surprise even when proofing.)

It's the maelstrom of the Textual, the music
of celestial spheres, the individual
genius each of these references exhibit
in the swirling,
that Poundian Vortex
never bettered.

Gaudier-Brzeska, also born
on the Fourth of October,
hammered & chiseled,
carved & burnished his way
into a new world, then the world
killed you, young Henri, the world,
whose inhabitants I described to her
yesterday
on our noontime waterfront walk
as mostly mediocre,
such a word, mediocre,
damn, sounds like tapioca,
which isn't mediocre, but fine
substance close to pearls I found
in oysters at Jorge's grass
shack on the beach
in Zihuatanejo,
no,
mostly mediocre
human
inhabitants
of this earth
with some underrated
brave souls on continents
we Americans have no notion of
like North Africa & Middle East, like Compton
& Watts, Bangladesh & Detroit.

Then there're the small
minority of Good
People,
(I mentioned Jessica, who
lent me off-the-cuff 50 cents
at Harbor Fish; Mike Mellor,
who quit
trick-or-treating
at Halloween, at 8-yo,
because at 7, slicked his hair
down, & wore a fake grey suit,
fake Republican saying, "Read my lips,"
to neighbors opening doors, mistaking the joke,
& taking him for a supporter of that party, the only party
I know he supports
is that of my own,
derangement
of the senses…)
who with his girlfriend,
Erin,
offered
to escort
us to
the new MFA
Goya exhibit
on All Saints weekend,
those days after Halloween.

Oh,
& then
I added another
segment of the population
of the world: the truly sinister,
evil bastards & bitches for lack
of better, more shocking blasphemies
to identify their corruption, these politicians,
(damn, seriously, I just had the damndest Time
even spelling that word, Politicians, a dirty word)
these soldiers willing to kill anyone

unlike them under orders,
these greedy
One Percenters,
hubristic lawyers,
millionaires, billionaires,
priests, poets & novelists, who
can't write, they, person-for-person could,
if you let them, erase the acts of the few good minority,
but we shan't
shall we?

What with Sonny Buxton right
this moment sending Sonny Rollins
on sax, along with Ray Brown on bass,
Shelly Manne on bass, across the airwaves
from KCSM Radio in San Francisco on "I'm an Old Cowhand"
from his 1957 album, *Way Out West*.

Yes,
I'm there today.

                                        ::::

I am led,
& at the same
Time, take the lead
in the Vortextual swirl.

                                        ::::

Not long after Barthes
says Beethoven was the first
musician to be free, he points out
that, "From this moment that the work
becomes the trace of a movement, of a journey,
it appeals to the idea of fate." Here, take it all down:

The artist is in search of his 'truth' and this quest forms
an order in itself, a message that can be read, in spite of its
variations in its content, over all the work or, at least, whose
readability feeds on a sort of totality of the artist: his career, his
loves, his ideas, his character, his words become traits of meaning…

::::

TIME IN THE FUTURE

Suffering was palpable on the way up Preble Street before the soup kitchen opened, & without any evidence of pride seen anywhere, unless on the face of the guy with the Mohawk & his worn-down female companion in leather proud to be with someone at all, while his was that of a warrior, totally outmoded & almost useless on the street. Wanted to pass there again on the way back across town, where once the sea is in view everything changes. Remnants of last night's dusk seemed floating on the stage of horizon. Both tankers, the *Mare Tireneum* & the *Northern Dawn* lent their names to the potential idyll of the day. Just before or after the wild apple tree, depending on the walk back or forth, there's a granite stone now slowly revealed by receding vegetation with a white quartz outline welded to the dark granite, which <u>I began to feel I could talk to at some point in Time in the future, if only I could get down to that mineral level</u>, & of course, the idea of Death quickly intervened, although the discussion with the granite & quartz stone is something I desire in life, on a walk in winter, when no one else is around. Rays shot forth from the top of the mackerel sky like some nave in a cathedral in France I also plan to see. Meanwhile, back on Preble, the poor & homeless put up a good front after lunch, but all the bad teeth in their smiles couldn't hide the same pain I saw on my way over to the waterfront.

::::

What with Brad & Rebecca on their way over in order to share
their planned itinerary down south to Alabama
with a long layover in Asheville to spend time
with my small press printer, Mark Olson,
check out Black Mountain,
& eventually join friends
near the Florida panhandle,

I transform the library table,
on which this myriad of sources
contributing to the vortextual swirl
has been stacked for months,
into a dining table
over which we can talk,
while serving up beet soup,
black lentils, arugula salad
topped with a fillet of salmon
baked with garlic, chipotle,
& maple syrup.

It's a minor
thrill the next day
to see the bare oak
of the library table +
coincidently
run into Jean Fields strolling
along East End Beach.

Jean who found this table
given away for free at one of the Yale libraries,
when her husband majored in architecture
there in the 50's, & a few years ago
scaling down her possessions,
thought I might make the best use of it,
this old oak trestle table
almost like a wide-awake Freudian writing pad,
so inviting, so damn Ivy League,
so that with the books moved to the bay window ledge
in the living room, unarranged, random,

a toss of the dice,
new sources surface,
& *Derrida and the Writing of the Body* glistens
in its stunning black & white cover
& X-ray image of the female form,
leading the author, Jones Irwin
of Dublin City University to examine Georges Bataille's
influence on Derrida,
leading me to my own copy of *Guilty*,
in which Bataille writes a letter
to his professor in Paris on December 6, 1937,
in which he refers to himself
as an "unemployed negativity," ha,
I'm laughing now Monsieur Bataille!!

Oui, I read your crazy biography
by Michel Surya, laughter in the face of Death,
your calling card, & in the letter to Alexandre Kojève,
(however unnamed here, rather, "Dear Blank,").

In fact, Kojève led the seminar
on Hegel's closed system,
which Olson said Keats hammered the nail
to wreck Hegel
with his concept of "Negative Capability,"
you oppose with your own metal:

> "I think of my life – or better yet, its abortive
> condition, the open wound that my life is –
> as itself constituting
> a refutation of Hegel's closed system."

How I identify with "unemployed negativity"
& "the open wound
that my life is,"
to the extent that
that laughter you came to advocate
in the face of Death is at least a grin,
no smirk, no grimace,

nor mere nod
of acceptance, but a smile
of welcomed defiance.

::::

In the dream tonight, up now
writing in the midst of the rain
banging on the backroom roof,
we saw the Quixotean taverna in
the dusty distance doors wide open
& the lone drinker hovering over his
reposada. However, when we wandered
in the place turned into an outdoor garden,
where the owners greeted us with open arms.

Mentioned connection to Manuel Ávila Camacho,
whom the owner knew only too well, but thought he'd recently let
himself go,
which not he, but in fact Death had.

We ordered the white wine.
The couple we sat with
were drinking, topping off
their glasses before filling our own.

I said this atmosphere reminded me of when we were kids,
alluding to times in Salem at grandparents', when adults were busy
with talk & drink & adult things,
while we children
were enthralled
with lilacs & horse
chestnuts against the sky,
enraptured & safe in the arms
of our mothers & grandmothers
& Mother Nature Herself, the rain
now so audible on the backroom's flat roof.

Good dream to dream vivid
just minutes ago, unable to sleep now
with the rain drumming on the tympan
skin of the flat roof, & huge oak trees on either side
of the house swirling
in the dark.

Out here writing in the middle of night,
not exactly *the* exact opposite
of enraptured & safe in arms
of our mothers & grandmothers
& Mother Nature Herself.

Returning to bed,
sleeping into the early morning,
dreaming of being at a party,
where a group of us want
to walk to the woods,
or shore, or mountain.

I forget the planned destination.
A walk interrupted by the tears
of two children who didn't want
their mother to leave. I said I'd stay
to take care of them, but the young girl
complained, clinging to her mother.

The others left. Upstairs, where the party
continued, a man came over to shake my hand
goodbye,
saying he'll never forget
the tilefish I caught, cut, cooked,
& shared with him, along with the splinter
I managed to take out of the very hand he shook with.

It wasn't exactly like meeting Jesus from Chihuahua in real life,
but this dream guy gave me his number
& spelled out the name of the remote
town on the Pacific coast of Mexico

he said was not near any city
I'd recognize.

Checking the maps just now, he's right,
the jumbled letters I have leftover
from the dream, placed
in whatever order
are nowhere
to be found.

THE GEOGRAPHY OF DREAMS

Lacan could have said the unconscious is structured like a geography as far as the series of dreams went last night with both pleasure & death drives emerging into a massive wave in the bay of Zihuatanejo, which I warned my swimming companion about before diving under it, submerged for a second or two just like those long, languorous days in the summer of '74. Glad to get past that threat, the next wave, also large, but only half the size of the first, I caught it good without the board my friend & I had at the start of the dream, riding the crest of it as it mounted toward the shore I now recall being reminded of when she & I watched *The Night of the Iguana* night before last. But that geography, now so personally mythological & ingrained in my body, was also called up by a note written to me earlier in the week by our daughter, who said she thought of me when served red snapper at the restaurant. I relayed to her the story of our ritual back then for three & a half weeks, ordering up the fish grilled whole (*Huachinango*) at 11:00 every morning at the shack on the beach. When the crest of the wave reached its peak I rose even a few more feet above it, & wanted people there on shore to see me in that old red bathing suit, thinking now how it mimicked the act of writing the autobiography, you know, the high-wire act of exposing oneself half-naked, but not bare-assed.

Or like the donkey with the broken leg, I suppose I could add as that image comes to mind from the same time on our walks into town. No one visible on shore anyway, just as there have been no readers of the work, but the work is not just for the here & now, just as the next dream carried me on to Boston waving out the driver's side window to the guy I recognized on the highway behind me. She warned me about the detour ahead with orange cones shunting us off to the right, where the survey team was mapping the area, demarcating it in a series of painted circles, protecting, as it were, something of particular geographic importance in the center. Now, surely, this landscape with which I was so familiar during my commute to work for so many years collided with my conception of what it must be like for my friends who make their annual trek to Tromsø, Norway, two hundred miles inside the Arctic Circle, where earlier yesterday I mistakenly believed they already were, but realized Bent & Camelia are not leaving until this week. So in the dream I stood on the small mound in the center of the geographic survey saying to the others around me, "Here, stand here, on top of the world." The others followed suit, standing there on the small mound, feeling what it was like, momentarily, to be on top of the world (a spot in my dream Boston so similar to the crest of the Mexican wave) then jumping off.

If that weren't enough, I found myself inside a boarding house constructed like the one we stayed at for a month in Mexico City, combined with the architecture of the rows of brownstones on Mass Ave. traversed so often on my way to work. As I exited the door leading down to the stone front steps, I brushed past Death without exactly touching his old overcoat, but excused myself with a certain amount of respect & reverence, & damn glad to do so. Found myself next inside the circulation desk of a library, where an Asian student requested a large atlas. Asked my young assistant if it were a folio, checking the spine for the call number. No, she said, but it was on reserve, & the student would have to pay to use it for an hour, but he declined. This surely emerged enmeshed, out my recent trip to Bowdoin College library for Barthes' *Camera Lucida*, which upon arrival learned both copies were on reserve. With just two hours to read it, I photocopied it, thinking I probably broke some copyright law, relishing my outlaw status. That book led me to Barthes' essay in my copy of *Writings on Cy Twombly*, a folio if there ever was one, where the author's lone phrase, *a man's spontaneity is his culture*, so fascinated me the whole weeklong. Hurried from my station at the circulation desk to write down the dream of waves in the bay in Zihuatanejo, standing on top of the world in Boston, brushing past Death with an "Excuse me," & all the geography enclosed in the atlas, when suddenly my father came by asking if he could cook supper for me, peering over my shoulder interested in what I'd already written down.

A FREE MAN

It's night & day for any poet worth his/her salt, so after reaping daylight images, some of which travel back in Time well over fifty years underground in memory, night brings on texts as various as Kerouac & Kristeva, the latter on the screen via a link from Mark Woods, "An Essay in Abjection," in which she examines attempts by writers to give voice to the abject: *The abject would thus be the 'object' of primal repression.* I get that. Then adds, *One does not know it, one does not desire it, one joys in it* [on enjouit]. *Violently and painfully. A passion.* In her critical assessment of some of my great ones, Dostoevsky, Proust, Joyce, she concludes that, *Death thus keeps house in our contemporary universe. By purifying (us from) literature, it establishes our secular religion.* That's just one example of what I'll take into bed tonight. Kerouac finally makes it to Denver. Locates Neal Cassady, & heads over to Allen Ginsberg's basement apartment where the poet reads him his "Denver Doldrums," & I dream:

Something lands upon the carpeted basement floor: nut, or root bole, with dangerous object sticking out of its round case, a beak, or tooth, or thorn, when suddenly this dangerous part of the object begins to grow, grow into a shoot, then longer stems, & as careful as I am in handling what is now more or less a thorn bush, I get stuck, & the venom, or ambrosia, (or juice I see as source) enters my veins, to the extent that I can feel the beginnings of the ecstasy of writing, & WANT more, so lift up what is now a bouquet of thorns (wounds) & bite into the lowest hanging root to chew & swallow IT.

Robert de Visée
Robert Musil
Robert Motherwell
Robert Hellman
Robert Rauschenberg
Robert Schumann
Robert Lee "R. L." Burnside
Robert James Ritchie "Kid Rock":
My name is Robert, too.

:::::

On Wednesday, in the midst of tracking down Barthes' essay, "The Grain
of the Voice," I got an email from my friend, Marilyn Crispell in response
to a recent review of my work. Knowing she'd recently given a series of
jazz piano concerts in Paris, I asked her how Paris was, & while she
composed her answer, which alluded to the fact that she also played in
Arcueil, where Erik Satie was born, attended a concert at La Java, where
Edith Piaf sang, & waited in line for an hour & a half in the cold for the
Basquiat exhibit, marveling that, *it was great to see the huge numbers of
people who still care about art!*, I read this sentence in Barthes, *As for piano
music, I know at once which part of the body is playing...*

:::::

Enamored as I am with names
& characters, accomplishments & shared wisdom
of Bataille, Derrida, Barthes, there are also days like a week ago
Monday when the anonymous man about my age
stood in the long express lane waiting
to purchase the *New York Times* & a potato,
a man after my own Soul
with my own pockets empty so often,
I was tempted to return
to that day to see exactly what, in fact, he'd spring
$2.50 for in the paper, & there,
pretty much one quickly gets an answer in the headline
regarding the Dallas nurse as the first person to contract Ebola

within the US.
Neighbors worry, & what with this being the US,
you know that panic will spread quickly across state lines.
I'm not saying the headline alone
prompted this anonymous guy
in a white tee-shirt to get the news,
remember, he said he was going to bake that spud
& read the paper, so I know he
got his money's worth & read it through
page-by-page,
all the bad
with nary a bit
of the good.

Exactly a week later it's the unknown,
to you, at least, Jack Daniels, right,
who works at Whole Foods in
grocery greets me with smile
& handshake + intriguing
answer to my question
when I ask how his
weekend was: just
back from 10 days
off & a 6-day
hunting trip
with friend
& the guy's
80-year-old
father, both
having lost
mother &
wife
respectively,
3 weeks ago,
an important trip
to have scored a moose
with hours left on the last
day of the license = Jack, half
Native American with roots in New

Brunswick, performed his sacred ritual
on the last night before the fateful encounter.

Asked to describe the rite, he said, he retreated
to his tent
because of all the rain,
preferring the outdoors,
but took out his hunting fetish,
a sculpted bear given to him
by the cousin of a Pueblo Zuni,
& practiced the language
that would plead with the spirit of the animal
to come to them,
that that's what one does
rather than necessarily tracking the animal down.

They couldn't hunt by night, according to state law,
but got out there half an hour before sunrise,
where within an hour the 600-pound
bull appeared.

Not long after on that same day,
the day I mentioned cleaning off the library table to make room
for dinner with friends heading out on their own road trip,
& saying the trestle table was a gift
from someone else unknown,
at least to you,
Jean Fields,
& there's Jean at 88 traversing the stones
on East End Beach walking her neighbor's dog,
saying she just returned from visiting her son in San Francisco
with an added visit to Port Townsend, Washington.

Told her we're just back from Denver
to see little Levi Marcus, who at 16-months
already tossed the football, digging the contrast of years
already lived & yet to live.

I had 9 raspberries bunched together
in my black corduroy jacket pocket,
which I'd found on tangled vines
behind a perfectly formed star
the skunk cabbage was straddling
the railroad track & galaxy of unknown brambles
holding down the output of wild fruit
this year more than last, & last year
more than the year before,
the total harvest
from the hidden patch
diminishing annually since I found it
back there in, say, 2008.

Split them down the middle yesterday,
5 for Kathleen, 4 for me to accompany
the cultivated & frozen fruits
for breakfast, but enjoying
a sacred harvest, at least
for me, as if digesting
the meat of a wild
animal I might
have reenacted
a rite, dialogue
in order to
coax its
spirit
into
Being.

::::

Barthes equates the *grain* of music with the body, or voice.
I believe he would have approved of the free two-hour
session performed by Abdullah Ibrahim on Monday
at the Schomberg Center for Black Culture,
& what was said about it by Ben Ratcliff
leaving out Barthes' loathsome parts of

speech to describe music: adjectives.
The critic saw the 80-year-old's
compositions "swimming
between islands of song
without becoming dis-
continuous... tension
in his work a matter
of weight, real or
metaphorical."
Ratcliff heard
old voices
seem to
speak
& saw
the pianist
not bother to
touch the keyboard,
as if there were ghosts
in the machine desiring
silence.

Know exactly what he means,
having had the privilege of hearing
the South African from Cape Town in
an intimate setting at the Iron Horse Tavern
in Northampton years ago, taking daughter, Thea,
along with us. There were no breaks.
Symphony with drummer & bass
without intermission, ancient roots
of the body from another hemisphere
there in evidence of the audible *grain*.

::::

Arcangelo Corelli streams over the waters from Venice
Classical Radio with his *Concertos da Chiesa in do Minore No. 3 Op. 6*

soothing my nerves against the nasty weather.
We're in the midst of a 3-or-4 day blow,
which I tried my best to stem the tide against
by getting up on the roof early the day
before yesterday about 5 hours ahead
of it, attempting to batten down the leak
with silicon spray I used twice before
to no avail.

Damn, if it isn't holding up, at least right now on the third day.

In Hemingway's short story it's also a Thursday on the third
day, when Nick & Bill say they want to get drunk watching
the autumn wind take down all the leaves in the orchard
where all the apples are already harvested. Damn, if
they don't talk about the World Series wishing they
could see one, say in St. Louis, but they all take
place in New York & Philadelphia, yet fishing
trumps baseball, they say, a chump's game.

There's Irish whiskey, a fireplace screen
against which Nick first plants his bare feet.
Got to love Hemingway's subtle masculinity,
bordering on Feminine, often
left invisible to the naked eye,
but this is a love story, nonetheless,
& memory of Marge, the hard
memory of losing
Marge defeats
the purpose
of whiskey,
sobers
him up
quick,
& they both,
Bill & Nick, go out
to hear a sole shotgun
blast resound against the wind in the distance.

She's proud of the fact that I've somehow plugged the leak, at least for now.

Earlier, propped my feet up,
but not touching the isinglass of the propane
Franklin stove. Black coffee,
but would have preferred Irish whiskey.
Those guys, Bill & Nick, were good with their hands,
could build things, set traps, catch fish.
I'm no handyman is my point, hate
the sight of a hammer, loathe the sound
of a saw, use screwdrivers only
in desperate circumstances.

I shut the lights out & let the fire inside
& downed leaves outside,
along with the rain itself be the only light,
thinking that while I'm no handyman in the practical sense
of the word, I've long been a bricoleur of words:

AN ACT OF BRICOLAGE

Wake up to the train, again, running right through town at 6:30 holding up
a whole line of 7:00 workers. Just flashed on how Seattle woke to the sun
curving round the mountain as I watched the homeless up before workers
in the stained-glass dawn. In the dream the woman in my arms remained
elusive. I remember hunkering down last night feeling good about myself,
but by morning had the task of reassembling all of that. An act of bricolage:
place this stone here, try abandoning that pattern, bookmark the page
where Freedom calls for novelty, brush the dust off the gladioli, garner a
certain selflessness in reassembling the Self.

This rain & wind adds
to the jostling force of
the vortextual nature

of the project, where
the man with newspaper
& lone potato returns
again & again, as if
some Mercurial figure
with a message, so
the subject of Ebola
returns as something
of an intrigue, & Hell,
the poor people of
Liberia, Sierra Leone,
Guinea, for the most
part stoically having
to deal with rampant
infection of the plague,
while panic sets in in
Dallas neighborhoods.

Early on looked into
scientific speculation
as to the virus's origin:
fruit bats in Central &
West Africa, where
segments of the society
traditionally hunt them
for food. On the ladder
in one of my 54 jobs
painting a house in
Haverhill, MA, a bat
fell from the top eave
of the corner of the roof,
where my ladder reached,
& bucket hung from a rung,
straight into the paint.

This mammal with face
of a child, (a mammal,
after all) eyes closed,
mouth open, gasping

for air out of the beige
paint was an unwelcome
sight to say the least, &
I could have toppled over
backward in the shock.

(What good would its
eyes open have done,
I now realize!) It wanted
out, not me, my neck,
nose so close to this
unexpected daytime
nightmare. For some
reason I turned brush
around, & handle first,
pressed against bobbing
head with ancient wings.
It's a mammal, not a bird.
I'm a mammal, not a bird.

::::

A new performance piece opened
in Brooklyn Sunday through Sunday,
again, from the Marina Abramović school,
possibly via precedents by Carolee Schneemann:
after all razor-cut blood covers the walls by the end.

Based on the heart-wrenching work
of Sarah Kane, British playwright,
who hanged herself in 1999
at age 28, *Psychosis*,
is a vortextual suicide note
composed of disparate, fragmentary
outbursts & lamentations, pleadings & disavowals.

We know the end.
Yet, our delayed, pent-up, empathic,
stubborn sense of unreleased catharsis

still rivets us to hope. In Polish with English supertitles,
the mix of languages barely helps cushion the real body
of actress Magdalena Cielecka, from falling
into our laps.

::::

.Is this the first sentence to begin with a period?

Speaking of Schneemann, now, astonishingly,
75, she had those garden snakes crawl all over
her torso in 1963 presaging Schechner's *Dionysus '69*,
she claimed not to know about the Minoan Snake Goddess
mythology ahead of Time, & of the film *Meat Joy* in 1964,
(reshown this year at the *Musée départemental d'art contemporain de
Rochechouart*, a museum three hours outside of Paris),
she claimed the mix of bodies
of human, fish, & other domestic animals
in close contact, (*The Bacchae*?) was an erotic,
Dionysian rite.

Claims she was first championed by poets:
Robert Kelly, David Antin, & Paul Blackburn.
Says she was influenced by the collage method
of Charles Olson's, "Maximus to Gloucester",

I come back to the geography of it…

       I have this sense
that I am one
with my skin
       Plus this-plus this:
that forever the geography
which leans in
on me I compell
backwards…

Asked in a recent interview what she means by "essences,"
septuagenarian, Carolee Schneemann, finished

her excursus with: "How are you in your skin?"

VOLCANIC TERRITORY
WITHIN THE HUMAN BODY

Struggling with an understanding of what Derrida calls the Archive Drive,
lifting it directly from Freud's references to the triple-named
Aggression, Destruction, or Death Drive,
the deconstructivist saying it is silent,
silent & unrecognized,
unless dressed-up, masked, made-up, painted, eroticized,
seduced, drummed-up, musicalized, bent,
fragmented, torn up out of the bowels
of the howling body,
the Archive/Death Drive
desiring to destroy itself
before it even erupts into view
like the volcanic territory within the human body
beyond the Pleasure Principle Freud discovered
& explored initially.

So it's no surprise, then, yesterday,
to receive a grand gift of mentorship
from David Anfam in the form of the postcard
sent from Madrid & the Prado
of that wondrous, delving,
plumbed reach of silent
Archive/Death Drive
in the image after Velázquez
by Francis Bacon of the *Screaming Innocent X*!

::::

I keep returning
to the Mercurial figure
in the express line, (did he

have wings on his ankles under
jeans & white tee-shirt, the guy about my age,
but looking youthful in a timeless, ancient way?),
whose name I should have asked, what with letting
him know beforehand I planned to include him here
(my own life become a poem months ago, his could,
if we talked more, say over a Guinness & a lone potato).

That's just it, though, since speculating on the reason
he bought the paper a week ago Monday was the headline
in pretty large bold **TYPE**, announcing:

**Dallas Nurse Contracts Ebola Virus,
Elevating Response & Anxiety**:
DALLAS – A nurse here be-
came the first person to contract
Ebola within the United States,
prompting local, state, and federal
officials who had settled into a
choreographed [get it?] response to
scramble on Sunday to solve the
mystery of how she became in-
fected despite wearing protective
gear and to monitor additional
places and people possibly at
risk.

As I said, that's just it,
because when they
announced in
the paper
today
that a doctor,
who'd treated patients
in Guinea is diagnosed with Ebola,
I couldn't help wonder when he entered
the port of New York = sure enough, the day after
my Mercury man here in Portland purchased the *Times*
with his meager stash, along with lone potato + let's face it,
not that many days after TSA in Denver patted down my wife's

& the 15-year-old's (also taken out of line) ass.

What a country. Speak out, shout out
against the powers that aren't
helping anyone, but
themselves!!

:::::

This morning new shadows danced & sang
with old leaves against the back fence.
Still vivid in mind at the same time
in the swirling vortextual world,
the bittersweet behind chain-
link just before East End
Beach begins fresh
from our walk
yesterday,
the yellow & red
of the vines enveloping
silver metal, while sun continued
to dig deep into the Atlantic water's
belly clear to the bottom rocks & sand.
Of course, Anne Carson's notion of *Eros:*
The Bittersweet surged around the vine as color
bypasses our internal censor, & her vision of him
as Pteros, or winged-one circled round me in my silent
language, or better yet, our constant talk,
as if together, our proximity
to each other, the yellow & red color
freely penetrating our Souls,
our walk, our gait in tandem
came as close to flight
as humanly possible.

Love had us.

SPLEEN TIME

Easier to turn the page of a book, (than one in life, I suppose, although they can go hand-in-hand,) I do, look: go over to the black canvas bag I carried all around town last night, first to The Snug where Michelle with her tattoos, in between cooing to her galfriends, pours as smooth a Guinness as this Gene Ammons version of *Cheek to Cheek*, then on down Washington Street to Tu Casa, where we both know you can't get real Mexican food in America, but hungry on top of thirst we splurged, & used our imaginations toward Veracruz & Zihuatanejo, no, I didn't open a book all night strolling around, but now, randomly, Benjamin addresses spleen Time, no less, in Baudelaire as reified & historyless. Dig this: *in spleen the perception of time is supernaturally keen. Every second finds consciousness ready to intercept its shock.* Didn't expect to stumble on anything that good like piano keys in *Cheek to Cheek* matching letters driven down here. More interested in turning a page in life last night talking deaths & dancing, bringing her & her daughter full-circle round in due recognition of their fathers, cheek-by-jowl, (just wrote jhowl), including tears of joy if need be. In Baudelaire seconds in Time engulf a person like a snowstorm, whereupon turning the page calls up the dream from last night, (internal screen Time), when I told the blonde she had intellectual ability, to which she did not respond, but then corrected myself to say what I'd meant to say, intellectual Beauty, whereupon she was all mine from then on in.

::::

In the dream this morning the word "lascivious"
& then, additionally "lasciviousness"
resounded audibly from a large,
blank, pink index card with
blue lines, as if from
someone taking

notes, & notes
invisibly written
turned into the hiss
of the word like a snake
walking on his belly as one
sometimes does in sleep in the dream
walk the reptilian walk on one's innards.

I'm sure it came from here:
the sound resounding
from a statement
by Schneemann
regarding her
Interior
Scroll:

> I thought of the vagina in many ways-- physically, conceptually:
> as a sculptural form, an architectural referent, the sources of
> sacred knowledge, ecstasy, birth passage, transformation. I
> saw the vagina as a translucent chamber of which the serpent
> was an outward model: enlivened by it's passage from the
> visible to the invisible, a spiraled coil ringed with the shape of
> desire and generative mysteries, attributes of both female and male
> sexual power. This source of interior knowledge would be symbolized
> as the primary index unifying spirit and flesh in Goddess worship.
> —CS
> http://www.caroleeschneemann.com/interiorscroll.html

Marguerite Duras in the midst
of the mind, when out of the blue
& black & white over Venetian airwaves
as if various pebbles picked up on an island
beach & placed on a paper plate, floated across
the sea in the form of Schumann's *Kreisleriana.*

Spaces between notes advance toward those by Bill Evans.

Based upon the 1819 novel,

The Life & Opinion of the Tomcat Murr
Together with a Fragmentary Biography of Kapellmeister Johannes Kreisler
on Random Sheets of Waste Paper, the music
& the approach to writing,
wherein a cat decides
to write his own autobiography
on the backside sheets of his master's.

It's pure vortextuality!
Becomes the only harmonious tone
I'm fond of, that which Gioseffo Zarlino
defined in 1558: harmony is the *concord of discords,*
meaning a concord of diverse things that can be
joined together. Ah, Schumann, who became
a composer as opposed to concert pianist,
when his father, a bookseller, broke his
son's right-hand ring finger with a
hammer handle when the young
man altered a note of Mozart's
Don Giovanni, yet the young
protégé was simply
experimenting
with what Kierkegaard
found in the music of the opera:
the sensuous erotic, or that which
is experienced immediately. An improvisation!

Suddenly I return to Marguerite Duras, for the Feminine,
for me, is the only shelter,
& Schumann's music, its space
like that of Bill Evans', is not masculine,
is no high-rise architecture,
but an embrace.

Two arms, ten fingers in the sound
of the Feminine voice, encircling one
in the spiraling vortex of Love.

Low notes, as well as high. Slow,

as well as rapid. Something Kristeva knows
about when she says that the writing of Marguerite Duras
is a thirst for suffering bordering on madness
revealing that mercy comes
with our most persistent despondencies...
The sound of a broken
ring finger is a delicious lamentation,
a Blues, a chord composed of discords,
thrown together to form the only form of harmony
I'm fond of: the atonal.

A melancholy with the holy hidden in the Word only
the flesh can flesh out,
as if one were led by a chain
of Sympathetic plexuses, the Solar
located behind stomach, in front of aorta,
& crura of diaphragm.

Wonderful to come full-circle round
in the swirling vortex in which a series of chords
floating over the ocean from Venice
like a plate of stones arranged
on paper brings
me to rendezvous,
again, with Marguerite,
whom I met in Paris,
& who says of one of her characters
that she is not just from Venice, but from all
the other places she has experienced along
the way via Julia Kristeva, whom I had
the privilege to meet in Cambridge
exactly this month a year ago,

& Søren, whom I discovered
in the pages of *Or*, the 2nd
of two volumes for a dollar,
used, in a Harvard Square,
bookstore, when at twenty-
years-old, his notion of the sensuous,

or *immediate-erotic* struck me like a hammer blow,
hard enough to crack the ring-finger on a right hand, & open
the secret to the world of language
in the body, organs, & bones.

::::

ANATOMICAL GEOGRAPHIES

We kept waking in pitch dark throughout the sleeping hours, as if reluctant to let go of the joys of the day & night before, whispering queries, exchanging verbal fragments, reaching way back in Times & places in between dreams. Purely anatomical, those geographies of Paris, Glasgow, Rome, Naples, Capri, Nice, Reims, the bed underneath us metamorphosing from the usual raft floating at sea to click-clack-click accompaniment of rail ties & coach-car sway. Yet we stayed there within the corporeal proximity that sent us far & wide, skin as brilliantly loquacious during those imagined journeys as tongue.

::::

No mere coincidence
that Bent sends new information
on a theory of writing based on the inclusion
of noise, e.g., creaking sounds emanating from wood
in the structure of Dogon looms.

Seriously, I like this, & let him know
we have a set of Dogon heddle-pulleys,
used to separate threads to ease the shuttle's
movement through warp runs in order to create
what other than, yes, *textiles*, pure, unadulterated

filled with noise & music.

Spirit carved on figurehead with bird atop
like ours, or tree. Heddle-pulleys singing
along one might say in the process of making cloth,
or in our case stanza, or paragraph,
the line's warp longitudinally up & down the length
of the page in the joy
of its own noise,
the pure *vortextuality*
Bent sent as yet another example
of at just the right Time, say,
as if Bill Evans were coming to town
as Kathleen once told me when we first met,
even though Bill was long gone.

She'd not gotten word of his passing,
& in her innocent remark drew closer to me,
a subtle hum of Love between us, say, like his
tune, "Quiet Now", from *The Paris Concert*.

::::

VORTEX OF DISCOURSE

Wander, without my Baedeker, past the amphitheatre in Pompeii, where
through smoke in the distance, I recognize two former contemporaries
reminiscing about their diverse experiences on Capri in the '20's, which
the dream allows us to eavesdrop on, or history, for that matter, (just as
one of the participants overheard the words of Adrienne Monnier & Léon-
Paul Fargue in the bookstore in Paris), here on the steps of the Temple of
Isis, Walter Benjamin continues his side of the discourse from the abstract
saying, *imagination is like the sun setting over the abandoned theater of the
world with its deciphered ruins… the unending dissolution of beauty, freed
from all seduction*, while D. H. Lawrence counters with his own corporeal
view that, *The human being has in his veins the blood of the wings of birds &*

the venom of serpents. All things emerged from the blood-stream…, creating a vortex of discourse, heaven-bent & earthward, at the same Time.

PLOT MARKS A GEOGRAPHICAL POINT

I.

It seemed late in the year, & cold, for the small white moth fluttering around stalks & skeletal remains of Queen Anne's Lace, but then the milkweed spore trailed it trying to imitate it? Suddenly made sense. Day of the Dead, after all. Souls up from underground manifesting themselves corporeally in any way they could.

That's where Time was when the clocks got turned back an hour: housed inside the body making every second count, not counting every second, no, not that. But at prolonged ease.

Three-hundred-million leaves from massive oaks on all three backyard sides, plus three maples out front can't defeat us. She raked swept shoveled all of them up as if cleaning lint off the living room floor. We should really let it all go to peat like the brick of it my grandfather's last sister made sure I added (a ritual) to the kitchen stove back there in Redford, Ballyhaunis, County Mayo, Ireland. They also gave me those iron tongs dug up from the fireplace foundation of my grandfather's birthplace in ruins. So that plot in writing marks a geographical point where character stays, or turns away from stasis, or stance, in ecstasy, say, or dance.

II.

Starriest of starry nights since the southern tip of Ireland itself, when I got up in the middle of it to check my email. Distance didn't end there with them either. Soon dream after dream took me to other & otherworldly worlds. A fish appeared with feathers. Sex in a corner room, violence on the water. A newborn suckled by surrogate mother named Deodora. Present within a gathering of musicians, (both jazz & marching bands), I tried to look up the word "frostbite," but the only two dictionaries in the library setting I could locate were **Dictionary of Christianity** & the **Real Estate**

Dictionary. Today, I pinpoint the Soul, internally, at the same 43-degree latitude Florence & Portland share.

Out there on my own today, it seemed I went too far, when temps neared freezing at the edge of Casco Bay. Thought of Belgrade in terms of once having gone too far, literally left out in the cold, wondering how to get home, or at least over the Adriatic to Venice. Then years ago, crawling on roof clearing gutters for winter, ice burning knees to blister pitch. Death must measure distance as much as mercury the cold.

I sidle up now to Venice Radio, vivid memories traveling back to dark alleys, glistening canals, as if it were, then at twenty, initial redemption from both death & cold.

::::

Took it as a sign, when before
Mike Mellor suggested he & his girl,
Erin Sutton, planned to escort us on the Day
of the Dead through labyrinthine lines of Boston's
MFA Goya exhibit, a postcard fell out
of the pages of a book I had
to return to
interlibrary loan: *End of the Glory of the World* by Valdes Leal.

Sent to me by David Anfam from Seville,
the painting is brilliantly gruesome
in its allegorical offerings.

Commissioned by the Brotherhood of Charity,
who made it its business to bury the poor,
often unburied & dead in the streets
from bubonic plague,
Leal portrays the tomb as life's inevitable consequence, dark
& damp, the meat & bones
of the Bishop decaying under insects before our
very eyes, while objects of vanity,
crozier, mitre, & robe are rendered useless,

while a stigmatized hand in the background holding a balance
reads on one side <u>NIMAS</u>, No More,
& on the other <u>NIMENOS</u>, No Less,
the former holding
a peacock (vanity),
dog (anger),
monkey (lust),
hog (gluttony),
goat (greed),
bat (envy)
& sloth,
while the right-hand pan
of the balance holds objects of salvation:
harp, scourge, nails, hair shirt, books, & rosary.

There's a prostrate knight in not-so shining armor.

This postcard sent on February 28th 2005.
I've kept it as a bookmark for all this time,
a fine reminder to remain humble
as possible, a trait I seem to have
no trouble holding onto,
an absolute necessity
to the act of writing.

Goya on
November 1st in Boston.

::::

In Mexico they celebrate Days of the Dead
on three consecutive days: October 31st -
November 1st & 2nd. Rained cats &
dogs the whole way down to
Boston from Portland on
Saturday morning,
having to call
ahead to

cancel
lunch
plans,
& meet
on site at
the museum,
but damn it, you can't
even enter the bookstore
directly without paying admission.

Which we weren't about to do, Hell No.
These museums have enough dough, do not
need mine, nor my wife's, nor friends of mine,
who sure as additional Hell, aren't part of the so-called
One Percent, you know the mitred Bishops of Valdes Leal's
End of the Glory of the World rotting right before our Climate
Changing eyes.

Look,
so Republican,
look, the Bushes want
Jeb, look hard while you
still have a chance to see through
the bushshit like Goya had, oh ya, just
as Goya had, as perhaps the most political painter
of all Time.

My Man, Goya,
who in his *Caprichos*,
or *The Disasters of War*
revealed man & woman to
themselves in all their hubris,
damned with a closed-fist view
of the powers that had been, Goya.

It was as if when finally entering
the exhibit innumerable lines later, cut
in front of thanks to Mike & Erin,
I knew the man, a bit.

Lines of people continued as lines of people
even as they entered the show, stood person-to-person
one-painting-to-the-next, if one
can belief that numbness,
whereupon
I bolted from the herd
& landed in the second gallery,
where this prose poem was on the wall:

Looking at Women:

Fashionable, devious, naïve, alluring, nude, at work, at play, at rest — Goya
was fascinated by women & their pursuits, regardless of their age or
position in life, no female type escaped his eye, whereupon he pointed
his pencil at pensive maiden, or exploited mother, or haggard crone. He
presented his women as he presented men, with dignity & ridicule in
equal, appropriate measure. And when it came time to the nude body,
Goya's approach was the same as with other subjects with unflinching
scrutiny; with imaginative improvisation, to create an intimate reality.

I lingered round the Feminine
as the crowd came & went wondering
what was so important it needed jotting down
notes, then they blinked away for something much bigger
& in color.

Huge guy in orange sweatshirt pushing baby carriage,
but no child, plugged into headphones listening
to the museum's added view of things, over
& above the prose poem on the wall.

He wouldn't budge. Plugged in
as he was, couldn't hear my,
"Excuse me," & stood
there more crowd
than crowd itself.

Symbolic
of what
I loathe
in the overbearing,
obtrusive masculine side
of humanity. Give me the prostitute
in, *She Prays for Her*, slowly harnessing
her stocking to garter belt, or the same pose
in, *Maid Combing a Young Woman's Hair*, yet
in modest attire, black tresses receiving bulk of ink,
more than the rest of the entire drawing, while the recto
of the piece shows her completely undressed, alone
with her mirror.

I'll linger here, again, in pages of the catalogue, far away
from any possible masculine obstruction,
other than my own
to overcome.

::::

She & I met up in the room
containing most of the images
from *The Disasters of War*, some
of which I've seen before in Portland,
but she steered me toward the final two
images from that series of etchings: *Truth
has Died* & *Will She Rise Again?*, the former
of which I chose as cover image for the first book
in the Trilogy, **This Time**, what with the bad taste left
in my mouth from the Afghanistan & Iraq invasions.

Any notion that politics can kill Truth,
(& as we know via Nietzsche Truth
is a Woman?), is devastating as
Death itself. Hell,
it's election day today, when it's difficult
to tell if anything at all has changed
since Goya's Time & the atrocities

of the Peninsula War?

Haven't yet seen all the carnage
suffered from nights & days
of Shock & Awe right up
to current drone strikes.

In *One Can't Look*, one looks hard & long.
All This & More depicts a pile of human bodies
the MFA attempts to compare to a stack of red fish.

Sure, I guess?
Americans since Vietnam
watching war on TV
with dinner.

GOYA'S TREES

Tree limb split in the storm last week made things more worrisome, when
placed in perspective. Goya resurrected trees as scenic ploys, backdrops for
lost body parts, stump altars to mutilated corpses, or war-torn camouflage
for stripping the dead of all belongings. My split tree limb in the backyard
caused by the storm last week bore strange fruit imagined in Spain, Black
Forest, Alabama, Nam, Afghanistan.

THE TONGUE OF PEACE IN A FEMININE VOICE

There is war. There is the girl in the yellow slicker riding her bike in the
snow with her faithful dog on a leash looking up to see what to do, where
to go next. There is always war, we must know that by now, which doesn't
lessen the need to halt this latest. If powers of perception saw the moment's

movement, the new. Two white houses across the street just changed color in the snow.

Rhododendron exhilarating the universe, while war wounds unfathomably, to depths out of reach of photosynthesis, where everything stays white in darkness. Sounds familiar. Bullet in the backyard sounds, while war exterminates music. When I saw Miles perform in 1969 his anger was silent in blue & black. When I heard Munir Bashir for the first time on his Baghdad six-string ud, it matched the tongue of peace in a feminine voice. In her book, *Rootprints*, Hélène Cixous says the world will ultimately forgive everyone, but war criminals.

The Third of May, 1808, heavily on my mind as we drove home from Boston in the snow. This business of politics & war.

Goya, witness to the start
of the Peninsula War,
or as it became known in Spain,
War of Independence.

From apartment #2 at 9 Puerta del Sol
at the corner of Calle de Carretas, Goya saw
his countrymen & women respond en masse
to the cruelty of French cavalry,
Turkish Mamelukes,
& Polish cuirassiers,
& the massacre
that followed.

Goya's rage is documented
by his gardener, Isidro, who recalled
26 yrs. later, that after the May 2nd insurrection,
his master fled to La Quinta del Sordo,
from where he witnessed,   through spyglass,
the executions taking place
on May 3rd at the Montana di Principe Pio.

Early that morning, in pitch dark,
the gardener says Goya, filled with black rage,

picked up his gun
& sketchpad,
& ordered his servant,
(quaking in his boots, he added),
to accompany him to the scene of the war crime.

Once there, he & Goya sat down
on a mound,
(there were bodies underneath them, he said),
& his master began drawing what he touched
& saw.

Thus began the first drawings for *The Disasters of War*.

Goya waited another six years before
documenting the monumental pieces
of May 2nd & 3rd.

::::

Perhaps there was an invisible,
stigmatized hand holding both extremes
of what Freud classically called the major root
causes of dreams, *fear & desire*,
when the woman exhibited
herself naked on the bed,
whom I watched,
& later touched,
but no sooner than waking
from that pleasantry in the middle of the night
last night, the next dream presented
the Red Dog of Death leaping at my face
& throat + three more, including a husky nipping
at my genitals until I managed to call out
out loud, so difficult to get the dream voice
to register in the dream, "Help me!"

Which she did,
gentle outreach

of her formerly
sleeping hand.

Call up, yet gain, the image of the Death of Truth,
which Geoff Gronlund & I asked Manchester City Galleries
for permission to use on the cover of **This Time**.

The link's right here: Barbara Rose,
(whose interview with Rauschenberg
I recall prompted the statement that
his *hand is one step ahead of his head
reaching for contact*), points out that
for the first Time during Goya's Time
Truth is Ugly fusing that Time to our own.

Black is the color of his & our Time.

Since the beginning
of my study of Goya
within the vortextual
world I travel, whether
to Boston, or the Still
Museum in Denver,
I've kept eyes & ears
open to the vibration
of the color black as
backdrop & foreground
of, if not Beauty, Truth
& Brutality.

::::

Received a couple of gifts of other's writing
before & after our second walk on Monday.
In the morning the postman rang bell as I've
asked in the past should this man of letters
(more often man of lettuce) receive anything
remotely hinting at the art. Big smile on his
face, knowing how often its only junk. This

had The University of Chicago Press on the
return address, so he guessed right that this
would put an equally big smile on my face,
which it did, thanking him at the threshold.

The review copy I originally requested two
years ago, & only recently followed up on
again, of Ben Bollig's **Modern Argentine
Poetry: Displacement, Exile, Migration.**

Sells for $150.

Distributed by The University of Chicago Press,
it's published by the University of Wales Press,
Cardiff. First off, open randomly to the middle
of Ben's take on Alejandra Piznarik, born Flora,
or in Yiddish, Buma Pozharnik in Buenos Aires,
(1936, d. 1972), she found exile in menial jobs
in Paris from 1960-64, where she used European
sources surrounding her there, an attempt by
"a writer from a less-well-endowed literary nation…
trying to create her own superior position through
the use of international quotation and reference."

A previously unknown, but now fellow compatriot,
who claimed the *word* was the poet's only home,
& that "Poetry is the place where everything takes place…"

Suddenly, a beautiful partner blooms before my reading
eyes in my vortextual world. Look, on the page chanced
upon = a poem collaged by lines from Henri Michaux,
Novalis, Kafka, Cecília Meireles, Sidney Keyes, &
Lewis Carroll, at once reminding me of my own recent
regression, when I wanted to abandon Derrida, Kristeva,
especially reading of Deleuze, for Beatrix Potter & Peter
Rabbit, who I only found out a week ago was naughty,
making me love the animal all the more, & who like
Alice (& Flora) "only wanted to see the garden."

My new *Queen of Spades* insists on returning
to Paris, although she's exiled even from there
she writes: "After years in Europe I mean Paris,
St. Tropez, Cap St. Pierre, Provence, Florence,
Siena, Rome, Capri…"
[sounds familiar]
"…not to mention New York and the West Village…"
"Everything is cunt, I've licked cunts
in various countries…" Ah, my new Queen
of Anatomy & Geography, a gift of CHANCE.

That gift arrived
in the morning before
our second walk, after driving
home in the snow, & the Goya show.
Second walk down to the promontory Victorians
called the Eastern Promenade, where the snow
knocked off most of the apples from the wild tree
right next the double-trunked elm, red still glistening
off green grass, a Persian carpet.

Took a half-dozen apples home.
Peeled & sliced one up. Ate it.
Not wanting just to see the garden,
but to be it.

After the apple,
open my computer to find word from young Patrick's
Uncle Clyde, who accompanied him down to Neruda's house
on Isla Negra: Dear Robert,

In response to Patrick's e-mail to me the fourth of this month, I'm putting
to print my recollections of our trip from Santiago to Isla Negra.

Don Jose Pena picked us up in his Mercedes and whipped down the road to
the seacoast arriving to a most bleak looking panorama. From left to right,
the scene was mostly shades of blacks and greys. Even the ocean seemed
grey as did the lowering clouds and sky beyond. Black boulders the size of
houses strewn along the grey beach blasted by dun colored surf. And then

the weirdest looking tree I'd ever set eyes on. Tall, fifteen to twenty feet in height; skinny with the craziest looking appendages which I imagine were branches and leaves, or maybe needles, together. Alternating on opposite sides of the spindly trunk, they stretched out a foot, maybe two at the most and hung upside down like a huge inverted flower blossom or a small umbrella blown inside out by the stiff ocean breeze.

Things only got weirder as we exited the vehicle and started inside. A smallish fishing boat with a forward cabin and assorted boat anchors in the yard. A rusted relic of an old steam powered tractor accented the myriad works of art and sculptures surrounding the seemingly haphazardly built structures that made up his most interestingly constructed house.

Things only got weirder as we went inside. My sense of sight panicked as I tried to assimilate the overwhelming number of objects everywhere. The stone and glass infused fireplace dominated one room. Hundreds of glass bottles of every imaginable size and shape stacked side by side like silent sentinels. All things nautical permeated the place: Spy glasses, brass portholes, brass rings and tie-downs for ropes along with nautical charts and maps. Ship logs, personal correspondence and books were highlighted by memorabilia galore collected by Pablo, the plenipotentiary, from his many world travels. Neither time nor page are sufficient to inventory all that was inside. I only wish that I could recollect a portion of what we saw inside that day.

Leaving Isla Negra Don Jose took us along the seacoast road to a restaurant alongside the beach in Vina del Mar. He had called ahead and reserved for us the best seat in the house...a cozy table in a bay window overlooking the beach. Feasting on scrumptious seafood, we washed it down with superb Chilean wine and Pisco's that our host insisted we try on the house. After all, it is the national drink of Chile and we hadn't tried one before. Then, down the road again to the seacoast port of Valparaiso and back to Santiago. A most memorable day indeed!

It has been a great pleasure for me to recount and remember the experiences of that day. Thanks for encouraging me to dig up and dust cobwebs off of treasures almost lost with the passage of time.

With best regards,

Clyde

Proceeded to share the coincidence of receiving his book,
& Clyde's recollections, with Ben Bollig, who responded:

Great news, Robert.
And I love the recollection of Isla Negra.
I visited in 2013, it's a marvelous place.
Neruda was a great collector - he called
himself a "cosista", or "thing-er", "thing-ist",
or maybe even a "stuffist".

Yours,
Ben

:::::

Out of the random,
chance, untitled music mix
I put on & listened to through headphones
walking the treadmill two days ago came Samuel L Jackson's
rendition of "Walking Around" by Neruda from the wonderful film *Il Postino*.

Seemed no coincidence
that two days before that,
out of the blue, from someone I've never met,
Clyde Campbell, sent a few paragraphs of his recollection
of visiting the poet's house on Isla Negra. Kathleen says these things
happen to me all the Time.

Baudelaire called them "Correspondences".
I gain a great deal of pleasure from the individual letters
of Correspondences, let alone lines, stanzas, whole paragraphs,
complete poems. "Walking Around" is the thingiest poem ever.
More so, perhaps, than even Francis Ponge?
Tempted, here & now, to list nouns,
(I know, Fenollosa stressed the verb,
saying all things move), but nouns

on a page move, too, especially
underpants on a clothesline
in the wind, or a nun
slain by a poet's
own pen.

My just correspondences.
Neruda & Ben Bollig, Clyde & his
Nephew, Patrick, & John Felstiner, whose
translations of "The Heights of Macchu Picchu,"
I solicited & published in *Janus Head* a few years ago
From the air to the air, like an empty net,
I went on through streets and thin air, arriving and
leaving behind,
at autumn's advent, the coin handed out
in the leaves, and between spring and ripe grain,
the fullness that love, as in a glove's
fall, gives over to us like a long-drawn moon… -PN via -JF

::::

She's gone
to Vermont for
an overnight. I'm home,
but not alone, Hell no, not alone.
May find solitude by the end of the day,
but in the meantime, look around, the backroom's
filled with friends & acquaintances, & when it comes
to art I don't distinguish between the two, I mean there's
Bird up in the air there on the shelf in the form of the vinyl
album *Charlie Parker – 1949 Concert*, a record I bought for two
bucks the second day we moved here.

Seriously, a guy had three banquet tables spread out in front of the house
next to us where good neighbors, Liz & David Margolis-Pineo used to live
(having moved to Munjoy Hill, we still see them, now & again), looking like a dream
image, really, all these jazz greats in crates & boxes, not coffins:
Mingus, *Me Myself An Eye*,
Coleman Hawkins, *Sirius*,

347

Miles, *Tutu*,
Keith Jarrett, *Facing You.*

Bought them all for ten bucks.
The record collector never reappeared, disappeared
like titles on the Magic Writing Pad, clear as Hell in the dream,
then erased, dreamlike finding Mingus & Bird, Jarrett, Hawkins, & Miles,
whom I saw & heard live in '69
leaving such an indelible imprint
even Freud's Magic Writing Pad
couldn't displace.

My good company today, listen in: there's William Carlos Williams
on the wall
behind me ensconced
in some blossoming tree, smiling,
wearing a black tie,
advertising his **Selected Poems**
by New Directions, a poster I bought framed,
when this bookstore, yet another,
went out of business on Pleasant St. back in 2004
when we busted the move
from Situate to Portland.

Across the room stands *Madame Edwarda*, back turned
on spiral staircase, hermaphroditic
by way of Hans Bellmer
portraying scrota galore
below anus in sheer
dress & high heels,
her hair in a bun,
bum prominent
in this original
engraving from
punched plate,
something
I picked up
in Cambridge
fresh out of school

348

& penniless, per usual.

Didn't steal it,
but it was a steal
from the Ferdinand Roten Galleries,
Baltimore, Maryland, back label reads: 27-19-127,
HANS BELLMER was born in Katowica, Silesia in 1902.

He studied at Polytechnic School in Berlin.
In addition to his painting Bellmer has executed
a number of engravings and has written several books.
Hans Bellmer's work has been shown widely including surrealist
exhibitions in Paris in 1934, the Gallerie Maeght in 1947,
and exhibitions in Chicago and Japan.
Bellmer died in 1976.

No, not alone.
May find Solitude
by the end of the day,
but No, not alone, what
with all this good company
here cheering me up, even in the abstract:
Duchamp's, *Etching for "Du Cubism"*, another
piece I picked up in Cambridge, fresh out of school,
penniless, per usual, a teacher of high school English, for
God's Sake, paying $115 a month for my apartment all utilities
included, there's Marcel Duchamp, recently deceased at the time,
having secretly constructed his masterpiece *Étant donnés*, in which
the figure's (Alajandra Piznarik has personally & posthumously given
permission) cunt is as prominent as Madame Edwarda's cheeks, anus, &
multiple scrota.

This etching toned
down in comparison,
also from Roten Galleries,
Baltimore, this Canceled Plate
Impression has Duchamp's signature
in the lower left etched into the paper,

while arrows of Eros fly past the makeshift
target, his vertical lines are narrow hatch marks
compared to receding, wider architecturally stacked
horizontals. A perfect Rembrantian circle crowns the piece
inside of which a flowing line in the form of the head of a bird
flutters above a single wing.

::::

Just back from a walk,
where the major premise
of the act is pure & simple
gratitude that one can amble,
gambol, stroll, meander.

Leaves strewn along sidewalks
on the 8th of November rival red apples
glistening out of green grass on Monday
for that rare metaphor allowed in here,
a Persian carpet

or anywhere else
in my writing (having banished them, along with
similes, iambic pentameter, alliteration, & academic
pretense: the finely woven, tight-knotted Persian carpet
Nature weaves, her own votextual composition filled
with nouns moving, animated before
a clear set of imagining
eyes.

Not to mention the catalpa
at the corner of James & Pleasant,
cousin to the massive-leaved tree we
made friends with in the center of Montpelier,
Vermont years ago, when Dan Carr & Julia Ferrarie
asked me to join them for a reading at the library,
& Kathleen, totally new to the scene then,

back up there now in proximate vicinity.

So I get connected to her there via the roots
I can feel underfoot
looking up
through the catalpa's
labyrinthine branches, bare
as they are twisting into the sky.

Those neighbors over there think,
"This guy's out of his mind,"
which in a way, I am, in Joy, in Ecstasy,
the tree linking me to her there now on the outskirts
of Montpelier, Vermont near the tree made such an impression
on us back then in 1989, & now here,
pulling sky down
to my grateful eyes
through limbs of this catalpa,
as if maybe they were her limbs
practicing yoga or dance.

"This guy's out of his mind!"
So I am. In Joy, in Ecstasy,
in Give & Take in Silent Conversation
with Two Similar Trees & These Two
Utterly Different Times.

::::

Add a few leftover drops of Bourbon to the black coffee
& the power goes out had me thinking superstitiously.

Taking a flashlight down to the fuse box
at 7:30 on Sunday morning, knowing
a few lights were on, along with electric heater,
music, computer, dishwasher, Hell,
I must have caused this
with a few of drops of Bourbon
added to black coffee on a Sunday morning

with her off visiting her brother
in Vermont, right?

I couldn't figure the fuse box out for the life of me.
Looked outside to see if streetlights shown,
or neighbors might find themselves
in similar straits: "Yo!"
to two guys on steps across the way,
"You got electricity over there?"

"No, it went out."
"Thanks," a bit relieved,
 pouring more coffee in the cup
while still hot, but no Bourbon.

Electricity out, no lights, coffee getting cold, phone out,
Hell, one begins to appreciate what one has: Luck.

By getting up early & starting that laundry
she wanted me to do yesterday, also turned on
the propane stove in the backroom, so
that remains on, but wouldn't have
started up without an electric spark
+ computer battery
now at 92%,
so although
I can't send an email,
or search the Web, I can jot down
my current
bearings.

Sidle up next to the stove
with green blanket over knees
reading Jim Harrison's *Introduction*
to Neruda's **Residence on Earth**, which includes
the entire original *Preface: Toward an Impure Poetry*.
Always loved Harrison's tough-minded approach
to the act of writing poetry, linking it to manual work
& the corporeal, animal body, anti-academic,

as well, surprised
when accepting invitations to read
on American campuses he doesn't see a procession
of coffins streaming out of English department offices.

Calling established MFA programs *anemic*,
he followed Chinese poet, Mao Tse Tung's lead
by suggesting poets first work for a year in the country,
(that up-before dawn hard labor),
then a year in the bottom-rung
grit of the city keeping
journals, notebooks
of their real-life experiences,
before finally being allowed to attend university in the third year.

There, that training would hone a fine, physical line,
where tools like shovel, ax, hammer, saw
get a man's hand ready to carve
observations into language
on the page.

Cut things short
regarding Harrison's take on Neruda
in order to trek up to the Black Cat Café on Stevens Ave.,
letting the barista know I have to try to get in touch
with friends to contact my wife visiting
her brother in Vermont
letting her know the power's out
in our area, & couldn't be reached by phone.

Wrote emails to Scott, Avry, Geoff, & Maureen to make sure
she got the message, which she did, of course,
by each & every one.
                         On my way back home, however, I notice other
houses in the area with lights now on, so have some hope
our power is back.
                         This Time: no Luck. Damn.
I must have fussed with the fuse box in my own inimitable way,
initially experimenting with the main

switch & others under
 a dull flashlight.

                                    Hell, get my reading glasses
on with the even now duller light
(dull as I am before all things
electrical technical, or mechanical,
but have used band saws could cut a man's
hand up to here, & lifted 77-pound boxes
of frozen fish ten-high
onto pallets
in the hold of a Japanese factory ship,
moved pianos, & sewn monograms of kids' bookbags),
but yes, equally dull in the dark before
a fuse box.

          Ah, said this blind man, that reads OFF, that read ON =
things start to click, & even a switch that wouldn't work after a short
circuit a week & a half ago now works, allowing the bulb near the bulk-
head + the one in the mudroom to go on =
                                    I'll be her new electrician!!

Leave the mudroom light on for her return, pour a glass of Bourbon.

Clean up from the night before all alone.
Restart dishwasher, laundry, reset clocks, etc.
Slice tomatoes & red onion, add anchovies.
Take out blue sheep cheese from the Basque area
of Spain, along with olives.

Take a shower. Put on best shoes & pants & shirt.
Say a prayer she gets home safe, wait.

                            ::::

OK, so I'm thankful to take my sources with me
down to the waterfront,
including two stray
notebooks recently fallen & ignored

on the bottom shelf of my bedside reading table.

Take hawk in gyre above Marginal Way as good omen, instinctual,
ancient reaction, pigeons scattering for dear life in droves,
just figure taking the left off Forest Avenue
is as meant to be as these notebooks
Harrison recommended poets
keep & draw from, so open spontaneously,
as impromptu a sax chord heard today never heard before,

Pee Wee, of all things, written by drummer Tony Williams,
& included on Miles' *Sorcerer*, Wayne Shorter's horn
in his 1962 debut with the group,
(although Miles sits out on this tune), still
borders on miraculous.

Random notebook page
has postcard of matador swiping muleta
before bull's eyes head horns neck back legs tail,
that grand animal machine,
whose courage needs
be matched, *Pase de muleta natural*, reads
the card in Spanish sent by David Anfam
from Madrid on September 16, 2009:
"Sun, vino, the Prado & dashing
Spaniards have proven the ideal
cure for the malaise of London."

Under postcard on random page
I find Julia Kristeva quoting
Roland Barthes:

> It follows that in any man who utters the other's absence
> something of the feminine is declared: the man who waits
> & who suffers from his waiting is miraculously feminized.

That's it!!! Waited
her return from Vermont
without mentioning the interminable length
of seconds.

This is a joy of an intersection of pages in the notebook brought along by
CHANCE =

> *The future will belong to the subject in whom there is something of
> the feminine.* —Barthes

> *The professor is the enemy of the artist – to speak without
> interpretation is to tell anecdotes to describe postures,
> atmospheres in order to erase the trauma that makes one
> speak.* —Kristeva

> *The copresence of sexuality & thought that characterizes the
> Freudian discovery of psychic life leads specifically to the fact
> that sexuality cannot say itself entirely, a hiatus – an asymptote –
> articulates sex to speech, the drive to thought.* —JK

> *From the Proustian child, who wants it 'deliriously' we mother
> each other reciprocally; we return to the root of all relations,
> where need & desire join.* —JK

All the way back to quote Proust himself:

> *What hammer blow has the person or thing that is lying there
> received to make it unconscious of everything, stupefied until
> the moment when memory, flooding back, restores it to
> consciousness or personality.* —Proust

Hawk as Sorcerer. Freedom for Freud reached back to the Greeks
as originally freedom of movement, to go where one wants to go.

Five pages on in the notebook, which is first dated 2/2/01,
another postcard of Etienne Carjat's Paris photograph
of Arthur Rimbaud taken in 1872, sent from friends
Brad & Rebecca wishing me I know not which,
"Happy Birthday," but marking pages reading:

A Little History: Freud & Lacan

Freud used the word freedom in relation to instinct & bound by
shackles of the human need to live in a community.

*Absolute freedom is nothing other than the realization of
desires.
*
*
*
*

The saint, like the writer, is alone — in absolute *Hilflosichkeit* —
expecting no one's help, on the verge of melancholy & atheism.

'Free' seems synonymous with an interior life, recreated in relation
to an exterior to be internalized; *Free not to resist the twin tyrants
of instinctual desire external reality, as Freud thinks, ** but free to
internalize the outside, if & only if this outside (to start with, the mother)
allows one to play, allows itself to play. ***** PLAY

My Game
My Own
FORT/DA

Freedom = Rebirth

::::

Twenty-fifth anniversary
of the fall of the Berlin Wall
came & went over the weekend
to a great deal of fanfare in the media,
front pages, TV coverage, Brandenburg Gate

prominent. In Alsace on November 9, 1989, Kathleen
swears she could hear (sense?) the commotion coming over
the border. It's a date to be remembered. However, what I kept
an eye out for was any recollection of Kristallnacht, which occurred
on the same date seventy-six years ago.

Kristallnacht, also known as Reichskristallnacht,
Pogromnacht, Novemberpogrome, by any name far
beyond shame, an event that marks the beginning of the Holocaust.

Sledge-hammers were used
to pummel Jewish hospitals,
schools, & most synagogues
in Berlin & Vienna. Nazi gangs
targeted healthy young Jewish men
for arrest, then sent to Dachau,
Buchenwald, Sachsenhausen.

Kept an eye out for any remembrance
of the event,
but saw none.

Walter Benjamin kept his head low
in profile there on the cover
of Eiland & Jenning's biography.

I'd bookmarked the page where the authors say
that Benjamin read Dostoevsky's *Crime & Punishment* for the first time,
only to come down with a case of nephritis resulting from his overly
sympathetic reading.

The bookmark? =
Photocopy of the Map
of the Original Dachau Camp,
marking main road, barracks, roll-
call place, gate into camp, administration
building, disinfection hut, green house, barbed
wire fence, guard towers, bunker (prison), crematorium
& gas chamber.

Sole reference to Kristallnacht in the biography
found Benjamin in Paris having all hope dashed
on getting word of the event. Goebbels officially
called an end to the violence on November 11th,
seventy-six years ago today, Veteran's Day, but
we know the end to that violence has never, will
never happen, resounding as it continues to do,
as if it were the interpretation of a watercolor by
Paul Klee, that Benjamin once owned, *Angelus Novus*,
in which the critic envisions the angel observing history
as one single catastrophe, the wreckage of present events
piling up at its feet:

> *The angel would like to stay, awaken the dead, and make whole*
> *what has been smashed. But a storm is blowing from Paradise &*
> *has got caught in his wings; it is so strong that the angel can no*
> *longer close them. The storm drives him irresistibly into the future,*
> *to which his back is turned, while the pile of debris before him grows*
> *toward the sky. What we call progress is this storm.*

It's as if for Walter Benjamin ~~twin wreckage~~ landed
before the Angel, at the same time on November 10th:
one universal, Kristallnacht, or initial Holocaust event;
the other personal = letter from Adorno, at the Institute
of Social Research in New York, essentially passing over
Benjamin's paper, "The Paris of the Second Empire in Baudelaire."

Adorno, famously declared,
"To write poetry after Auschwitz
is barbaric." That sentence. This essential
rejection [TA denied it was one] of the material
as presented by one of the great scholars of all time
is a sentencing [he knew WBs economy depended solely
on stipends from the Institute] & it's no wonder
Benjamin must have heard railcars in his ears
& in the distance, after reading Adorno's letter
condemning the essay's lack of theory

for "wide-eyed presentation of mere facticity…" or
for being "at the crossroads of magic and positivism."

Adorno, (the month before,
driving around Mount Desert Island in Maine
in his new Ford convertible), sentencing
Benjamin to the sound of railcars
in his ears, or, as the latter
had expressed earlier
in fears for his brother, Georg,
already in the prison of Bad Wilsnack in Brandenburg:

The greatest nightmare for those in his situation, as I often hear from people in Germany, is not so much the dawning of each new day behind bars as the threat of being sent to a concentration camp after years of imprisonment.

George will die in Sachsenhausen, in 1942.

::::

Two & a half years ago I expressed awe at the tragedy
that occurred between Benjamin, stuck in Paris,
& the Institute of Social Research in New York.

Ironically, this was published in *The Killing Floor*.

WALTER BENJAMIN'S 'CENTRAL PARK'

I.

Perhaps the recent stay in NYC with only The Dakota standing between our apartment & Central Park, or by the consistent perspective marginality offers, what with recent attempts to house over forty-years worth of my papers, I'm drawn toward the utterly tragic circumstances literary theorist Walter Benjamin found himself in in Denmark & France from 1938-40. He's got his eye on New York. Hears Death in the form of Gestapo jackboots. Gets interned as a foreign national at an outdoor stadium in Paris. Argues against the threat to cancel his small stipend from the Institute of Social Research at Columbia University, writing to Max Horkheimer, that the latter did not fathom the difference between reduction for his New York colleagues & cessation for him in Paris, "We are all isolated individuals. And for the isolated individual the perspective opened by your letter, with its terrifying earnestness, overshadows all other plans." But he continues to read & write. Before leaving Paris, in hopes of getting to America, he leaves much of his archive with Georges Bataille, fellow writer & librarian at the Bibliothèque Nationale. The last work to be located there was found in 1981, a tract he'd been writing in 1938-39, what editors of the four-volume *Selected Writings* published by Harvard call, "the most advanced drafts & notes for the partially completed *Charles Baudelaire: A Lyric Poet in the Age of High Capitalism,*" also known as *Central Park.*

II.

Imagine, Central Park. He tailors his findings on Baudelaire writing during his Time in Paris by attempting to apply the same principles to New York City, where friends & colleagues had offered to find him work & an apartment near Central Park. One of his initial correspondences was to define Baudelaire's "Modernity" as *giving expression to extreme spontaneity,* which he refers to, after Jules Laforgue first broached it as Baudelaire's "Americanism." This does my heart good, seeing Baudelaire as the father of the prose poem, & knowing it is, first & foremost, at least for me, an act of revolt. I continue to hear jackboots of Death haunting Benjamin, hoping to house his archive & find a job in New York. He sees New York as one of the great cities of the world, which possesses a "labyrinthine character" with "an image of the Minotaur at its center." "…he [the Minotaur] brings death to the individual… is the image of the deadly power he embodies…" (His ambivalence to the chance of ever making it to New York?) Benjamin points out the facts & obsessions of Baudelaire's Time as the fetishization of commodity, prostitution, & the marketplace. Adds here, for his own purposes, again, in *Central Park*, "Emigration as a key to the big city." Are his Columbia University colleagues listening? Toward the end of the 46 loose-leaf sheets that make up Central Park, Benjamin asks almost rhetorically regarding Baudelaire's belief or non-belief in progress, "Walt Whitman?" The editors point out that additionally, in preparation for his ill-fated trip to America, Walter Benjamin reads William Faulkner's novel, **Light in August**.

https://thekillingfloor.typepad.com/kfb/2012/06/time-capsule-here-walter-benjamins-central-park.html

::::

Benjamin, masterful Encyclopedist.
In the essay, rejected by Adorno,
(although Adorno denied it was
an outright rejection), [more
life sentence], "The Paris
of the Second Empire
in Baudelaire,"
Benjamin cites:

Charles Dickens
at Lake Geneva looking
fondly back toward Genoa
for its miles of gas-lit streets;

Karl Marx jesting with the term

"commodity-soul" over & against
Baudelaire, whom he calls an *eroticist*:
"That holy prostitution of the soul which gives itself completely,
poetry and charity, to the unexpected that appears, to the unknown
that passes."

Stroller, walker, flâneur.

Charles Fourier imagining the Paris
barricades (those magic stones, which for Baudelaire
rose up to form fortresses) as an example of unpaid,
but impassioned labor.

Tax-free wine
of the barricades
I continue to keep an eye out
for = this La Bergerie Sainte-Croix, Syrah-Merlot,
vin-de-pays-doc at $4.99 close to the 1-franc a bottle refill
I'd find in Nice at twenty!

Benjamin invoking *force*
via Gustave Tridon as the *Queen*
of the barricades that shackled prisoners reach
out toward her from behind bars.

Alexandre Dumas as sellout
to tens of thousands of francs newspapers
paid for stories over & against Baudelaire narrowly
escaping landlords & creditors by sleeping in the "risky beds"
of friends.

Edgar Allen Poe, of course,
throughout the essay, not only on man
walking around streets, but ebony darkness
above gas-lit luster.

Honoré de Balzac on Fenimore Cooper's
"…poetry of terror that pervades the American woods…"

Even cites E. T. A. Hoffmann
as an author who could not pass by
a wine tavern without checking who might
be inside.

Frederich Engels on the brutal
indifference of men on the streets
of London.

Benjamin suspected/theorized
that commodities of the new Capitalism
of mid-19th century civilization erased empathy
for one another, unless possessed of
such sensitivity as Baudelaire.

Shelley on the Hell of London.

Just noticed by CHANCE
in sync, in tune Poe's
ebony darkness
quoted above
along with
Miles in
the background on
Bye Bye Blackbird.

RESOLVED TO SOLITUDE

Conquered agitation experienced earlier in the week at the scheme of
things this country impacts on more than just sensibilities, but Soul. Soon
as gone, wanted it back. The ire Nietzsche advocates one needs to fight
against one's Time. Brutal acceptance. Brutal rejection. Here I am in the
midst of territories, distance, & Time stretching from the Archaic through
Crucifixion, as Holbein laid things out in the 16th century, to Goya three
hundred years later pulverizing Truth into just so many splintered black

lines of horror the eye can swallow in one hard gulp. No room for coddling, taking things for granted, or sing-song spoon-fed pablum masquerading as poetry & art. Resolved to Solitude, I spend all my Time alone, or with stones.

::::

A notebook
long abandoned
as useless, ugly,
essentially empty,
fell to the floor off
the corner of the now
crowded writing table
two days ago, so seemingly
useless, I ignored it overnight
before putting it back in a less
precarious place, only to wonder
if gravity might be sending a message?

First thing I open to is a note composed
on all four sides of 2X2-inch scrap paper
latched together with a small piece of tape.

It's from Pattie Russo, who resurfaced just
before leaving for Denver on my birthday, the day
after I finished **Book II** of "Anatomy & Geography"
& a couple days before beginning this project: Dear Bob,

> Strange after so many years... to find such a beautiful spot
> & to know that you have helped -> -2. make it so... David
> noticed the book... we learned of how you first came here
> even sat at the same table. There are no accidents. Perhaps
> another day -> -3. we'll meet at Sophia's. I am remembering
> the Christmas the tree fell & we watched it slowly tumble.
> I also recall you being the first one to visit in the hospital ->
> -4. a radio as a gift under your arm. The radio has long since
> gone but the memory of your generosity remains. I wish you
> well. David too.   Love, Pattie

Written as the result of the CHANCE
event ("There are no accidents."?) of them
having lunch at Sophia's on Market Street years
ago, & seeing my new book back then, *Body of Time*.

"It's a little handmade collage work of art," I wrote to her
yesterday, when after meeting up again, she took my email address
& we began, again, to correspond. It's funny, I added, that she alluded
to each of the same events mentioned in the note,
when she said they came to Portland
more recently "in order to bump into Bob Gibbons,"
which they did in the hot pepper aisle, where I'd purchased
a bag of chipotle to go along with the mango for salsa.

More blank pages in this <u>Mead Fat Little Wireless Neatbook 200 sheets</u>
notebook than any I own, but there in the first few pages, what other than
notes taken while reading Leo Bersani's, *Baudelaire and Freud*, no less!

It's dated 11/03/04, so we were fairly new to Portland ourselves,
& far away from Bob Slate's stationary store in Cambridge,
where I could score my favored French notebooks,
vaguely recalling that I must have picked this one up for cheap at CVS,
of all places, but I needed something, because I for one can't retain
contents
of difficult texts like this Bersani,
or most of those cited throughout this project
without scratching them down by hand, which etches
them in the cerebral cortex, & perhaps other organs, & Sympathetic
plexuses.

Bersani, skeptical of recent, so-called revolutions in consciousness,
favors "the indeterminacy of being" found in Baudelaire's greatest poems,
quoting:

The Artist's Confiteor

How penetrating is the closing day of autumn! Oh! penetrating
to the very point of pain, for there are delicious sensations,

which, ~~while imprecise, are not without intensity~~; & no blade
has a keener tip than that of Infinity.

How great a delight it is to drown one's gaze in the vastness of
sky & sea! The solitude, the silence… ~~these things thinks
through me &I through them (for in the grandeur of reveries~~,
the sense of self soon fades!); they think, as I say, but in music
pictures…\\\\\\\\\\\\\\\\\\\\\

…My over-stretched nerves now produce only clamorous &
painful vibrations.

…The study of beauty is a duel in which the artist screams with
fear before being defeated. 9 = 33, respectively

Vibrations,
nerves, cathexions,
drives, sensations, animistic
visions into language on which
I ride, sail, trek, walk, train, tread,
view that sky through limbs of catalpa,
as if it were my Woman's lap, say, most
Immediate, Intimate, Infinity, this photograph
of her seated half-naked next open French doors
in Nice, again as if she were not just ideal Muse for me,
but model for Matisse!

Leo Bersani claims in the pages
of this fat, ugly, previously abandoned
notebook taken up by gravity,
that artistic attention produces ecstasy
& dissipates the self's integrity.

[He must mean simply wholeness,
as opposed to integrity as any moral stance…]

In accordance with Baudelaire's artistic enterprise,
"to go outside oneself" is equivalent
to allowing the self to be

penetrated, invaded,
congested, & shattered
by the objects of its attention:

The Objects
of
Its Attention

Bersani talks of Baudelaire's "pleasurable nervous shocks"
as if they were Kristeva's own *cathexions* igniting words
from flesh itself.

Then alludes to his **Intimate Journals**, a volume I stumbled on
on my to meet Barney Rosset for the first time,
the day after opening the hotel window
to the hole,
which was Ground Zero.

In Bersani's interpretation, "the shattering of the artist's integrity
is also seen as a momentous sexual event. In order to be possessed
by alien images, the artist must open himself in a way which Baudelaire
immediately associates with feminine sexuality."

First return to true
self often a shock,
not always pleasant,
not even a safe, or
familiar harbor. But
ultimately the pain
that drives us there
recedes, subsides
like a rhythm of
the tides. At the end
of the island's farthest
reaches ledges are
marked with glyphs,
a fish, say, white
quartz dug long ago

out of grey granite,
& at the edge of matter,
where the ethereal sea
offers up cool refuge,
there the self most
resembles the island
& one can long again
for companionship,
another lone visitor,
or seasoned explorer.

SCYTHED, I IMAGINE

Night of cruel diversions, labyrinthine gauntlets, cuttings, reductions, shatterings, fragments of paintings & sculpture strewn on the floor, even stalks of grain, scythed, I imagine, by Death itself, when afterward I woke from the dream with the phrase, "My redefined Self."

WOMAN MARRIED TO THE SUN & WIND

Though it reeks of it in that grand sequence of prose poems, *Paris Spleen,* Baudelaire uses the word prostitution only three times. He seems to equate the phenomena with generosity of spirit, a creative sharing of the self with the crowd. I suppose most of us are secretly fascinated by it, through our propensity for idealization of it as much as that for Love. In one piece of his, *The Beautiful Dorothea,* sun beats down on everyone in the seaside town. At noon dogs yelp for mercy from the heat, but Dorothea, cool in her billowing dress, as if the waft of air were a wave of water. Walking, she's working.

In Nice once, as a young man, I watched my own independent like a study for weeks. Her routine, clockwork. A five-day week in fact. At 11:00 sharp she'd roll out her rattan mat on the pebbles of the public beach. Red bikini, black, white. She's etched in a young man's cortex exactly thirty-five years to this coming summer. Classically Nicoise, dark, petite, she may have come from a long line of ladies & sailors. I was always close to her on the beach. No one ever approached her there. Not a Soul. She never entered the Mediterranean. Drank water, perhaps a piece of fruit. Certainly never read, but the sun, the horizon. At 1:00 she'd put her white shirt back on, gather her mat, ascend the stone stairs home. From the bar on the street she owned, I'd watch her stroll from the corner halfway down the street, then back. Many men, some as young as I, approached, talked, made offers. She was selective, or expensive, I'll never know. If I was jealous, it wasn't of the men, but of Baudelaire himself, who'd written *his* woman into history. More than speaking to her, more than touching, I wanted to transcribe her grace, her spirit that cannot be wizened with time, my anonymous woman married to the sun & wind of Nice, I desired what I have here.

WHEN ONE CARVES OUT FREE TIME

All that wine. Did I really need all that wine? I might as well have been Li Po teetering precariously, while standing up in a thin boat addressing the moon. Not today, no, no more wine, no just the river & the boat. If there is no procession of young women, that's ok, I've seen them in the dream. Nothing, but real life for me today. I've already heard from someone in the north of Spain, which did my heart good. Wrote to an Irish editor, & a fellow writer in Ann Arbor. To my right, Walter Benjamin exhibits his postcard collection in a chapter marked by Lucas Cranach's *Eve*. No kidding, randomly, there's Ibiza & Mallorca. Both in black & white. I'm traveling via airmail today. This is nothing, but a postcard. Aren't those the finest moments of travel, when one carves out free time, to sip coffee at the little table, write to friends telling them how grand Cannes is, how welcoming Nice, how rapturous Florence with its exotic *Eve* in the Uffizi? Color never seems so vivid as when seen through the eyes of freedom. No color better than that of flesh, whatever the shade of skin.

I WANT TIME [NOVEMBER 14, 2008]

Whereas earlier in the week I walked *inside of Time*, in pain, today I walked *inside of Light*, without it. Much of life boils down to the courage to suffer, which I've long tried to avoid; instead, carrying a tiny, broken, black cross made of obsidian in my watch pocket, letting it carry the monstrous load, while I hum along, language reeling. Splotches of sunrise on metallic surfaces through bay kitchen window begin the day, read as signs, good signs for a successful day. Success judged by strength of language voiced on the page, or filled with compassion in conversation with friends, strangers, or favorite fishmongers. Today, *in that Light*, Benjamin compared Proust's **Search** to that of a fisherman casting *...nets into the sea... his sentences are the entire muscular activity of the intelligible body; they contain the whole enormous effort to raise this catch*. Sacred hake down at the docks from both Dans. Walk east as far as I can until, suddenly, turning around, a ray of blood falls down out the sky next to my eye, female cardinal following right after her mate. Color, shape mimicking staghorn sumac protecting the pair above underbrush of thorny rose hip & bittersweet. Turn again in Time to catch the stern of the tanker *Aqua* flying the Maltese flag, transporting my longing toward parts unknown.

::::

Snowed overnight
a bit of which I caught
sight of just after the paper
arrived when I shut the outside light out,
then headed back to bed.

Suggested we get dressed, put towels on the Adirondack rockers,
& watch this year's second snowfall.
We did. Got dressed. Grabbed towels.
But it stopped. The snow stopped
snowing, but you know, by the time the sky changed

from pitch dark to faint light, I turned my head away
from keyboard & screen just in time to catch the black
of the crow fighting the cold in flight, a tracery that lingered
long afterward in opposition to the halting of the snow
the vaulting of the crow.

::::

Shared a few lines
from recent references
to Baudelaire with publisher,
Geoff Gronlund, mentioning my copy
of *Intimate Journals*, at the same time
asking if he could send the gift
he'd given me last time
we got together, Sartre's **Baudelaire**, a volume
I got a lot too high to remember to carry home,
leaving before 6:00 in the morning the next day.

[Only thing I'd known about Sartre's take
on Baudelaire was that the philosopher felt
that poets reinscribe their utter failings!]

Sure, he said, then sent email images
of title pages of Arthur Symonds' translation
of Baudelaire's **Letters**, & another volume titled,
On Wine and Hashish, wondering if I might like to
borrow them as well.

Hell, ya!! So wouldn't you know,
even though he headed into Boston
to hear Dylan tonight, he & Angelina
detoured to drop off the lot. Bonne Chance
is all I can say to myself, what I have, Good Luck
is what I have, & Friends who are also Good!

Hoped I could put something to Good Use: USUFRUCT,

that useful word Olson adored.

Hell, Ya! [*The right to enjoy the use & advantages of another's property
short of the destruction or waste of its substance.*]

Geoff also let me know he hasn't read the letters, yet.
Of course, soon after they left, delved into them.
Here's some kind of priceless volume:

New York: Albert & Charles Boni, 1927.
Gold endpapers. Told Geoff, Symonds
was a famous Symbolist poet,
friend of Yeats, etc., but
there's a minor glitch:
although the previous
owner's name is
signed on
flyleaf,
most
pages are not cut,
just like volumes in bookstores
lining the perimeter of Luxembourg Gardens.

It's hard to find any number of pages in a row uncut
enough to read an entire letter! Damn, USUFRUCT, indeed,
I can't take it upon myself to use a letter opener to read what I want
to, & risk the possibility of reducing the value of the volume, now, can
I, Charles, & Charles, & Geoff? & Arthur??

Who suddenly reminds me that during my first teaching stint
there was a guy with the same name, [Symonds], teaching
French, who told me his father arranged a liaison
for him a with a young girl [Hell ya, jealous!]
for their initial [initiation?] sexual encounter.
His first lay, one might say.

I digress. Nevertheless.

Laughed while reading
Baudelaire's 1861
Christmas letter
to his mother,
but tears
welled
up later
when we dovetailed
the reading, paragraph-
by-paragraph aloud to one
another, his *melancholy* (with
holy hidden) destroying his faculties.

Ouf! He wants to talk about something
else. Hah! He wants to write a humorous
book about the meetings & intrigues he's had
with members of the French Academy, *those old
fools* he underlines in the letter,
naming them one-by-one,
as if knowing that even without a humorous
book, this letter will forever condemn them: M. Viennet,
M. Villemain, Thiers, Guizots, the whole list begins to read
like Proust, & let's not forget that Marcel uses Charles as yardstick
to measure & judge great writing,
endeavoring in his final volume
"to recall the poems of Baudelaire,
which are based in similar manner on a transferred
sensation, in order definitely to place myself again in line
with such noble literary heritage."

Baudelaire, so familiar with poverty,
that in the second half of the 1861
Christmas letter to his mother,
he broaches the topic
of the dumb cashmere shawl
he's pawned a number of times,
& now has it back again having lost
200 Francs on the previous transaction,

& now being told by *all* the pawnbrokers that at this
time of year they have such an abundance of cashmere
shawls that they warn patrons they will take on no more.

Charles, who has already mentioned suicide as the only,
or at least easiest way out
of his battle
with the Academy,
stating to his mother that only
the *trifling emolument* attached to the chair
is the sole reason for his *accursed canditature,*
a distraction
that keeps him
from his work.

Baudelaire, whose work provided him
with the highest reaches of intoxication, that ecstasy
beyond hash, wine, or laudanum, then
asks his mother to offer him
other expendable goods of hers,
which are, of course, of no use to her,
in fact: *they must be objects, which are absolutely USELESS
to you, and which have no sentimental value of any kind.*

Poor beggar
bastard son poet!!!
To have to write such things!!!
Humiliating things to say to beg
for poetry of so little monetary value,
yet, when the body yearns for spirit it turns TOWARD
THE WORD.

::::

November 16, 2002 Scituate, MA

Dear Kathryn, (Kathryn Rantala, publisher of lit mag, *Snow Monkey*)
       ...outside it's raining either water or stars. —Cesare Pavese

It's grey on this coast today. Waves high, nor'easter impending. I think of you there on Puget Sound, this electronic medium linking us. Poetry links us. Somehow, Pavese, too. Right now, with the comfort of my books piled high, I'm in front of the screen reading poems by Pavese exiled from his wonderful book **Hard Labor**. The online mag Slope http://www.slope. org/ has managed to locate a new translation of these rare poems. Death has a lot to say. It must. Often I've tracked the drive Freud found beyond pleasure. Pavese's anguish, his suicide sitting next to him like a shadow from a reading lamp. If death is this honest, why cower from it?

I really don't want to belabor the point here, but I just read the perfect poem, a prose poem by him, translated by Richard Jackson there in *Slope*, "Street Song" makes my point. It's "about" a man who appreciates life to the fullest because he's just gotten out of prison. Maybe prison's the closest thing to death in life, & not subtle like the death drive. Upside-your-head obvious, the deprivation prison orchestrates. The gates open, senses rejoice: "It's a joy to meet people on the street that talk to us and to speak with them alone, and grab some girl with a push. It's a joy to whistle while waiting in a doorway for girls and then walk arm in arm and take them to movies to smoke on the sly, and press against their beautiful knees. It's a joy to talk to them, to fondle them and laugh."

In between these previous paragraphs I ran outside, first spatterings of rain on the window urging me to gather some wood from the pile, split a few logs. Talk of Death got me thinking, appreciating, heightening senses. Death does that to me, for me. It's a big black Cadillac, Death, pretty obvious to us poets. Yet, it took Freud's thoroughly scientific genius to define it in **Beyond the Pleasure Principle**, that extremely difficult text proving the drive back toward inorganic matter. The joy of riding both drives at the same time. How? Writing. The sentence. "And at night, to feel yourself pulled onto the bed, and feel two arms pull you down; and to think of the day that you are out of prison and it's cool even in the sun. From morning till evening to circle around drunk, and to look laughing at the people who pass by and enjoy everyone - even the dumb ones - feeling alive on the streets."

You'll be drinking your Champagne today, I'll have red, the weather suits red. Talk, that's joy. Rain talked. The wood. Said, "I'm dead. But not unhappy."

THE DYING LEAF

He who has kissed a leaf
need look no further. —WCWilliams

Focusing
its tenuous hold
on the natural world, the desire to return, Freud said,
(Eros with dust on his tongue)
to inorganic matter,
the leaf captured by Man Ray
in an act of transformation,
substance to shadow.

A state no less vibrant
than before: Calyx
to Vortex!

After the workout I went feminine, picking roses, pricking me the white & red roses yelling, "Take us, take us inside, inside your senses where Beauty resides." Quiet down roses, November roses, quiet in your sacrifice. No, an African daisy over there, orange, clamoring to join in the chorus. Choric. The sound Kristeva says gurgles in us before forming a syllable. It's African & Greek. When I think of her, too, I think of her great respect for Dostoevsky, the importance she lends to the oppressiveness of his father causing the utter sternness of his superego forcing him to speak, to write, & of course the last-minute word of reprieve from the Death sentence in prison.

When are we happier than jotting down the words, feeling the words rise up, putting our ears to the edge of the well of the unconscious? We prayed to write, right? Seven, eight years old, praying to write. Writing praise. "Street Song" is the perfect title! What Whitman, what Kerouac, what Rimbaud, what Max Jacob walking around Paris with Picasso, what James Wright around Venice? What we want! Songs, walking. Or paragraphs, lines. Breaking out of the prison of not talking. Not appreciating the grandness of life. Adding to the grandness of life by considering its alternative. I hear you're toasting me later today, across a continent, uttering a word or two of praise for someone you've never met, except on the page, on the screen. Thank you for that, thank you for recognizing my work. Work, joy, wine, death's reminder, wind, roses, oak, maple, rain, which is the perfection of seconds.

Yours truly, Robert Gibbons

REACHING BACK THROUGH TIME

How often I've gotten to a point of having had enough of men, men themselves in congregate, say workplace factory hands, especially where meat revealed its gruesome hierarchies, fetid floors, & bottom lines, let alone leather, fish plant, or cold, deep hold of Japanese trawler, on further back to football locker rooms, even then, however, prescient enough not to attend an all-boys school. So, too, Melville with the gang & catalogue of ships & men gets wearingly masculine, & for such a one as me whose preference has long since been the Feminine, or Solitude. So maybe Melville felt it, too, at Times, at least at the juncture in the novel, where he introduces "The Virgin," but foolish she may be out of Bremen, a station I, too, stopped at in my Passion early on. The gist of the chapter is not Woman, it never is for him, but sacrifice of the blind, hobbled old Sperm Whale for the oil that will, ironically, light many a bridal chamber. Monstrous whale whose final death throes are compared to "a waning world" itself, turning up "white secrets" & whose carcass shows evidence of a stone lance embedded deep inside it, reaching back through Time to Northwest Coast Natives before discovery of the so-called new world.

Geography & the body,
so well aware of my bearings
today, November 16, 2014, light
at the end of the tunnel on this long
project, three volumes, my heart somehow
still intact, my liver, the sympathetic chain of nerves
from Solar Plexus all the way up through chest to brain.

FUNNEL OF TIME

I.

Boiling eggs. The white cat found on Boulevard St. Michel, while doing laundry a few streets over from Picasso's rue des Grands Augustins studio, woke me this morning with a purr & the usual query, "Are you writing?" Funnel of Time. Between dream & reality. (Hell, I was in Gascony, again, last night.) From Paris the slow, five-hour train headed southwest to Cahors. It's not that I'm here, now, trying to remember, no, these fingerprintless fingers know their own way to do things. Hotel de France, a short walk from the train station in pouring rain. Deeply in love. Hung our socks over the balcony to dry the next day. Rain can't deter our determination. Two things brought us there: the Black Wine of France, made with the Auxerois grape, equal to ink one can draw, or write with; & the prehistoric cave of Pech Merle, where extinct horses 25,000 years before the present merge with negative handprints, & an ochre fish of the pike family swims above them against the wall.

II.

Contemporary Cahors. Spent a late night at the bar, *37°2 le Matin*, named after the film *Betty Blue*, written & directed by Jean-Jacques Beineix, parts of it filmed here on the Aubrac plateau. That, too: the magic geography.

After figuring out the difficulties [there's no stop at the cave] of the bus schedule, after an omelet downtown in the dark before dawn with a glass of red wine, the bus dropped us off eleven kilometers short of the cave forcing the trek to Conduché, Cabrerets, & Pech Merle under thousand-foot cliffs, past fields of flint, following the River Célé. Our sense of exploration, the width of the unknown came close to the wanderings of Cro Magnon 25,000 years ago. Free. We hugged the unknown exemplified in the expanse of the road ahead, sky & cliffs above, the dead below. The unknown turns into dance, into music, language, ritual. Dust the chartered buses roiled up behind rear wheels & exhaust got in our eyes, nose, & throat, taught us the ineluctability of the body.

::::

Proofing this manuscript recently
I came across the image of the grass
at the foot of Munjoy Hill below
Eastern Prom the day after
the snowstorm littered the earth
with shimmering wild apples
in a pattern resembling some
ancient Persian rug, recalling
that I'd peeled & eaten one
of the half dozen, & cooked
the rest in a compote, making
the fruit & the image of the day
resonate that much more inside me.

All of a sudden (as if the spirit of the flesh
of the apple was now also the spirit
of the flesh of my self) it reminded
me of the time on my lunch half-
hour off from yet another temp job
in Boston, when I spotted this
apple tree on the corner
of Gainsborough Street
with that lone, shiny
temptation hanging

there on bare limb = I leapt up
reaching with umbrella
& back down to sidewalk
to no avail a number of times
the Fool in muddled middle
of the city making six bucks an hour,
a cut of which the agency took out
at the end of each week, major ratio
of the pittance.

Suddenly, these two guys appeared asking
what I was doing
(other than playing the Fool?) =
"I want that apple so my wife can include
it in the pie she plans to make this weekend,
& I can have the spirit of the tree inside me."

No sooner that said than the smaller of the two
leapt upon the bent over shoulders of the taller guy,
grabbed the apple, tossed it in the air
toward my free hand.

Turns out one was a painter, the other an actor.

These younger, artistic, impromptu acrobats
asked if they could buy me a cup of coffee,
which they did, & for weeks after we met
& talked. I saw the painter's marginal work
filling his little apartment. Read the manuscript
of the play the actor worked on. But what I recall
most was the latter's reference to Jerzy Grotowski's
invention of theatre stripped down to bare essentials,
not only scenery stripped bare, music abandoned
in favor of silence, but most importantly actors
themselves trained to move without convention,
rather on the shock of impulse, nerve, antennae,
one could say.

Here, in the volume I picked up as soon as this
recollection hit, *An Acrobat of the Heart*,
the author, Stephen Wangh, begins
with the introduction of Grotowski
at a workshop at NYU in 1967.

Introduced, no less, by then Editor of *The Drama Review*,
Richard Schechner, who Wangh says, stayed for the workshop,
& a year later created The Performance Group leading to the
extremely experimental *Dionysus '69*!

In a way it may seem crazy that here, I've been at this project,
"Anatomy & Geography" verging on six straight months now,
& recently saying I'd seen a bit of light at the end of the tunnel,
to turn in the dark back full-circle one could say toward the same
subjects that have obsessed me all along: body, walking, trauma,
poverty, stones, sex, death, Holocaust, performance, CHANCE,
color, jazz, black, classical, spontaneity, silence, language, letters,
perception out of more than the eye, but organs, nerves, plexuses
like the Solar located behind stomach in front of aorta & crura of
diaphragm, & here's Grotowski reducing the stage to naked man,
woman, actor.

An apple leads
me to the knowledge
that Grotowski produced
a "play" titled *Akropolis*, based
on a 1904 text by Stanisław Wyspiański,
collaged by a process of coincidentia oppositorum
with language found in a contemporary collection of stories,
This Way for the Gas, Ladies and Gentlemen by Holocaust survivor
(& yet another suicide) Tadeusz Borowski, the initial tale
of which begins with the image of naked men
wandering barracks of a concentration camp
in the sweltering heat, while kommandos
delouse their bedding & clothes at once
with the narrator's overview of the F.K.L.
– *Frauen Konzentration Lager* –
where twenty-eight thousand women

have been driven out of the barracks
for delousing by the same gas
used to kill lice & old men.

Grotowski staged
Akropolis at Auschwitz.

Grotowski compared the work
of his troupe to that of a shoemaker
implementing hammer & nail. Actors
(inmates) performed the play without contact
with spectators, appearing everywhere among them,
as if in nightmarish trance.

Grotowski compared the text to a scalpel
opening the actors up
to unknown interior realms,
a kind of self-dissection,
thus "Theatre Laboratory" as the name
of the troupe.

Physical action in *Akropolis* is set to the daily rhythm
of work in the concentration camp, in this case the constant
movement of large pipes from one place on stage to another,
that monotony of Time.

Grotowski was less interested in Wyspiański's original 1904 text than issues
surrounding the Holocaust, thus whittling down the poet's words to bare
bones.

The action of Wyspiański's *Akropolis* takes place
within Krakow Cathedral, but Grotowski's set
at the crematorium at Auschwitz
attempts to reenact the tremor
of the camp, the awe
surrounding lost memories.

Here, Ladies & Gentlemen,
is what we found

when resurrecting
the disinterred, the smoke
of Auschwitz framing Poland.

The apple
at the corner
of Gainsborough
in Boston, which actor
& painter, transformed instantly
into a pair of acrobats, picked for me,
& which my wife added to the pie she planned
to cook that weekend, implanted the spirit of the tree
into me, & that memory led me here to the staging of *Akropolis*
at Auschwitz.

Celan & his graves in the sky, his refrain of "black milk".

There is no deeper dissection of the human Soul
than the witness of Holocaust.

::::

I have my hearing aid on today,
a day, when researching & writing this
no soundtrack was allowed, no jazz,
no classical, just as Grotowski would
have it, no music at all, when all I hear
today glancing at photographs of his production
of *Akropolis* at Auschwitz, the players undressed
in rags mimicking wounds, catatonic stares,
movements in sync in rhythm with daily labor
of the camp.

Wedding procession of Rebecca & Jacob
in which a stovepipe stands in for the Bride,
a (masculine) stovepipe wrapped in a rag
for a veil in place of the Feminine.

All I hear. That's all I hear.
Baudelaire's & Benjamin's,
Lorca's & Celan's, Goya's,
Neruda's, Apollinaire's,
Lamentation of the World.

::::

Portland, 10:30 a.m., 11/21/2014

CODA

IMMENSITY OF TIME... DISTANCE ITSELF

Immensity of Time... distance itself. Trod over millennial stones trying to pull into view the newest ship from overseas. The *Elka Delos* propelled its way from Amsterdam two weeks ago down to the mouth of the IJ at Ijmuiden, a fairly recent town in Holland, formed in the late nineteenth century to make way for the North Sea Canal expanding the port of Amsterdam, granting access to the open sea. Take in the stern's white letters from the edge of Fish Point in Portland, where the age of man's relation to fish & the sea is evident in scars & markings below me. Those white letters, D-E-L-O-S, transport me, yet again, to an island dear & mysterious to my heart ever since I learned, decades ago as a young scholar, the island had been abandoned for lack of water, its cisterns run dry, & that fallow ground itself was the goddess Leto's need for giving birth there to twins Artemis & Apollo. Jane Harrison's Artemis, & Károly Kerényi's Apollo: austerity & abstraction. Ground underfoot connects me exactly across through the isthmus of Ijmuiden to the island close to my Soul. I stand on Delos via the Immensity of Time... distance itself.

::::

POSTSCRIPT

*When we all walked together at night, Bill would constantly
be pointing things out he thought were terrific: a big gasoline
stain on the sidewalk… or a billboard… or graffiti on the
wall.* —Elaine DeKooning

*…yet simply to walk, walk on, did not seem nearly enough for my
rabid nerves…* —Frank O'Hara

Unlike the dilemma certain Abstract Expressionist painters faced, whether
the work is finished, or not, is one problem I've rarely encountered. Perhaps
a matter of medium, I'm not sure, but a work made of language, as opposed
to a work made of paint, perhaps it has a better chance of speaking up? "I'm
done." That's what happened with repetition of the word "Lamentation"
at the end here. In fact, a chorus of voices chiming in: Goya & Baudelaire,
Lorca & Celan, etc., just as it was 'round noon, when at the end of the first
set, Monk came on with *In Walked Bud*, & at the end of set II when Carlo
Crivelli's painted wounds appeared as actual mouths desiring to speak.

However, an inevitable inertia played a role in more poems being written,
but recognizably not part of the ongoing *Anatomy & Geography*. Sure,
continued to walk around taking things in turning into language, but
the tenor of that language far different than that crescendo leading
from Grotowski's Poor Theatre performance at the Crematorium to the
Lamentation of the World. A lightness, one could say, relief, not weariness
accompanied me after this six-month project led to three manuscripts,
some 300 pages of a single work.

Succeeding fragments rang with a similar air as previous pieces, that mix
of mourning & desire, Eros & Thanatos, such as Vasari reporting the
anecdote of Donatello witnessing Uccello unveiling a work over the door
of the church in Florence depicting *Thomas reaching into the wound*. Or
when observing a number of perfect chevrons of Canada geese, she & I

walked hand-in-hand in gratitude & grace. Or a few days later with Shonda Howard on the phone, when she spoke of wings, reminding her that both wings of Souling are patience & courage, (not that I named Lacan in our conversation as source of the concept). Only fragments of a corporeal approach to language & the world continued to emerge.

As well, certain readings appeared as validations to what went on before. When the online version, **Boom: The New York City Flâneur in Postwar American Literature and Art** led to my own copy of Susan Buck-Morss's "Aesthetics and Anaesthetics: Walter Benjamin's Artwork Essay Reconsidered," I heard resonate at least a potential **Postscript**. She cites Benjamin advocating Art's full use "of the corporeal sensorium to restore the instinctual power of the human bodily sense for the sake of humanity's self-preservation." Then adds her own take: "The senses maintain an uncivilized and uncivilizable trace, a core resistance of cultural domestication." In many ways I see the entire six-month project of *Anatomy & Geography*, as an act of revolt, that aspect essential to Kristeva's ground of art, while at the same time in accordance with Terry Eagleton's notion that, "Aesthetics is born as a discourse of the body."

Not that at any point in time were abstract proscriptions adhered to, rather, harnessing internal drives, heightening senses, remaining open to chance. The day after the work said something like, "I'm done," I found myself at the waterfront gazing at this oily black sea, dark indeed, a salty brine roiling up into redolent air, whereupon I opened randomly to Rilke's *The Prodigal Son*,

> Who can describe what happened to him then? What poet has the eloquence to reconcile the length of those days with the brevity of life? What art is broad enough to simultaneously evoke his thin, cloaked form and the vast spaciousness of his gigantic nights?

Even now, weeks later, after receiving the third Preface to this lengthy poem from Peter Anastas (to whom, along with Ben Bollig & Bent Sørensen, I'd be hard pressed here to articulate my gratitude for such generosity toward, & illumination of the work), CHANCE drops sources off their shelves, as if a toss of dice. In this case **Robert Motherwell: What Art Holds**, out there in the back room, temps below freezing cracks its casebound spine in half in order to hear Emerson say that, "we are responsible *for finding the journey's end in every step of the road*, in our own gait."

Mary Ann Caws goes further on, examining what she calls the artist's American Epic, that self-same painting, *Reconciliation Elegy*, I walked past at least once a workday leaving the confines of the library at the National Gallery of Art during years 1990-94 to wander amid the permanent collection of the East Wing. She compares Motherwell's, "engagement with the massive body of white unprimed, or 'raw' canvas" to Melville's encounter with the White Whale. What I find fascinating in Motherwell's approach to this work is his claim that, "I had to paint the ultimate work while walking on it, inside its perimeters."

That's it. I walked inside *Anatomy & Geography*, scratching lines on blank pages. Hope the reader can hear footsteps, see handprints against a cave wall. Draw a similar conclusion: We're within.

WORKS CITED IN ORDER OF REFERENCE, BOOK III

Benjamin, Walter. "Unpacking My Library" *Walter Benjamin Selected Writings, Vol. 4* (Cambridge, MA: Belknap Press) 2003.

Goya, Francisco. "Prospectus for Caprichos" *Goya: The Disasters of War and Selected Prints from the Collection of the Arthur Ross Foundation* (New York: The Spanish Institute) 1985.

Kerouac, Jack. "The Great Western Bus Ride" *Good Blonde & Others.* (San Francisco: Grey Fox Press) 1994.

McMurrich, J. Playfair. *Leonardo da Vinci: The Anatomist* (Baltimore: Carnegie Institution of Washington) 1930.

Herbert, Zbigniew. "Lascaux" *The Collected Prose: 1948-1998* (New York: Ecco Press) 2010.

Stegner, Wallace. *The Spectator Bird* (New York: Penguin) 1976.

Olson, Charles. *'West'* (London: The Golliard Press) 1966.

Hemingway, Ernest. *In Our Time* (Paris: Three Mountains Press) 1924.

Gibbons, Robert. *The Degas* (Asheville, NC: Innerer Klang Press) 2013.

Kerouac, Jack. *On the Road: The Original Scroll* (New York: Viking) 2007.

Kristeva, Julia. *Desire in Language.* Trans. Thomas Gora, et. al. (New York: Columbia University Press) 1980.

Kerouac, Jack, *The Subterraneans* (New York: Grove Press) 1958.

Duras, Marguerite. "The Black Block" in *Practicalities*. Trans. Barbara Bray (New York: Grove Press) 1987.

La Belle, Jenijoy. *Herself Beheld: The Literature of the Looking Glass* (Ithaca: Cornell University Press) 1988.

Gibbons, Robert. *Streets for Two Dancers* (Macon, GA: Six Gallery Press) 2004.

Esselmont, Brigit. "Eight of Swords Tarot Card Meanings and Description" Biddy Tarot. http://www.biddytarot.com/tarot-card-meanings/minor-arcana/suit-of-swords/eight-of-swords/

Sartre, Jean-Paul. *Being and Nothingness*. Trans. Hazel E, Barnes (New York: Citadel Press) 2001.

Kerouac, Jack. "The Railroad Earth, Part I" *New American Story* (Harmondsworth, UK: Penguin Books) 1971.

Bollig, Ben. *Activismo Poetico: Enasyo Sobre la Poesia Argentina Contemporanea* (Chubut: Espacio Hudson) 2013.

Bollig, Ben. *Modern Argentine Poetry: Displacement Exile Migration.* (Cardiff : University of Wales Press) 2011.

Barthes, Roland. "From Work to Text" *Image Music Text*. Trans. Stephen Heath (New York: Hill and Wang) 1977.

Baudelaire, Charles. *The Intimate Journals of Charles Baudelaire*. Trans. Christopher Isherwood (Boston: Beacon Press) 1957.

Walker, T-Bone. *Goin' to Chicago* (London: Pablo Records) 1966.

Barthes, Roland. "Musica Practica" *Image Music Text*. Trans. Stephen Heath (New York: Hill and Wang) 1977.

Pound, Ezra. *A Memoir of Gaudier-Brzeska*. (New York: New Directions) 1970.

Rollins, Sonny. "I'm an Old Cowhand" *Way out West* (Contemporary Records)1957.

Irwin, Jones. *Derrida and the Writing of the Body* (Burlington, VT: Ashgate) 2010.

Bataille, Georges. *Guilty.* Trans. Bruce Boone (Venice, CA: The Lapis Press) 1988.

Surya, Michel. *George Bataille: An Intellectual Biography.* Trans. Krzysztof Fijalkowski and Michael Richardson (London: Verso) 2002.

Olson, Charles. "Equal, That Is, to the Real Itself" *Collected Prose* (Berkeley: University of California Press) 1997.

Barthes, Roland. *Camera Lucida.* Trans. Richard Howard (New York: Hill and Wang) 2010.

Barthes, Roland. "Non Multa Sed Multum" *Writings on Cy Twombly.* Edited by Nicola del Roscio (Munich: Schirmer/Mosel) 2002.

Kristeva, Julia. *Powers of Horror: An Essay in Abjection.* Trans. Leon S. Roudiez (New York: Columbia University Press) 1982

Barthes, Roland. "The Grain of the Voice" *Image Music Text.* Trans. Stephen Heath (New York: Hill and Wang) 1977.

Ratcliff, Ben. "One Song Can Contain Multitudes", *NYTimes*, October 14, 2014.

Hemingway, Ernest. "The Three-Day Blow" *The Short Stories of Ernest Hemingway* (New York: Scribners) 1938.

Olson, Charles. "Maximus to Gloucester, Letter 27 [withheld]" *The Maximus Poems* (Berkeley: University of California Press) 1983.

Frank, Priscilla. "Carolee Schneemann, Feminist Performance Artist Talks 'Olympia,' Deodorant and Selfies. *Huffington Post*, 12/11/2013.

Derrida, Jacques. *Archive Fever: A Freudian Impression.* Trans. Eric Prenowitz (Chicago: The University of Chicago Press) 1995.

Carson, Anne. *Eros: The Bittersweet* (Princeton: Princeton University Press) 1986.

Ammons, Gene. "Cheek to Cheek" *The Big Sound* (Prestige) 1958.

Benjamin, Walter. "On Some Motifs in Baudelaire" *Walter Benjamin Selected Writings, Vol. 4* (Cambridge, MA: Belknap Press) 2003.

Hoffmann, E. T. A. *The Life & Opinion of the Tomcat Murr Together with a Fragmentary Biography of Kapellmeister Johannes Kreisler on Random Sheets of Waste Paper.* Trans. Anthea Bell (London: Penguin Classics) 1999.

Berger, Karol. *Bach's Cycle, Mozart's Arrow* (Berkeley: University of California Press) 2007.

Kierkegaard, Søren. *Either/Or: A Fragment of Life* trans. David and Lillian Swenson (Princeton: Princeton University Press) 1946.

Kristeva, Julia. "The Malady of Grief; Duras" *Black Sun: Depression and Melancholia.* Trans. Leon S Roudiez (New York: Columbia University Press) 1989.

Evans, Bill. "Quiet Now" *The Paris Concert* (Blue Note) 1983.

Benjamin, Walter. "Imagination" *Walter Benjamin Selected Writings, Vol. 1* (Cambridge, MA: Belknap Press) 1996.

Lawrence, D. H. "Etruscan Places" *D. H. Lawrence and Italy* (New York: Viking) 1972.

Cixous, Hélène, *Rootprints: Memory and Life Writing.* Trans. Mireille Calle-Gruber (London: Routledge) 1997.

Tomlinson, Janis A. "Women Served and Observed" *Goya: Order & Disorder* (Boston: MFA Publications) 2014.

Goya in Perspective. Edited by Fred Licht (Englewood Cliffs, NJ: Prentice-Hall) 1973.

Goya, Francisco. *Prints from the Collection of Manchester City Galleries* (Manchester, UK: Manchester City Galleries) 2009.

Rose, Barbara. "Goya Then, Goya Now" *Goya: The Disasters of War and Selected Prints from the Collection of the Arthur Ross Foundation* (New York: The Spanish Institute) 1985.

Bollig, Ben. "On Exile and Not-Belonging in the Work of Alejandra Pizarnik" in *Modern Argentine Poetry: Displacement Exile Migration* (Cardiff: University of Wales Press) 2011.

Neruda, Pablo. "Walking Around" read by Samuel L. Jackson. *Il Postino*, 1995.

Neruda, Pablo. "Heights of Macchu Picchu." Trans. John Felstiner. Janus Head, Vol. 10/1, Fall 2007.

Harrison, Jim. "Introduction" in *Pablo Neruda's Residence on Earth*. Trans. Donald D. Walsh (New York; New Directions) 2004.

Davis, Miles. *Sorcerer* (Columbia Records) 1967.

Kristeva, Julia. *Intimate Revolt: The Powers and Limits of Psychoanalysis*. Trans. Jeanine Herman (New York: Columbia University Press) 2002.

Proust, Marcel. *Cities of the Plain*, quoted in Kristeva's *Intimate Revolt*.

Benjamin, Walter. "On the Concept of History" *Walter Benjamin Selected Writings, Vol. 4* (Cambridge, MA: Belknap Press) 2003.

Adorno, Theodor W. "Cultural Criticism in Society" *Prisms*. Trans. Samuel & Shierry Weber (Cambridge, MA: MIT Press) 1981.

Eiland, Howard and Jennings, Michael W. *Walter Benjamin: A Critical Life* (Cambridge, MA: Belknap Press) 2014.

Benjamin, Walter. "Central Park" *Walter Benjamin Selected Writings, Vol. 4* (Cambridge, MA: Belknap Press) 2003.

Benjamin, Walter. "The Paris of the Second Empire in Baudelaire" *Walter Benjamin Selected Writings, Vol. 4* (Cambridge, MA: Belknap Press) 2003.

Davis, Miles. "Bye Bye Blackbird." *'Round about Midnight* (Columbia Records) 1956.

Bersani, Leo. *Baudelaire and Freud* (Berkeley, CA: University of California Press) 1977.

Baudelaire, Charles. *The Intimate Journals of Charles Baudelaire.* Trans. Christopher Isherwood (Boston: Beacon Press) 1957.

Baudelaire, Charles. *The Prose Poems and La Fanfarlo.* Trans. Rosemary Lloyd (Oxford: Oxford University Press) 1991.

Benjamin, Walter. *Walter Benjamin's Archive.* Trans. Esther Leslie (London: Verso) 2007.

Benjamin, Walter. "On the Image of Proust" in *Walter Benjamin Selected Writings, Vol. 2* (Cambridge, MA: Belknap Press) 1999.

Sartre, Jean-Paul. *Baudelaire* (New York: New Directions) 1950.

Baudelaire, Charles. *The Letters of Charles Baudelaire.* Trans. Arthur Symonds (New York: Albert & Charles Boni) 1927.

Baudelaire, Charles. *On Wine and Hashish.* Trans. Andrew Brown (London: Hesperus Press) 2002.

Olson, Charles. *Call Me Ishmael* (San Francisco: City Lights Books) 1947.

Proust, Marcel. *The Past Recaptured.* Trans. Frederick A. Blossom (New York: Albert & Charles Boni) 1932.

Pavese, Cesare. "Street Song." Trans. Richard Jackson. *Slope*, Issue 16, 2002. http://www.slope.org/archive/issue16/pagepavese.html

Freud, Sigmund. *Beyond the Pleasure Principle* (New York: Boni and Liveright) 1924.

Kristeva, Julia. "Dostoevsky, Suffering, Forgiveness." *Black Sun: Depression and Melancholia*. Trans. Leon S Roudiez (New York: Columbia University Press) 1989.

Melville, Herman. *Moby Dick or, The Whale* (San Francisco: Arion Press) 1979.

Grotowski, Jerzy. *Towards a Poor Theatre*. Trans. T.K. Wiewlorowski (New York: Simon & Schuster) 1968.

Wangh, Stephen. *An Acrobat of the Heart* (New York: Vintage) 2000.

Borowski, Tadeusz. *This Way for the Gas, Ladies and Gentlemen*. Trans. Barbara Vedder (New York: Viking Penguin) 1967.

Romanska, Magda. *The Post-traumatic Theatre of Grotowski and Kantor* (London: Anthem Press) 2012.

Flaszen, Ludwik. "Akropolis: Treatment of the Text" in *Towards a Poor Theatre*. Trans. T.K. Wiewlorowski (New York: Simon & Schuster) 1968.

DeKooning, Elaine. "Edwin Denby Remembered," *Ballet Review*, Spring, 1984.

O'Hara, Frank, "Petit Poème en Prose" *The Collected Poems of Frank O'Hara* (New York: Knopf) 1979.

Vasari, Giorgio. *Lives of the Artists*. Trans. George Bull (Harmondsworth, UK: Penguin) 1965.

Lacan, Jacques. *Feminine Sexuality*. Trans. Jacqueline Rose. (New York: W. W. Norton) 1982.

Gelhawat, Monika. *Boom: The New York City Flâneur in Postwar American Literature and Art* (Ann Arbor, MI: UMI Microforms) 2008.

Buck-Morss, Susan. "Aesthetics and Anaesthetics: Walter Benjamin's Artwork Essay Reconsidered," *OCTOBER: The Second Decade, 1986-1996* (Cambridge, MA: The MIT Press) 1997.

Eagleton, Terry. *The Ideology of the Aesthetic* (London: Basil, Blackwell) 1990.

Rilke, Rainer Maria. *Selected Poetry.* Trans. Stephen Mitchell (New York: Vintage International) 1989.

Caws, Mary Ann. *Robert Motherwell: What Art Holds* (New York: Columbia University Press) 1996.

::::

ALSO BY ROBERT GIBBONS

Under the Great Divide with Ed Dorn
Old Orchard's Palace
Old Orchard Beach Cycle
Spent Some Time with Lorca in New York
Animated Landscape
To Know Others, Various & Free
Traveling Companion
This Time
Jagged Timeline
Travels Inside the Archive
Beyond Time: New & Selected Work, 1977-2007
Body of Time
The Book of Assassinations
Streets for Two Dancers

The Degas
Olson/Still: Crossroad
Rhythm of Desire & Resistance
This Vanishing Architecture
Of DC
Lover, Is This Exile?
Ardors
The Woman in the Paragraph
Yellow & Black